FUNDAMENTALS OF MODERN MANAGEMENT

FUNDAMENTALS OF MODERN MANAGEMENT

by

J. S. DUGDALE, M.A.

Docteur en Sciences Economiques
Associate Member of the British Institute of Management
Member of the Institute of Office Management
Fellow of the Institute of Linguists

This book is approved as a basic text for the
Certificate examinations of the Institution of Works Managers

© JAMES BRODIE LTD., BRODIE HOUSE
QUEEN SQUARE, BATH
SOMERSET, ENGLAND

First published, 1964

Second edition, with corrections and index, 1965

Third impression, 1968

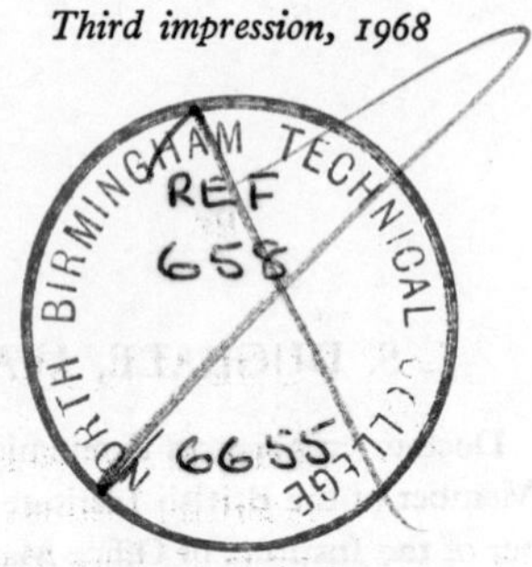

I keep six honest serving men,
(They taught me all I knew),
Their names are What and Why and When,
And How and Where and Who.

RUDYARD KIPLING.

Made and Printed in Great Britain by
COWARD AND GERRISH LTD., LARKHALL, BATH, SOMERSET

FOREWORD

The aim of this book is a modest and severely practical one: to supply in brief compass some of the ideas relating to the management process which have developed in the last half-century or so.

The requirement of brevity has often meant bald, unqualified statements, but this is regarded as an advantage, since the student must think for himself about these matters. Nearly all the questions given at the end of the various sections have been chosen with a view to encouraging the critical thinking of the reader rather than the mere uncritical regurgitation of book-matter.

The material is that which the author has himself used with senior students from middle management and supervisory levels. A section should be read ahead of the class meeting, so that the time can be used for analysis and discussion, and not wasted in note-taking.

A special feature is the detailed guide to further reading: numerous suggestions are given so that the student can read different arguments and expositions and widen his point of view. It is not expected that a student will read everything suggested, but he must make an effort to drape more flesh round the skeleton here presented. The footnote references, many of them to periodical literature, will also be useful to students who wish to pursue a special topic.

Whatever the author himself understands about this 'subject' has been gained not only from the writers who are collectively acknowledged in the reading lists and from his own experience in several large organisations, but also from numerous discussions with people in industry and commerce and, not least, from the students whom he has tried to lead through the thickets.

J. S. D.

London, 1963

ACKNOWLEDGEMENTS

Grateful thanks are expressed to the following for allowing the use of copyright material.

Messrs. Longmans, Green & Company Ltd. for a diagram from Brech's *Principles and Practice of Management; Time and Motion Study* for a table by K. Shone; Professor Asa Briggs for summary of lecture; Organisation de Co-operation et de Développement Economiques for diagrams in *Modern Management;* Professor R. W. Revans for 'Science and the Manager', from *Management International;* The Editor of *The Manager* for various extracts; Messrs. McGraw-Hill Book Co. Inc., New York for questions from Laird: *The Techniques of Delegating.*

CONTENTS

PART ONE

INTRODUCTORY

THE PERFORMANCE CAPACITIES OF EVERY MAN ARE DETERMINED BY

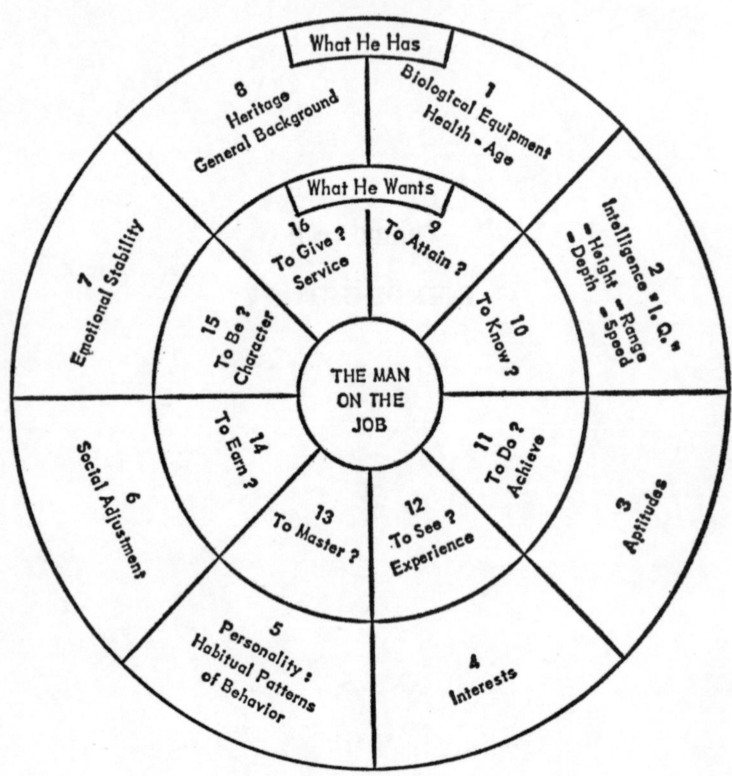

There is no improvement except through change
Wanting constitutes the motive power that propels improvement : within the scope of potential capacity

WHAT THE JOB OF MANAGEMENT REQUIRES
Every Top Executive Should Know

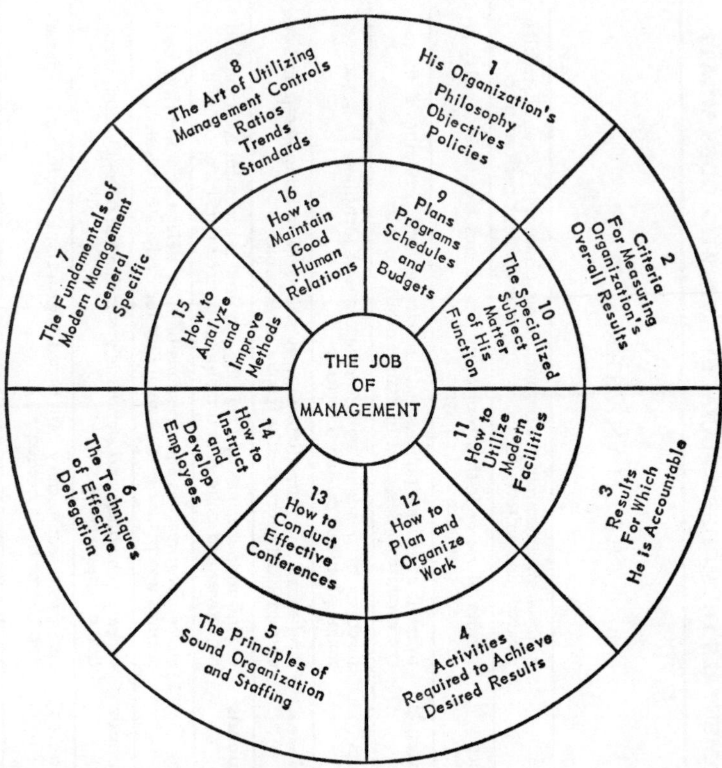

Productivity, morale, and over-all results decline whenever management doesn't KNOW; can't DO, or doesn't CARE about every item listed above

FUNDAMENTALS OF MODERN MANAGEMENT: WHO DOES WHAT?

The Board of Directors	THE MANAGER		*Within his Functional Area each Department Head*
Concurs	**1. Clarifies**	*viewpoints*, interprets the organization's philosophy, over-all results desired, and criteria for evaluating management performance	**Interprets**
	2. Appraises	results of *research* that project producer and consumer needs; of marketing studies and analyses	**Understands**
Approves	**3. Recommends**	over-all *objectives*, policies, and programs, and prescribes management controls designed to assure desired results	**Develops**
Reviews	**4. Interprets**	forecasts of *trends* in significant areas and identifies, in sequence, major problems related thereto	**Interprets**
Concurs	**5. Determines**	long-range and immediate *strategy* necessary to bring about and/or sustain satisfactory results insofar as possible	**Develops**
Approves	**6. Recommends**	organization *structure and key staff* required to accomplish established objectives and policies and maintain desired performance	**Recommends**
	7. Activates	*major programs*, assigns responsibilities, delegates authority, and secures acceptance of accountability for designated results	**Supervises**
Approves	**8. Recommends**	*budgets*, schedules, and standards governing the over-all administration of approved programs	**Initiates**
	9. Co-ordinates	*activities* in conformity with broad approvals; looks for and initiates improvements as needed	**Directs**

FUNDAMENTALS OF MODERN MANAGEMENT: WHO DOES WHAT?—*continued*

The Board of Directors	THE MANAGER		*Within his Functional Area each Department Head*
Reviews	**10. Presents**	*summary reports* of results for conformity with established objectives, policies, and related management controls; effects remedial action as required	**Prepares**
	11. Examines	*periodic survey reports* of member and employee attitudes and directs appropriate action wherever need is indicated	**Understands**
	12. Directs	*communications*, up and down and across, as necessary to keep everybody affected adequately informed and to maintain high morale	**Maintains**
Approves	**13. Reviews**	*adequacy* of objectives, policies, standards, and other basic controls and recommends improvements wherever possible	**Initiates**
	14. Conducts	individual *appraisals* of immediate subordinates' performance and follows through until desired results and job satisfaction are maintained	**Conducts**
	15. Leads	*staff conferences* as needed to utilize most effectively the power of 'group thinking' in the solution of management problems	**Leads**

CHAPTER ONE

MANAGEMENT AND EDUCATION

The report of the National Economic Development Council, *Conditions Favourable to Faster Growth* (London, H.M.S.O., 1963), significantly begins with a section on 'Education and Economic Growth'. Paragraph 15 (page 3) states: "To achieve the increase in productivity necessary for growth will call for highly skilled management throughout the economy not only in industry but in every type of organisation. The term 'management' covers a wide range of responsibility and function, from the boards, lower levels of management and supervisors of companies, large and small, to the principals of 'one-man businesses'." The next paragraph continues: "The most successful managers are those who are most conscious of the need to improve still further and who have a constant urge for progress, and a quick response to changes in demand and environment".

The report emphasises the fact that a good manager must possess "*innate qualities of leadership and initiative* which, whilst they *cannot be implanted*, can be *developed* by the *right kind of practical and theoretical training*"; "the *actual techniques* of most management jobs can be taught". The report insists on the need for education not only for young men who are just beginning to climb the managerial ladder but also those already in executive positions. The main subjects of study should be the new analytical techniques which can "provide a more accurate basis for *decision-making* and improve *control* over the various functions of the business"; human relations; communication within and outside the firm; and the problems of industrial relations. Other aspects of management education which need to be developed are: a better working knowledge of languages; methods of marketing and the assessment of future trends; financial and operating ratios and inter-firm comparisons.

According to an estimate made by an industrial consultant there are in Britain some 450,000 'managers', of whom less than one per cent have received "any form of management training" (quoted *The Financial Times,* May 7th 1963). The purpose of the syllabus for the Certificate in Works Management is to supply a student with a training in the basic features of the theory and practice of management. There is at present only a small corpus of managers trained either in critical thinking about the nature of management or in the new skills and techniques, such as communication, demand forecasting, costing and financial programming. It is not, therefore, surprising that Britain has in recent times lost her industrial lead. The 'industrial revolution' is not a single once-for-all process, but is "a *permanent* revolution in which the pioneer country can retain its original advantage by selling to others the tools and techniques for the next stage of advance".[1] It is not enough to have *scientists* and *technologists*: we must also have competent *managers,* and scientists and technologists trained in management.

The traditional bias of the English educational system has been towards the classics and the humanities—a liberal education suited to the more leisurely atmosphere of the previous century. It is not suggested here that liberal studies should be neglected; indeed, the potential manager should take every opportunity of reading widely in literature, history and philosophy. (An interview of forty American business 'presidents' revealed that thirty-two advised less specialisation in education if a person would prepare himself to be a good company president; all forty suggested more liberal arts study.)[2]

The educational background of British managers is in process of changing: the number of managers with a university degree is increasing, the number with elementary education only is decreasing and greater emphasis is being laid on professional qualifications. The following table shows changes in the educational background of managers in a steel plant:

[1] Michael Shanks: *The Stagnant Society,* Penguin Books (1961), p. 207.

[2] H. B. Maynard (Ed.): *Top Management Handbook,* McGraw-Hill, New York (1960), p. 159.

CHANGES IN THE EDUCATIONAL BACKGROUND OF MANAGERS IN A STEEL PLANT[3]

Educational background	*Top managers*		*Middle managers*	
	1935	*1954*	*1935*	*1954*
University degree . .	3	8	0	4
Professional qualification .	2	3	3	27
Neither of above . .	7	10	39	84
TOTAL . . .	12	21	42	115

In an analysis of the factors related to promotion in management, it was found that the possession of an Arts degree or non-technical qualification was more advantageous than a science degree or technical qualification; this suggests that there is a concentration in selection on the technical man for the *specialist, technical* post and the Arts man for the *top, co-ordinating post*, "in which a background in the humanities is believed to be of greater value than an intensive training in a specialisation".[4]

It is only in recent times that management has come to be recognised as a distinct profession or a social institution. This new recognition may be said to date from the publication in 1941 of James Burnham's *The Managerial Revolution*, though before that time some managers, especially in the U.S.A., had viewed themselves as professionals. One of Burnham's main contentions[5] was that in recent decades a partial separation of *ownership* from *control* has taken place, so that "income and power have become unbalanced". Control over the instruments of production has been shifting away "from the capitalists proper towards the managers". This move towards social dominance of the managers constitutes the 'managerial revolution'.

Although the theory of the managerial revolution as put forward by Burnham now seems untenable, there has undoubtedly been a movement towards a 'managerial society' since 1900. The

[3] I. McGivering, D. Matthews and W. H. Scott: *Management in Britain*, Liverpool University Press (1960), p. 66.

[4] *ibid.*, p. 67.

[5] James Burnham: *The Managerial Revolution* (available in a Penguin edition), especially chapters VI, VII, VIII, X).

reasons for this are: the *growing size and complexity* of industrial production; the combined process of *separation of ownership and control*; the principle of *limited liability* and all it implies; and the need for all kinds of *experts* within industry. This growth of an increasingly managerial society, as distinct from the old family employers' society or the independent shopkeepers' society of the 19th century, has changed the context of industrial relations as much as the new power of the Welfare State has done.

QUESTIONNAIRE

submitted by the Institution of Works Managers on the Factors which limit Productivity

THE FACTORS LISTED IN THE QUESTIONNAIRE

The 52 factors from which members made their selection were shown on the questionnaire as follows:

A) Management

Aa Complacency in the board room, induced by full order book—no urge to raise productivity.
Ab Quality of management—lack of management training.
Ac Innate distaste of change, in management.
Ad Frustration at all management levels, due to lack of clearly defined sphere of delegated responsibilities.
Ae No effective joint consultation.
Af Lack of feeling of national unity in family firms.

B) Finance & economics

Ba Antiquated costing systems which discourage the use of highly productive equipment.
Bb Insufficient cost information to indicate the best areas for improvement in productivity.
Bc Undue concentration on *labour* productivity to the detriment of capital productivity.
Bd Reluctance to spend money for new equipment—plant, tools, buildings and services.
Be Lack of appreciation of value of cost reduction.
Bf Lack of courage in preparing budgets to force methods improvements.
Bg Too rigid control from the top, and in too much detail—stifles manager's initiative.

C) Marketing

Ca Lack of market research and sales forecasts.
Cb Inaccurate sales forecasts.
Cc Not enough standardisation—resulting in short runs and overload of design and production engineering staff.
Cd Too rapid changes in production plan.
Ce Orders not appropriate to the plant skills available.
Cf Price maintenance arrangements remove incentive for methods improvement.

D) Supplies: buying and stock control

Da Buyer cannot cope with needs of production.
Db Poor stock control.
Dc Production delays due to inadequate forward appraisal of availability of supplies.
Dd Ineffective control of inventories.
De Too much importance given to low level of inventory.

E) Industrial engineering techniques

Ea Under employment of industrial engineering techniques.
Eb Lack of any real form of production planning.
Ec Lack of detailed shop-floor planning.

Ed Systems which require paper rather than product.
Ee Lack of trained and experienced industrial engineers.
Ef Failure to "sell" work study to shop-floor.

F) Personnel

Fa Disinclination of workers to work.
Fb Innate distaste for change, in men.
Fc The natural human desire to get what you need by giving the minimum.
Fd Unsatisfactory wage structure.
Fe Unsatisfactory "incentives".
Ff Staff departments not receptive of need for productivity.
Fg Staff conditions too easy/hours too short.
Fh Overstaffing due to fear of labour shortage.

G) Management/labour relations

Ga Lack of good human relations.
Gb Full employment—excessive labour turnover—high and continuing cost of training labour.
Gc Full employment—reduces ability to discipline and lowers level of effort.
Gd Absence of national policy on "sharing the productivity cake".
Ge Not enough job evaluation.
Gf Time lost in industrial disputes, official and unofficial.
Gg Restrictive practices — management and labour.
Gh Poor communications—upwards and downwards.

H) Trade unions

Ha Distaste for something thought to put money in the bosses' pockets.
Hb Demarcation between trades and between unions, i.e. craftsmen/general workers.
Hc Leaders have no genuine desire to promote productivity.
Hd Irresponsibility of members.
He Communist infiltration subverts harmonious relations.
Hf Will not accept improved methods.

The Questionnaire* was answered by 656 persons, but 169 replies could not be used in the analysis for various reasons. The following list shows the top 15 adverse factors selected:

THE TOP 15 PRINCIPAL DRAWBACKS SELECTED

The top fifteen adverse factors in order of their selection by members were:

1) Quality of management—*lack of management training*.

2) Not enough *standardisation*, resulting in short runs and overloading of design and production engineering staff.

3) Insufficient *cost information* to indicate the best areas for improvement in productivity.

4) Frustration at all management levels, due to lack of clearly defined sphere of *delegated responsibilities*.

5) Poor *communications* — upwards and downwards.

6) Full employment — reduces ability to *discipline* and lowers *level of effort*.

7) Lack of *market research* and *sales forecasts*.

8) Reluctance to spend money for *new equipment* — plant tools, buildings and services.

9) The natural human desire to get what you need by giving the *minimum*.

*The full report, entitled *Spanners in the Works* can be obtained from The General Secretary, Institution of Works Managers, 196 Shaftesbury Avenue, London, W.C.2.

10) Unsatisfactory "*incentives*".

11) Too rapid changes in *production* plan.

12) Lack of any real form of *production planning*.

13) Under employment of *industrial engineering techniques.*

14) Inaccurate *sales forecasts.*

15) Lack of good *human relations.*

The main point to be made in the present context is that hitherto ownership and management were regarded as two sides of the same coin, and the discussion of the matter usually centred on the privileges and obligations of *ownership*. The distinction between a man's action as *owner* and his action as *manager* was rarely made. This state of affairs reflected the comparatively late development of the social sciences: there had been no intellectual disciplines which studied the behaviour of people and enterprises. As a result, however, of the rapid development of the social sciences in the 20th century, the process of management has been identified as a crucial one in society. Executive action is a socio-psychological process. The most recent discussions of the field of management imply knowledge and techniques which are assumed to have *universal* properties and which can be applied not only to *different kinds* of organisation but also in any of the *functional areas* (production, finance, marketing and personnel) and at any level of the hierarchy from managing director down to foreman. The essential elements of *executive action* are *decision-making*, *communication* and *leadership*. Recent studies of executive action draw upon numerous fields of study or disciplines and the approach is therefore termed *inter-disciplinary*: such subjects as economic theory, sociology, semantics, information theory, budgeting, quality control and so on are each made to yield a contribution which is synthesised with the others.[6]

It is not improbable that future managers will receive much more training in the social sciences. A factory, it is now recognised, is not only an *economic* system but also a *status* system. The workers at all levels may be interested not only in their wages or salaries, or their job satisfaction, but also in their *rôle* in the factory—their relations with other people. The system of communications is also important: there is both a *formal* and an *informal* communication system, and the latter is just as real and important as the former in influencing the 'inner life' of the

[6] A readable introduction to the 'inter-disciplinary' approach is Henry H. Albers: *Organised Executive Action*: *Decision-Making, Communication and Leadership*, John Wiley, New York (1961).

factory. The 'folklore' of the factory, the attitudes of people to one another, are just as important as inter-departmental memos and orders pinned to the notice-board. What might be called, then, the social organisation of industry is an important field of study, and such books as Brady's *Business as a System of Power*, Elliott Jaques's *The Changing Culture of a Factory*, Homans's *The Human Group*, Schneider's *Industrial Sociology*, Bendix's *Work and Authority in Industry* and Whyte's *The Organisation Man*, to name some of the more important studies, have shown how sociology and allied disciplines can be applied to the study of industrial organisation and industrial relations.

Management, then, is now being recognised as a subject for *systematic* study, and is beginning to exert greater influence as a *distinct social institution*. Whether or not management can be regarded as a profession is a different matter. The definition of a profession is itself no easy matter, but Hyman has suggested a good working definition:[7]

> "A profession is concerned with a *body of established knowledge*; it involves the *training of recruits* in this knowledge; it concerns itself with the *extension of this knowledge* and it demands a *sense of responsibility* towards the clients."

Even management consultants can as yet hardly claim to possess established knowledge about the theory and practice of consultancy and, if such knowledge does not exist, recruits cannot be trained. It has recently been suggested by an American writer[8] that management cannot yet be regarded as a profession, in spite of the fact that a long line of 'business educators' have classified business as a profession. "The professional image is artificial and synthetic, not based on the reality of learning and tradition". Donham's definition of profession includes four basic elements:

1. A profession is characterised by a *systematic body of specialized knowledge* of substantial intellectual content.
2. It is further characterised by a *motive of service*, by *standards of conduct* which govern all professional relationships.

These are the basic elements; two further elements seem also to be important:

[7] See S. Hyman: *An Introduction to Management Consultancy*, p. 89 (my italics).

[8] Paul Donham: 'Is Management a Profession?', *Harvard Business Review* (September–October 1962).

3. A recognised *educational process* and *standards of qualification* for admission.
4. An organisation devoted to the advancement of the profession's *social obligations* and the enforcement of *standards of admission and membership*. (See also pp. 45-6.)

As regards the first element, there has been wide divergence of opinion and disagreements as to what *kinds of knowledge* are required. (The present writer has spoken to managers about the 'social organisation' of the factory and it was obvious that they did not understand this phrase and thought it had something to do with sports' clubs or whist drives). There are signs that in the future there will be much greater agreement on the scope and aim of management studies, but one must agree with Revans that management, by and large, is still in the 16th century, awaiting its Galileo to stimulate the *study of facts*, its Kepler to encourage their *measurement*, its Huygens to investigate the *instruments of measurement*, and its Newton to enunciate the *fundamental laws* of these facts.

Business administration, says Donham, certainly contains the second element; the third element, he thinks, has no relevance to *general* business administration, since the manager can come from all levels of education and may, in fact, have no formal education at all; as regards the fourth element, there are no professional associations or organisations for the business-man in the U.S.A. The heart of the matter, Donham concludes, is lack of "a rigid code of ethics and conduct, together with the prompt disciplining of those who transgress that code; but in business the legal minimums are the ethical minimums". This is not to say that there are not "thousands of business executives who have a high sense of ethics which governs their business conduct . . ." Donham believes, then, that business is not a profession and cannot be one, until a body of knowledge is developed and agreed upon, until standards are developed for admission to and maintenance of professional status, and until executives in the mass accept a code of ethics to which they will adhere.

The aims and work of such a body as the Institution of Works Managers should go far towards meeting some of these objections. It is worth while here to quote the professional code of the Institution of Works Management (my italics):

INSTITUTION OF WORKS MANAGERS PROFESSIONAL CODE

The Institution of Works Managers is a professional organisation, the members of which believe that good leadership must be allied with technical competence, and that the works manager's aim should constantly be:

1. To improve the *Efficiency* of the organisation he controls;
2. To promote *Goodwill and Understanding* within the organisation;
3. To assist individuals to *Develop* to the best of their ability, and to place on each as much *Responsibility* as circumstances will reasonably allow:
4. To avoid endangering the *Future Performance* or security of the undertaking for the purpose of achieving *Immediate* Results;
5. To set an example of *Justice and Loyalty* within his company and to take the lead in establishing *Relationships of Mutual Respect and Sincerity*, so ensuring that *Similar Standards* are observed by *All* in *Subordinate command;*
6. To conform to a *High Standard of Personal Behaviour* and thus, by example, to engender in others a sense of *Good Citizenship*;
7. To maintain a *High Standard of Loyalty* to *Other Works Managers and The Institution*, so that the *Dignity* and the *Status* of the *Profession of Works Management* may be enhanced.

It has frequently been asserted in the past that management cannot be taught.* It is obvious that in any sphere of human endeavour natural talents and temperaments are of great importance, but the statement that "nothing which improves a person's understanding of management, and therefore his speed of learning and his proficiency, can be taught" would be "plain nonsense: it would put administration in a different category from every other art; it would imply that nothing of the lessons learned by one generation would be passed on to the next. Formal instruction in administration can help to develop understanding as well as the speed at which lessons of practical experience are learnt."

* One argument runs: since there is no generally accepted definition of management, it may be impossible to teach it. But even if no *a priori* definition exists it may still be possible to teach—by trial and error—a body of useful knowledge. (*Cf.* E. Dale's 'comparative approach' to discover the best results of earlier successful business-men—*Planning and Developing the Organization Structure*, American Management Association, New York, Research Report No. 20 (1952).

ADDITIONAL READING ASSIGNMENTS

1. National Economic Development Council: *Conditions Favourable to Faster Growth*, London, H.M.S.O. (1963).
2. Michael Shanks: *The Stagnant Society*, Pelican Books (1961), especially chapter 8, 'Can We Compete?'
3. I. McGivering, D. Matthews and W. H. Scott: *Management in Britain*, Liverpool University Press (1960), 'Managers', pp. 62–77, and 'Managerial Characteristics and Organisation', pp. 133–141.
4. Paul Donham: 'Is Management a Profession?', *Harvard Business Review* (September–October 1962).
5. L. Urwick: *Is Management a Profession?* 2nd edition (1958).
6. Stanley Hyman: *An Introduction to Management Consultancy*, London (1961).
7. *Human Sciences: Aid to Industry* (pamphlet produced by D.S.I.R.), H.M.S.O. (1961).
8. E. F. L. Brech: 'The Profession of Management' in *The Principles and Practice of Management* (ed. Brech), 2nd edition (1963), pp. 1016–1038.
9. C. Vincent: 'The Consultant and his Image', *The Manager* (Sept. 1962).
10. W. R. Dill, T. L. Hilton, W. R. Reitman: *The New Managers: Patterns of Behaviour and Development*, Prentice-Hall, New Jersey (1962). Three interesting case-studies on the experience of young Americans "on their way up" the managerial ladder. Worth reading *in toto*.
11. H. C. Metcalf and L. Urwick (Eds.): *Dynamic Administration: The Collected Papers of Mary Parker Follett* (paper on 'The Profession of Management').
12. L. F. Urwick: 'Management and the Administrator', in *The Making of an Administrator* (ed. A. Dunsire).
13. L. W. Norris: 'Moral Hazards of an Executive', *Harvard Business Review*, Vol. 38, No. 5 (Sept.–Oct. 1960).
14. R. A. Goldwin and C. A. Nelson (Eds.): *Toward the Liberally Educated Executive*, Mentor Books, New York (1960).
15. David Granick: *The European Executive*, London (1961).

TOPICS FOR ESSAYS/DISCUSSION

1. "Until the calibre of management improves we cannot hope to get the full value out of our investment outlays. This calls for a major reform of our educational system, to break the present exclusive dominance of the humanities." (M. Shanks).

2. Consider training for management under the following headings: (*a*) General Training; (*b*) Practical Training; (*c*) Training to develop the 'Whole Man' (see, for example, Hooper's discussion in *Management Survey*, 6, 'What Makes a Man a Manager?').
3. What do you understand by a 'profession'? How in your view can management become a more professional activity?
4. "Perhaps the most illuminating place to start thinking about organisation is with one's own job". (H. A. Simon: *Administrative Behaviour*, Introd. to Second Edition, p. xvii).

   Examples: What are one's attachments to goals and organisation units? What are the important situations in one's work where one has to choose between competing goals and loyalties? What do the choices which one has made in such situations reveal about one's own values and the values that others in the organisation will impute to one? How have these goals and loyalties come to be and who maintains them?
5. How can the 'human sciences' aid industry? Discuss under the heading of either (*a*) Studies of Human Efficiency; (*b*) Studies in Social Organisation and Human Relations (See D.S.I.R. pamphlet).
6. In what ways does management: (*a*) resemble; (*b*) differ from, the profession of medicine or law?
7. Whether or not management is regarded as a profession depends largely on the criteria used. An important criterion would be a period of special training. What are *your* views?
8. Do you consider T.W.I. to be an adequate system of training supervisors today?

CHAPTER TWO

APPROACH TO THE STUDY OF MANAGEMENT

§ 1. An Elusive Subject

One of the reviewers of Roger Falk's *The Business of Management* (Pelican, 1961), wrote: "For less than the price of a packet of cigarettes you can at least discover that management simply should not be written about". Falk himself good-humouredly admits that, though management tends to become obscured in *cliché* and good intentions, "yet a lot of good, sensible stuff has already been produced". He goes on: "That no giant has yet emerged in the field of management writing is perhaps not hard to understand. If it is accepted that the art (or craft) of management consists in striking a balance between what is technically and humanly valid, it will not seem strange that those who feel the urge to put down their ideas on paper do it in a somewhat tentative manner". At best, says Falk, management is "the most elusive and tenuous of subjects".[1] It is, however, of its very nature, a subject which "strikes at the heart of social behaviour."[2]

§ 2. Aim of this Book

The present writer holds with Falk that plenty of "good, sensible stuff" has already been written on management, and a major aim of this book is to guide the student in a critical approach to such writings. The book must not be regarded as a "text-book", the different sections of which simply have to be learnt and regurgitated in an examination. Its essential aim is to foster in the student critical thinking about management and to encourage him to read more detailed discussions of the matters treated. For this reason, the reading lists have been carefully compiled, in many instances with individual chapter indications. The lists are also fairly comprehensive, so that alternatives are available; there is no suggestion here that the student will read everything, but it is hoped that he will make a careful selection from the lists, and not only in those matters which particularly interest him. Where possible, it is hoped that courses will be arranged so that the student can read in advance and come prepared to spend the class-time in discussions and case-studies.

[1] Roger Falk: 'Writing About Management', *The Stock Exchange Gazette*, January 18th, 1963.

[2] *idem: The Business of Management*, p. 12.

§ 3. Case Studies

A fair selection of case-studies is now available in this country; they afford good practice in the careful analysis of business situations and in decision-making, but, however 'realistic' they may be, the participants in a case do not have to bear the responsibility for the consequences of their decisions. An American book[3] is very useful in this respect, in that it has case-studies attached and related to each of its six Parts, with questions in each case classified under the following main headings:

1. ORGANISING: STRUCTURAL DESIGN
2. HUMAN FACTORS IN ORGANISING
3. PLANNING: ELEMENTS OF DECISION-MAKING
4. PLANNING: DECISION-MAKING IN AN ENTERPRISE
5. LEADING
6. MEASURING AND CONTROLLING

It is recommended that the student should study one or two of the cases in this book to learn something of the *systematic* approach to case-study. Students who have not done any case-study frequently wish to rush to the end of the case and "solve" it. In many cases there will not be any firm solution, and much of the value of case-study consists in the detailed analysis and assessment of evidence, and the arguments with fellow-students whose "reading" of the evidence and whose ideas and attitudes differ from your own.

§ 4. Rational Decision-Making

After you have read a case once or twice, the first step is to *identify and clarify the problem, i.e.* make a diagnosis. A good diagnosis will (i) state what is wrong (or apparently wrong); (ii) identify the *causes*; (iii) offer a *tentative 'solution'*; and (iv) indicate any important *limits* within which the 'solution' may be applied. The discovery of the real problem in a case is the first important exercise (some cases, of course, indicate what the problem is). Einstein wrote: "The formulation of a problem is often more essential than its solution, which may be merely a matter of mathematics or experimental skill". The next step is to suggest what might be done to overcome the obstacles or snags revealed by the diagnosis. The student (or the case-leader) should then

[3] William H. Newman and Charles E. Sumner: *The Process of Management, Concepts, Behaviour and Practice* (Prentice-Hall International Inc., London. 1961).

assemble all the pertinent data—opinions as well as facts—which are related to the problem in hand. The pros and cons of *alternative* lines of action should then be considered with some indication of the relative advantages and disadvantages of each alternative. It will be rare that any one alternative is so patently superior to the others that analysis will supply a single incontrovertible solution.

§ 5. The Question of 'Principles' or 'Fundamentals'

The real meaning of 'principle' is *foundation* or *beginning*, and the word is, therefore, applicable to any fundamental truth which is regarded as universal in its particular field, *e.g.* moral, economic, physical, mathematical, legal principles. The practical meaning of *principle* is "any underlying cause of more or less correlated facts in any particular field of investigation".[4] Another definition is "a general law or rule adopted or professed as a guide to action".[5] Most of the so-called *principles of management* are near to the latter definition in that they purport to be *guides to action*: they are not fundamental truths or propositions which form part of a comprehensive system of business behaviour or of the people in businesses. Similarly, if one talks about the 'laws' of human behaviour, such a usage does not correspond with that of the natural sciences (*cf. Oxford English Dictionary* definition of 'law': "In the sciences of observation, a theoretical principle deduced from particular facts, applicable to a defined group or class of phenomena, and expressible by the statement that a particular phenomenon always occurs if certain conditions be present"). 'Laws' of business management are "*conditional* statements which are qualified by such adjectives as 'primary', 'usually', 'largely' and 'normally'."[6]

Megginson[7] has distinguished between *principles* and *fundamentals* as follows:

> A *principle* is "a general proposition *sufficiently* applicable to the series of phenomena under consideration to provide a *guide to thought*".

[4] Mooney & Reiley: *Onward Industry!*, p. 17.

[5] *Oxford English Dictionary*.

[6] George Copeman: *Laws of Business Management and Executive Way of Life*, London, 1962. "Introduction".

[7] Leon C. Megginson: 'The Pressure for Principles. A Challenge to Management Professors', in H. Koontz and C. J. O'Donnell: *Readings in Management* (1959), pp. 13–18.

A *fundamental* is "a statement that serves as a *basis of action*". Hence, principles or fundamentals are not injunctions to be followed blindly, but to serve as a guide or point of departure. A body of knowledge can be built up by trial and error, but there must be reliable *feed-back*. If persons who teach management are to proceed by trial and error, they must know when they are on the right or wrong track.[8]

A *full* corpus of management principles which would furnish formulae for the solution of all managerial problems does not exist now nor is it likely to exist in the future. Yet it seems possible to learn from experience and transfer what one has learned from one case situation to another: what can be learned are the fundamentals which are involved. "There are seldom two business cases that are alike in all respects, nor are there many techniques of managing that apply in the *same* way in *different* circumstances. In fact, there are dangers in assuming that such similarities exist. However, if one can seek out and apply the *fundamentals* in different circumstances, and if these fundamentals can be resolved by resort to principles, the solution of problems or the application of techniques can be made more effectively. . . . The value of seeing management as a conceptual scheme of principles is that it lets one see, and understand, what would otherwise have remained unseen."[9]

This difficulty over the term *principles* is not confined to management. Even accountants have complained that the term 'accounting principles' is misleading, and suggests a degree of *precision* not actually attained. "More important than arguments about terminology, however, is the development of underlying postulates and definitions."[10]

Some of the 'principles' put forward in the past have been more in the nature of methods for better management practice, but *method* refers to the means whereby principles could be put into practice. Although some management principles could be *deduced* from the nature of the management process itself (if the latter could be defined) a body of principles *drawn from practice* is likely

[8] See Nigel Farrow: 'Management Educators: Lost Explorers in a Blackboard Jungle', *Business* (May 1963).

[9] Koontz and O'Donnell: *Principles of Management*, p. 11.

[10] See George R. Catlett: 'Factors that Influence Accounting Principles', in *Studies in Accounting Theory*, ed. W. T. Baxter and S. Davidson, London, Second Edition (1962).

to be accorded more acceptance. Such principles would be drawn from a comparative study of observed strengths and weaknesses, and this would require much first-hand research that has not so far been attempted: a good example is Guest's study of participative, permissive leadership in works management.[11] At the end of his study of administration Simon[12] admits that no *definitive* administrative principles have emerged: the next step forward will be the development of adequate case-studies of existing administrative situations, and the development and improvement of techniques for *measuring* the success of particular administrative arrangements.

§ 6. The Qualities of a Manager

Many attempts have been made to list the qualities required of a good manager, but these tend to add up to a picture of an archangel rather than that of a fallible human being. It is a good thing to exclude *business acumen* from such discussions, for strictly speaking this is not a management skill at all, but a *specialised commercial expertise*.[13] A person who has a flair for buying and selling may not have sufficient management skills to ensure the continuing effective accomplishment of his business.

Some *mental ability* the manager must have; he must also be able to see the *other person's point of view* and must possess the power of self-criticism; he must be able to *discriminate* between important and less important matters; he must be able to *use specialists*, since business is becoming so complicated that no one man can possibly know all the answers; he must have judgment to know when to lay down a *standard* procedure and introduce 'red tape'. In addition, he must have organising ability, persistence, integrity, a balanced temperament and a sense of humour. He must be able to distinguish between *true policy matters* and questions of *day-to-day practice*. The knowledge a manager requires lies in four fields: the *technical*, the *economic*, the *human* and the *administrative*.[14] Strictly speaking, technical knowledge is not part of management, but the other three fields comprise the elements of the management process. Drucker stated that

[11] Robert Henry Guest: *Organisational Change: The Effect of Successful Leadership*, London (1962).
[12] Herbert A. Simon: *Administrative Behaviour*, p. 247.
[13] Brech (Ed.): *The Principles and Practice of Management*, p. 1019.
[14] *ibid.*, pp. 1020–25.

"the function which distinguishes the manager above all others" is his educational one—his job of giving others "vision and ability to perform".[15] For this the manager has a specific tool—*information*; yet of all the skills which the manager requires the average manager is least equipped in reading, writing, speaking and the language of numbers.[16]

The acquisition or development of these skills must, therefore, constitute an important part of the manager's training, and every opportunity on a management course must be given to students to practise speaking and writing, as well as reading as widely as time permits. A book such as the present provides scores of topics for group discussion or for short 'papers' by individual students.

§ 7. Group Discussion

It is suggested that the present subject can best be studied in group discussion, in which the students face one another and the lecturer takes the rôle of critical listener instead of the main speaker. In this way the collective experience and attitudes of the students can be utilised. Freedom and spontaneity are essential if such a group is to be effective.[17]

Sweeping statements will be heard in group discussion; they may arise out of mental laziness or a desire to impress. The habit of making such statements must always be checked, and the lecturer himself can set an example of exactness. (The words *tend* and *tendency* are useful ones). The distinguishing feature of scientific work is a readiness to co-operate, to listen to criticism and to admit that one's point of view may be wrong, however sincerely it may be felt.[18]

§ 8. Logic and Reasoning

(i) *The Syllogism* is a method of argument whereby two statements are made (major premises and minor premise) and a conclusion is drawn, *e.g.*

15 P. Drucker: *The Practice of Management*, p. 309.

16 *ibid.*, p. 306.

17 See M. L. Johnson Abercrombie: *The Anatomy of Judgment*, chapt. 5, 'The Nature of Free Group Discussion'; and R. W. Revans, 'Discussion in Industry', in *Discussion Method* (Bureau of Current Affairs, London (1950), pp. 60–66; Josephine Klein: *Working with Groups: the Social Psychology of Discussion and Decision*, London (1961).

18 H. Bondi: 'Why Scientists Talk' in *Guildhall Lectures 1961*, London (1962), p. 39; excellent examples will be found in such books as R. H. Thouless: *Straight and Crooked Thinking*; S. Stebbing: *Thinking to Some Purpose.*

All men are mortal (*major* premise) = A is B
Smith is a man (*minor* premise) = C is A
Therefore, Smith is mortal C is B

There are various ways in which the syllogism may be falsely stated, *e.g.*

All Italians speak Italian = A is B
I speak Italian = C is B
Therefore, I am an Italian C is A

(ii) *Argument from Analogy* is often heard in discussion, and seen in its cruder form in advertisements. By *analogy* is meant similarity of function or relationship; it has been a very important tool in the advance of science, a fruitful guide to the formation of hypotheses and suggesting lines of research, *e.g.* the wave-theory of sound, the theory of natural selection. By itself, however, analogy establishes nothing, in spite of the so-called "proof by analogy", which runs as follows: Suppose a phenomenon (or class of phenomena) P is observed to resemble some other phenomenon (or class) Z in respect of a certain feature F; from this similarity it is concluded that P also resembles Z in respect of some *other* feature, G, which Z is known to possess but has not yet been observed in P. This conclusion would only be justified if it can be shown that, directly or indirectly, F and G are connected by some law, and this connection can only be shown by inductive methods.

(iii) *Begging the Question* or *Arguing in a Circle* is another common fallacy. If we say that chopping wood makes a person tired because it induces fatigue, we have made no headway at all, for we are still in the position of wanting to know why chopping wood makes a person tired or fatigued.

(iv) *The Fallacy of the False Cause* ('*post hoc ergo propter hoc*'). If one event immediately precedes another there is no proof that the former was the cause of the latter.

(v) *Misuse of Statistics.* It is always necessary critically to examine averages and percentages given as 'proof'. Values may be widely dispersed, grouped round the lowest and highest, and the average does not give any indication as to the degree of dispersion.

This is not a textbook on logic; it is merely being suggested that members of a discussion group pay attention to the *nature of the evidence* they adduce, and the *form* of their arguments. The habit of sound reasoning can best be developed by examining, in the light of logical principles, particular beliefs and particular examples of reasoning, both sound and unsound. Every true belief implies the *falsity* of *some other* belief, and the formulation of the *contradictory* of a proposition will often lead to the discovery of a fallacy. Arguments should also be examined and dissected in order to try to make clear what is being asserted in each of its propositions. The procedure in argument and thinking should be:

(i) To *withhold our judgment* if we are not sure what precisely is being maintained, or what exactly is required to prove it.

(ii) To be willing to consider arguments and beliefs *on their own merits*, with a view only to their rational justification or rejection.

(iii) To acquaint ourselves by a study of logic with the conditions necessary for an argument to be *valid* and with the *methods for procuring evidence* in support of beliefs, the truth of which is under examination.

§ 9. A Note on Induction and Generalisation

The simplest form of *inductive procedure* consists of four well-defined stages:

(i) OBSERVATION of a number of facts that are summed up in an EMPIRICAL GENERALISATION.

(ii) FORMATION OF A HYPOTHESIS. Suggested by the generalisation considered in relation to the knowledge already attained;

(iii) DEDUCTION. The investigator *infers* the consequences which follow from the hypothesis when entertained as true;

(iv) ANALYSIS OF THE OBSERVABLE FACTS relevant to the deduced consequences with the object of trying to establish the truth or falsity of the deduction, and hence of the hypothesis itself. When a hypothesis can be confirmed by phenomena that are susceptible of *quantitative measurement* it is generally possible to re-formulate its original statement more exactly. It must be emphasised that a general risk incurred in the first stage of inductive inquiry is that of 'finding' what we *expect to find*, or what we think might be useful in upholding our preconceptions. Empirical generalisations are based upon personal observation and the testimony of others; the next step is that of forming a *provisional explanation* or *plausible generalisation*. Every generalisation was formerly an hypothesis; the next step is confirmation or rejection by appeal to *observable fact*, and no scientist will seriously entertain an hypothesis unless its character is such that it can be *tested*, either directly or indirectly, *by observation*. Although a hypothesis may sometimes be formulated on the basis of a simple enumeration of observed resemblances, the latter can never *verify* the hypothesis. If the probability of the hypothesis is initially low, it may be slightly increased by argument from analogy, but the most important task is to bring in empirical evidence in a form suitable to demonstrate the truth of the hypothesis with a fairly high degree of probability.

§ 10. What is a Theory?

One frequently hears in discussions, "It's all right in theory, but . . .", which shows that many students do not understand what a theory is. ("There is nothing so practical as a good theory", say the scientists). A theory is an attempt to explain how a group of separate facts are related to one another; a theory is a *unifying concept*, providing a *single* scheme of interpretation for a whole group of *apparently disconnected facts*. The importance of a scientific theory lies in the attempt to fit many facts into one single, meaningful picture, and the provision of workable concepts. When a theory has been subjected to experimental test over a long period of time, it is elevated into a scientific *law* or *principle*.

What is needed in management studies is more and more realistic case studies, so that good theories can be based upon them. An example is Guest's study of works management, a "study of change in a complex human group".[19] What is lacking in this new

19 Robert H. Guest: *Organisational Change. The Effect of Successful Leadership*, London (1962).

area of scientific inquiry, says Guest, is "a comprehensive framework within which to operate". He deplores the fact that management investigators still have "no unifying concept around which to make further refinements and discoveries", and that there is not sufficient empirical material and real life studies of organisations. The subject of Guest's study is, briefly: one factory in a group has such a poor record of performance that a new manager is appointed. As a result, there are changes throughout the factory in "inter-personal relationships, feelings and perceptions", and in three years this factory goes from bottom to top position in most indices of performance (p. 103). In this study, Guest did not oversimplify the situation by assuming that certain matters were constant, but examined such matters as the factory's organisation and its supervisory personnel, before deciding that they had nothing to do with the change, which was due to the new manager's style of "permissive leadership".

An excellent English example of such an empirical study has recently been made in England by T. Lupton;[20] it deals with factors affecting the behaviour of industrial workers, and provides a detailed analysis of the influence of technological, administrative and social factors on the level of output of two groups of workers, in an electrical engineering workshop and a garments assembly workshop. Behaviour in these workshops is studied by means of a simple conceptual framework based largely on social anthropology, and the author works out a *general* method for explaining and predicting industrial behaviour. The student is advised to look at these two books as good examples of recent 'field' work.

§ 11. The Study of Politics and the Study of Management

Politicians, like managers, must possess certain *specific skills* if they are to succeed, including those of decision, explanation, negotiation, public relations and opposition—skills which come mainly from natural aptitude and from experience, not from books. Managers also, like politicians, need *flair*—"the ability to see situations whilst immersed in them, and to grasp opportunities whilst they occur".[21] Professor J. B. D. Miller has discussed the different answers that have been given to the question 'Why

[20] T. Lupton: *On the Shop Floor*, London (1963).

[21] See J. B. D. Miller: *The Nature of Politics*, London (1962), chapt. XIV, 'The Business of Study'.

should we study politics?' which are also of relevance and interest to the student of management. He eventually decides that "the way to study politics is to discover what is actually the case, to penetrate falsehoods and to seek for generalities and causes whenever they can be found . . . only the broadest generalities will be possible; and even these will be approximate". But the combination of *sound generality* and *detailed knowledge of particular systems* will provide a far better basis for understanding than no study at all. It is admitted that there are great difficulties in political study, but that "these can be tackled with some hope of success, so long as the student does not expect miracles and is not led into the trap of claiming to be able to perform them".[22]

ADDITIONAL READING ASSIGNMENTS

1. E. F. L. Brech: 'Introduction', Management in Principle' in *The Principles and Practice of Management*, Second Edition, London, 1963.
2. George R. Copeman: *The Laws of Business Management*, London (1962).
3. E. F. L. Brech: 'The Profession of Management'. chapter VIII of Part v of *The Principles and Practice of Management.*
4. Peter F. Drucker: *The Practice of Management*, chapters 27, 28, 29 and 'Conclusion'.
5. R. H. Guest: *Organisational Change: The Effect of Successful Leadership* (1962).
6. T. Lupton: *On the Shop Floor* (1963).
7. Case Studies (obtainable from the Institution of Works Managers).
8. *How to Lead Case Studies* (B.I.M., 1963).
9. H. A. Simon: *Administrative Behaviour*, Appendix, 'What is an Administrative Science?'.
10. W. Puckey: *Management Principles*, London (1962), chapt. I, 'Science or Art'.
11. Sir F. Hooper: *Management Survey*, Penguin Books (1960), chapts. 2 and 3.
12. H. B. Maynard (Ed.): *Top Management Handbook* (1960), chapter 4, 'The Art of Managing', by Robert C. Hood.
13. J. D. B. Miller: *The Nature of Politics*, London (1962), chapter XIV, 'The Business of Study'.
14. D. E. Butler: *The Study of Political Behaviour*, London (2nd edit., 1959), chapters I–VI.
15. Lionel Robbins: *An Essay on the Nature and Significance of Economic Science*, chapter V, 'Economic Generalisations and Reality'.

[22] *ibid.*, p. 273 (my italics).

TOPICS FOR DISCUSSIONS/ESSAYS

1. Are there any 'principles' or 'fundamentals' of management? Clearly explain the sense in which you are using the words.
2. "Surely management is largely a question of decision-making" (R. Falk).
3. A manager "does not 'handle' people; he motivates, guides, organises, people to do their own work. His tool—his only tool to do all this—is the spoken or written word or the language of numbers" (P. Drucker).
4. Strictly speaking, business acumen or entrepreneurial flair "is not a management skill at all" (Brech).
5. On what "essential minimum human qualities" is success in management founded?
6. Write a reasoned analysis of any case which has interested you.

PART TWO

OUTLINE OF THE DEVELOPMENT OF INDUSTRY AND MANAGEMENT

CHAPTER THREE

THE DEVELOPMENT OF INDUSTRY AND MANAGEMENT—(I)

§ 1. The Meaning of Industrial Evolution

It was John Stuart Mill who drew attention to industrial history simply as a record of devising skill, "the unlimited growth of man's power over nature", an increasing physical knowledge which is "converted by practical ingenuity into physical power".[1] Machines, new working processes and better organisational devices are part of the history of human skill which can be studied simply as part of the records of human achievement. Such a study would, however, mask the real problem of industrial evolution which is the growing pressure of material requirements. There are two opposed forces in history, the growing pressure of population and the lessening fertility of land, and all invention and organisation can be viewed as attempts to overcome this fundamental opposition and to achieve a balance. Hence, "the root idea of the evolution of industry is invention. . . ."[2]

§ 2. The Development of Management

Organisation and management are co-extensive with human history; even in primitive hunting-tribes there was some organisation and control of the tribal unit, some division of labour. The problem of controlling men, materials and machines obviously arose in the earliest civilisations. Think, for example, of the detailed planning, organisation and control which must have been necessary for the construction of the stone pyramids of Egypt. Remember, also, that the horse was unknown in ancient Egypt, and 100,000 men are said to have worked for 20 years on the Great Pyramid; the most advanced tools were copper saws and copper tubular drills.[3]

There is even written evidence relating to the problems of management and organisation going back to early times. Thus, the Egyptian papyri (going back to 1300 B.C.) indicate the importance of organisation and administration. In China, the

[1] Quoted D. H. Macgregor: *The Evolution of Industry*, chapter 1.
[2] *ibid.*
[3] See I. E. S. Edwards: *The Pyramids of Egypt*; S. Clarke and R. Engelbach: *Ancient Egyptian Masonry* (1930).

parables of Confucius (551–479 B.C.) contain practical suggestions for public administration. In ancient Greece Socrates (469–399 B.C.) defined 'management' as a skill separate from technical knowledge, a remarkably modern attitude. In Rome the magistrates had 'functional areas' of authority; it was through the use of the *scalar principle* (Latin *scala*='ladder') and *delegation of authority* that Rome became an imperial power with a degree of organisational efficiency hitherto unknown. Again, the efficient formal organisation of the Roman Catholic Church was based upon the development of a *hierarchy of authority*, *functional specialisation* and an early use of the *staff device*. It must be emphasised that most early civilisations were based upon slavery, even the so-called Greek democracy. In Britain the position of coal-miners and salt-miners up to the beginning of the 19th century was not far removed from slavery.[4] The organisation of the American cotton plantations up to 1885 was based upon slavery.

§ 3. Middle Ages

These can conveniently be studied with reference to the example of England.

Feudalism was based upon land-tenure by a *contract of service* to an overlord. In England it corresponded to the manorial 'system' (11th–15th centuries). Feudalism slowly died out after the Black Death, and with the *commutation* of labour dues *villeinage* disappeared. The 16th century saw the virtual extinction of villeinage, apart from a few freakish attempts at its enforcement. The relation of the peasants to the lord of the manor was that of *serfs*, *i.e.* they were 'bound to the soil' and had no legal right to leave their holdings. The Norman maxim was 'no land without a lord' (*nulle terre sans seigneur*). The manor was managed by officials: the *seneschal*, the chief official, sometimes overlooking several manors; a *steward* for each manor; and a *bailiff* or foreman, who controlled the organisation of the agricultural work. Serfdom may be regarded as occupying an intermediate position between slavery and freedom.[5]

[4] See Taylor's essay on 'The Sub-Contract System in the British Coal Industry' in *Studies in the Industrial Revolution* (ed. Pressnell).

[5] For further details see J. S. Dugdale: *Economic and Social History*, London (1963).

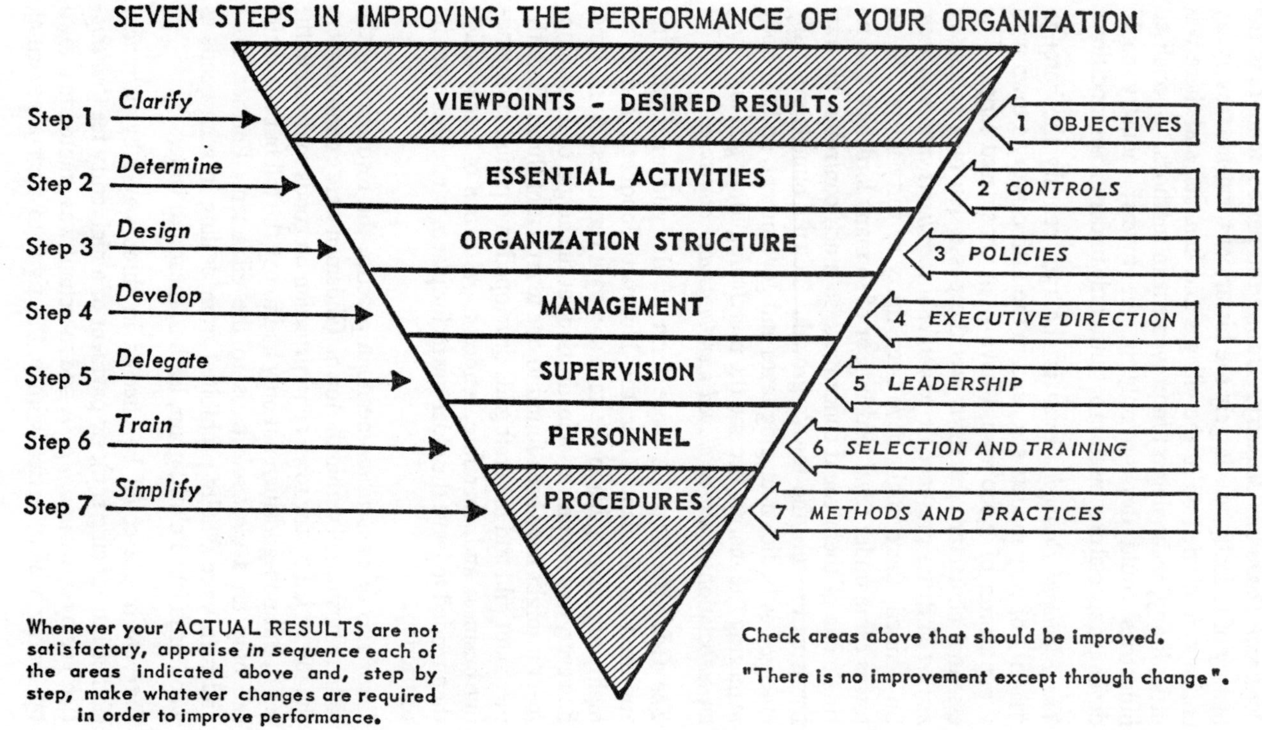
SEVEN STEPS IN IMPROVING THE PERFORMANCE OF YOUR ORGANIZATION
Step 1 Clarify
Step 2 Determine
Step 3 Design
Step 4 Develop
Step 5 Delegate
Step 6 Train
Step 7 Simplify
VIEWPOINTS - DESIRED RESULTS
ESSENTIAL ACTIVITIES
ORGANIZATION STRUCTURE
MANAGEMENT
SUPERVISION
PERSONNEL
PROCEDURES
1 OBJECTIVES
2 CONTROLS
3 POLICIES
4 EXECUTIVE DIRECTION
5 LEADERSHIP
6 SELECTION AND TRAINING
7 METHODS AND PRACTICES
Whenever your ACTUAL RESULTS are not satisfactory, appraise in sequence each of the areas indicated above and, step by step, make whatever changes are required in order to improve performance.
Check areas above that should be improved.
"There is no improvement except through change".

Medieval Towns and Industry. During the period 1066–1485 the history of industry was largely the history of town-life. Everyday crafts were carried on in the villages and hamlets, and there was little, if any, technological improvement in methods. Specialised industries could develop only in the towns; industry could develop a special organisation or status only under urban conditions.

The Medieval Borough. Even in the 13th century the borough was still of very modest size, and in the 11th century a town with a population of 2,000 would have been considered large. The essential character of a town was the possession of a *permanent market* and the presence of *professional merchants and craftsmen*. So defined, there might have been thirty or forty towns. Some towns came under royal lordship, or of so many lordships that no single one of them could concentrate so much control in his own hands as to stifle the town's growth. Town Councils gradually emerged as bodies managing taxes and government, and the body managing the market became the merchant gild, or *gild merchant*, an association of *self-employed merchants and craftsmen*.

The Gild Merchant. A loose form of the gild merchant first appeared in England after the Norman Conquest, and more highly organised gilds in the 12th and 13th centuries. At no time, however, was it a universal institution: at the height of its development it might have been found in one town out of three. Both the merchant gild and the craft gilds developed in a period of expanding business and, therefore, tended to *restriction* of trade, which then tended to leave the older towns for places where there was no restriction.

Restriction of competition meant in practice the restriction of the right to buy or sell within the town. Gildsmen were exempted from the toll levied by the town administration on goods sold within the town, but non-gildsmen not only had to pay the toll but also could sell only on a *wholesale* basis to the gildsmen. Further, non-gildsmen were wholly prohibited from dealing in such goods as wool, unfinished cloth, grain, leather, meat and wine.

Entry to a gild could be effected in three ways: by *patrimony* (father introducing son), by payment of a high entry fee ('*redemption*') or by *apprenticeship*. A gild merchant was granted to a town by *charter* which carried with it the right to elect a governing body for the town. Entry fees were used partially to provide rudimentary social services, such as the maintenance of hospitals and almshouses. A gild was, roughly speaking, a corporation in its economic aspects, but the corporation and the gild did not always coincide: it was possible for a man to be a *burgess*, and not a gildsman, and the converse. In general, however, the gild and the borough were run by the same people.

The *economic functions* of the gild merchant were:

(i) the *regulation* of the borough trades;

(ii) the reservation of this trade for its *own members*;

(iii) the right of *lot*, *i.e.* a gildsman who made an advantageous purchase of goods had to share the bargain with fellow-gildsmen;

(iv) the promulgation of '*assizes*' with regard to *prices, weights, measures* and *qualities*;

(v) the establishing and enforcing of the 'just price', *i.e.* a fair price based mainly on the cost of production of an article;

(vi) the forbidding of such practices as *regrating* (buying goods in order to re-sell them in the same market at a higher price), *fore-stalling* (purchasing goods on their way to the market or before the market had opened in order to get them at preferential prices), and *engrossing* (buying up the whole or a large part of a stock in order to form a 'corner' and force up the price;

(vii) *controlling the trade* between its own town and others, and trying to obtain for its members the right to trade *toll-free* whilst levying tolls on strangers who wished to trade within its own jurisdiction;

(viii) the gild itself sometimes made *bulk purchases* and re-sold the goods after making a small profit for itself, to its members;

(ix) the gild helped its members in the *collection of debts*.

Medieval Industries. These were typical crafts catering for the needs of a rural economy, such as wheelwrights, cartwrights, saddlers. At the other end of the scale were luxury crafts, such as goldsmiths and furriers. In addition there were mining and quarrying, building, the manufacture of armaments, and ship-building. Mining and masonry were free crafts, and many miners were self-employed, paying only a 'royalty' to the landlord. The leading medieval industry was the *woollen* industry: woollen cloth was the product of a number of technical processes. The general pattern of *ownership and control* found in the cloth-towns was that of a small, wealthy group of 'clothiers' who controlled the industry and a growing number of cloth-workers—masters or journeymen—who had no share in the management of the industry, nor freedom to change their conditions. In the mid-13th century the industry began to shift from the towns to the countryside because costs were lower and organisation less rigid than in the towns. Another reason for this locational change was the technical improvement known as the *fulling-mill*, which could be set up whenever there was a good water supply.[6] The erection of such a mill called for heavy capital investment and, with the great expansion of the industry in the 15th century, signs of capitalistic organisation appeared. The country clothier bought wool or homespun, put it out to local weavers and fullers, employed his own cloth-finishers and then arranged for the sale of his cloth ('domestic' system or 'putting-out' system[7]). There was a tendency for former historians to give an over-idealised picture of the domestic system. "It has been depicted almost in the light of a golden age where the artisan was his own master, working as he pleased at his loom or bench, and where *no rift* between capital and labour marred as yet the social harmony" (Lipson).

There was, however, little that was idyllic about it. "It suffered from many of the evils of the sweated domestic system of cities, such as London, at the end of the nineteenth century, which was organised in a similar way" (Court). The domestic system continued until after the mid-19th century.

The Origin of Modern Business Methods. The origins and genesis of capitalism go back to 11th century Italy. Already in 1338 there were eighty firms doing a banking and exchange business in Florence (*e.g.* Bardi, Peruzzi). In Germany there were great banking and mining companies, such as the Fuggers. In some Italian states of the 15th century there were organisations similar to the joint-stock companies of later times. The oldest treatise

6 E. M. Carus-Wilson: 'An Industrial Revolution of the 13th Century', *Economic History Review* (1941).

7 For a summary of modern views on the domestic system see D. H. Coleman: *The Domestic System* (Historical Association pamphlet 1960).

on *book-keeping* was published in Italy in 1494, and, with the expansion of trade, Italian methods of book-keeping spread to northern Europe. All the main book-keeping terms, such as *account, debit, credit*, are of Italian origin. The first treatise in English was James Peel's *Art of Italian Merchant Accounts* (published 1569). The development of *double-entry* book-keeping constitutes an important landmark in the history of management; by the end of the 17th century it had become the accepted means of control.[8]

§ 4. The Industrialists of the Eighteenth Century

The 18th century may be regarded as a 'watershed' in history, dividing the era of production in small, scattered units from that of large-scale organisation. The increase in size was due to the steam-engine, power-driven machinery and technical advance, though some industries (iron and steel, shipbuilding, paper-making, non-ferrous metals) had been relatively large in their units since the sixteenth century or earlier. Some 18th century industrialists ran one-man businesses, others favoured associations in partnerships, companies, even cartels.[9] The main method of raising capital was by partnerships, *e.g.* in the iron industry, or by industrialists allying themselves with landed gentry and aristocracy. The beginnings of personnel management are to be seen in the Durham factories of Sir Ambrose Crowley, or the New Lanark factory and model village of Robert Owen.

It was an age of rapid technological advance, and the industrialist had to keep abreast of changing techniques of manufacture; hence, industrialist and inventor were often one and the same man, *e.g.* Hargreaves, Huntsman, Abraham Darby, John Wilkinson. There was a strong connection between industrial management and nonconformity, especially Quakerism. The success of the Quakers "lay in their attitude to their working life. Believing fanatically in the virtues of hard work, honesty and sobriety, as well as in the need for straightforward dealing and plain humanity

[8] The earliest known published treatise was that of Luca Pacioli. Double-entry techniques in the 17th and 18th centuries included balancing of accounts, anticipation of profits and valuation of assets. See Yamey, Edey and Thomson: *Accounting in England and Scotland 1543–1800*, London (1963).

[9] See the excellent study by M. Flinn, 'The Industrialists', in *Silver Renaissance: Essays in Eighteenth Century English History* (1961), pp. 57–80; see also A. Redford, *The Economic History of England 1760–1860*, chapter iv, 'The Industrial Capitalists'.

in their relations with each other and with their workpeople, they avoided excessive risk and combined persistent vigour with cautious enterprise" (Flinn). Captains of industry were becoming commoner in all branches of industry, their success being mainly due to general business capacity, manipulation of capital and labour management. Apart from a few exceptions such as Watt, Boulton and Wedgwood, they were not men of good general intelligence, moral fibre and wide culture; on the contrary, they were mostly ill-educated and coarse and intellectually "in most cases not markedly distinguishable from their foremen, save in their knowledge of business method and their ruthless determination to make money quickly". The industrialists, however, were aware of their common interests and, in the later eighteenth century, numerous agreements and organisations for collective action were formed. In most of the iron trades, employers' organisations were being established, and in 1785 the General Chamber of Manufacturers of Great Britain was formed.

§ 5. The Industrial Revolution[10]

This term was popularised by Arnold Toynbee,[11] who emphasised not so much the *economic* gains of large-scale industrialisation as the *social* dislocations and losses. The same essential approach was adopted by the Hammonds in their books.[12] Other writers, however, emphasised *technical* progress. In 1832 Charles Babbage[13] had written his essay on *The Economy of Machinery and Manufactures*. In 1835 Andrew Ure published his *Philosophy of Manufactures*, a eulogy of the new machines which had enabled man greatly to increase the output of raw materials and finished products. Ure's attitude to the machines of his time was rather naive, but later writers studied in detail the histories and uses of particular machines, and the Newcomen Society produced valuable research papers on the development of the new technical environment associated with coal, iron and steam.

The main feature of the 'Industrial Revolution' was a new relationship between men, materials and resources. As a result

10 The student is referred to Ashton: *The Industrial Revolution*; H. L. Beales: *The Industrial Revolution*; J. D. Chambers: *The Workshop of the World*.

11 In his *Lectures on the Industrial Revolution*, delivered 1881/2, published 1883.

12 e.g. *The Village Labourer* (1911), *The Town Labourer* (1917), *The Rise of Modern Industry* (1927).

13 On Babbage, see Urwick and Brech: *The Making of Scientific Management*, Vol. 1, 'Thirteen Pioneers', pp. 20–27.

of the growth of population in the 18th century there was an increase in demand, and mechanisation was the means whereby this increased demand was met.

What was the relationship between technical invention and business initiative? The inventors by themselves could accomplish little; the effectiveness of inventions and the better use of resources depended upon the businessmen who had to display an unusual combination of qualities. They needed, firstly, the ability to see an opportunity and the drive to exploit it. One should distinguish between businessmen who are genuine *innovators* and those who are content to follow in the steps of the pioneers.

A man like Arkwright was in the first category, and enjoyed 'monopoly profits'. Secondly, businessmen had to pay careful attention to *forecasting* and *planning*. Since there was no local or national capital market, and limited liability did not yet exist, they had to plough back a large portion of their profits to expand their plant and machinery. Hence, the early economists associated capital with what they called 'abstinence', and made the virtues of *thrift* and *self-help* central in their philosophy of business. Thirdly, they had to be able to manage and supervise the daily routine of their enterprises and develop new ways of working into *routines*. Fourthly, they needed a flair for *selling*.[14] Some businessmen were paternalistic in their relations with their employees; others were fiercely competitive, and relied upon strict discipline.

Inventions and businessmen needed improved transport and banking facilities if the new industrial society was to operate efficiently. A word may be said here on banking: in the mid-18th century banking and credit facilities were very restricted but, from the late 18th century onwards, there was a great increase in the number of country banks,[15] the bank partners being recruited from the industrialists themselves, financial intermediaries (*e.g.* attorneys), and remitters of funds between London and the provinces. Between 1825 and 1844 many reforms were introduced, including the authorisation of *joint-stock* banking. In 1844 the Bank Charter attempted to put English banking on a sound basis.

[14] See N. McKendrick: 'Josiah Wedgwood: An Eighteenth-Century Entrepreneur in Salesmanship and Marketing Techniques', *Economic History Review*, Second Series, Vol. XII, No. 3 (April 1960).

[15] L. F. Pressnell: *Country Banking in the Early Industrial Revolution.*

The 'Industrial Revolution' changed the character of work for a large number of employees who had hitherto employed personal skill and craftsmanship in their work. A new group of engineers and mechanics began to replace master craftsmen and individual handcraftsmen. The new industrialists were largely deficient in any sense of *social obligation* or responsibility to their workers. There were a few exceptions, such as the Strutts, who did their best to create communal facilities in the neighbourhood of their factories; Pilkington Brothers, who began to show that the spirit of enterprise was not inimical to a sense of social responsibility; and Boulton and Watt, who introduced a mutual insurance society.[16]

The age of handicrafts gave way to that of mechanical production. The lack of educated managerial control was reflected not only in the social plight and penury of factory employees, but also in the debased character of many of the products. Labour was regarded as a *commodity* and machinery as a cheap method of *mass-production.* Mass-production probably began in the 1840s in the sense of a *standard product* produced in a continuous flow on a large scale. The devices employed, such as the Archimedean screw and the bucket-conveyor were not new: the novelty consisted of the *combination* of a human assembly line, the mechanical transport of the product, and the arrangement of both workers and machines in a *sequence of operations.* (There are examples of mass-production in early times, *e.g.* the sun-dried bricks of ancient Egypt, the pottery of Greece and Rome. The desire for mechanical repetition of forms and patterns is reflected in the architecture of Egypt, Assyria, Greece and Rome).

The discontent of the working classes expressed itself in *machine-breaking* (the 'Luddites', 1811–12), organised *trade unionism* (especially in 1833–5), the growth of *friendly societies*, the *Chartist movement* (1837 to the early 1850s) and in the *Co-operative Movement* (founded in Rochdale, 1844). "Contemporary objections to the new industrial conditions were real and well-grounded, despite the material advantages factories usually offered to individuals in the form of higher wages, and to the nation in the form of greater output. They were not simply manifestations of irrational opposition based on the worker's inability to accept the

[16] See E. Roll: *An Early Experiment in Business Organisation. Being a History of the Firm of Boulton and Watt 1775–1805*, London (1930); see also C. Wilson: 'The Entrepreneur in the Industrial Revolution', *History* (June 1957).

discipline of the clock or the overlooker. The greatest objection to the factory was a perfectly rational one, that the factory worker was under the absolute and uncontrolled power of the capitalist. . . Out of the distinction between the capitalist, sole owner of the new machines, and the worker, entirely dependent on the sale of his labour power, socialism developed as a new political economy. It grew up as a counter doctrine to that of the businessmen, who increasingly demanded 'laisser-faire', the right to manage their own enterprises without any outside intervention on the part of the state" (A. Briggs).

Did effective management have any place in the 'Industrial Revolution'? Certainly the need for effective executive control, as distinct from technical competence, was recognised. In the early phase management, in the sense of control, must have been a very important consideration. Above all, the early managers needed the capacity for mobilising and co-ordinating large quantities of both capital and labour; neither task was easy, but the *recruiting and management of labour* was, perhaps the more difficult. Other problems lay in the field of marketing and salesmanship, since industry was becoming international in scope. As already stated, a few of the early factory masters were 'community builders' as well as organisers of production; they brought their imagination to bear on the human problems of machine industry and showed that they possessed at least rudimentary notions of welfare, *e.g.* Arkwright, the Strutts, the Gregs, Benjamin Gott, Heathcoat, the Ashtons, Ashworths and Whiteheads. In New Lanark Robert Owen initiated radical changes in factory management and, on the assumption that employees were vicious because of their environment, he improved their housing, cleaned up the streets, opened a cost-price shop and established a school. He also advanced the minimum working age to 10¾ years, provided dining facilities and services, and improved the physical environment and layout of factories. Here can be seen the beginnings of personnel administration.

Both the industrial towns and the factories grew rapidly, with little or no forethought or planning. There were many problems of health, hygiene and safety, but gradually Parliament confronted them and worked out an industrial code. Exceptional employers emerged also in the later 19th century, *e.g.* Courtauld's had a day-nursery in 1852, Coleman's started a works-kitchen in 1868, Salt built a model village at Saltaire in the 1850s. Lever's started at Port Sunlight in 1888, the Bournville village and Rowntree's new factory appeared in the 1890s, the Hull Garden Suburb in 1908. Great changes are signalised here in the conception of what was not merely desirable but practicable. Some firms had long been giving sick-pay, but Cadbury's opened a surgery with a doctor in daily attendance, an Ipswich firm had a day-nursery and Adams, the Nottingham lace-makers, introduced rest-pauses. House-journals were started, such as that of the Thames Iron-works (1895), and Lever's (1899).

A new kind of manager emerged, at first called the Social Secretary (after American usage), then Welfare Manager. A start was made on holidays with pay, *e.g.* in 1888 the London Gas Light and Coke Company began a week's holiday with pay for those who had been employed in the carbonising department during the previous year; the South Metropolitan Gas Company also announced double pay for a week's holiday for men with three year's service. Constituted pension schemes came in first for clerks, with the Gas, Light and Coke Company apparently leading the way with a contributory scheme in 1842; the same company also had the first scheme for manual workers in 1870. Siemens Brothers of Woolwich adopted a pension scheme from their German parent in 1872. In 1904 Lever's began a fund to provide widows' pensions and also retirement pensions for men with twenty years' service.

The long hours of the early factory system had been necessitated by the desire to *spread the fixed cost* of expensive equipment over as many units of output as possible; further, in the days when mills had depended upon water-power there was the further motive of crowding as much work as possible into those periods when power was available. The first landmark was the *Ten Hours Act* (1847). In the 1890s several firms went on to the 48-hour week, but most industrial wage-earners remained on a normal working week of over 50 hours until after World War I. The few firms on a 48-hour week constituted a movement known as Industrial Betterment, the importance of which was its demonstration that an industrial town need not be a bad place to live and work.

An important landmark in 19th century history was the development of *limited liability*; British economic prosperity owed much to this principle, which led to the establishment of a well-organised banking system and the development of joint-stock enterprise. Limited liability enabled the small investor to help industrial expansion at a comparatively small risk to himself; firms could determine the scope of their activities without being severely restricted by financial stringency.[17]

§ 6. Science, Industry and the Professions

Science began to develop between the 15th and the 17th centuries, and without this development the 'Industrial Revolution' could not have taken place. It is obvious that science, industry and the professions are inter-dependent, all related to the use and acquisition of knowledge. A few professions, notably the law, the Church, architecture and medicine, have long histories, but at best, before the scientific age, they were rudimentary. The real foundations of professional bodies were not laid until the 18th and early 19th centuries, *e.g.*

The Law Society: formed in 1729, re-formed in 1825, granted a Royal Charter in 1845.

Institute of Nursing: established 1840.

Civil Engineers: first met in 1818, received a Charter in 1828.

Architects: received their Charter in 1837.

In the second half of the 19th century the great growth of engineering technologies led to the formation of new societies which have lasted into our own times, *e.g.* Mechanical Engineers, Electrical Engineers, Sanitary Engineers, Naval Architects, Heating and Ventilating Engineers, Chemists, Surveyors, Accountants, Actuaries. In the 20th century came the Automobile Engineers (1906), Structural Engineers (1908), Aeronautical Engineers (1920).[18]

The development of the professions meant that new elements of control were available to managers, both on the technical and commercial sides; after the mid-century specialists were to become increasingly available. With the growth in size of the industrial unit fundamental management problems began to emerge:

(i) The *owner-manager* found that he could not keep an eye upon everything, and the problem of *delegation* arose.

17 See H. A. Shannon: 'The Coming of General Limited Liability', *Economic History* (1931).

18 For a general survey see A. M. Carr-Saunders: *The Professions.*

(ii) Delegation could not solve everything, because of the limited 'span of management' or span of supervision; hence, sooner or later the device of *departmentation* had to be adopted.

(iii) The third problem related to the question of *what kind of authority* should be allocated to different persons in the organisation. This is the problem of line-and-staff organisation. It seems legitimate to suppose that in the early 19th century line organisation only—and then in a very crude form—existed. *Staff* relationships developed much later and *functional* authority—the power of an individual over specified policies, processes or practices—later still, with the growth of specialised branches of knowledge.

§ 7. Changes in Business Organisation in the Twentieth Century

The legal forms of business have changed: at the beginning of the century the usual type of business organisation was the *unincorporated partnership* or *sole trader*. There were only 29,000 registered companies and most of these were private, *i.e.* did not invite public subscription to their securities. Today, however, industry is largely in the hands of the joint-stock companies of which there are some 331,000, the majority being private companies. Secondly, there has been a growth of giant companies; it is usually said that this has meant a divorce between *ownership* and *control*, or conditions in which shareholders can exert little influence on management, and which managers form a *salaried class*. Yet, in at least one-quarter of the very large companies, with over £3 million capital was, in 1957, controlled directly or indirectly by the large shareholders. Hence, the divorce between ownership and control in very large companies is by no means so common as is often assumed. There are also numerous small firms in which ownership and control are congruent. Nevertheless, the growth in the size of firms and the increased concentration of production have greatly affected the problems of direction and management. New problems of administration have also resulted from the growth of the public sector: the main problem is how to reconcile the claims of *economic efficiency* and *democratic control*. Allen believes that during the past decade there has been a strong tendency in the nationalised industries for the commercial principle to be subordinated to political considerations.[19]

ADDITIONAL READING ASSIGNMENTS

E. Roll: *An Early Experiment in Industrial Organisation: the Firm of Boulton and Watt (1775–1805)* (1930).

T. S. Ashton: *The Industrial Revolution* (1948).

H. L. Beales: *The Industrial Revolution* (new edition with 'New Introductory Essay') (1960).

W. Ashworth: *A Short History of the International Economy*, chapter III, 'Business Management and Organisation'.

J. D. Chambers: *The Workshop of the World* (1960).

M. Flinn: 'The Industrialists' in *Silver Renaissance: Essays in Eighteenth Century English History* (1961).

A. Redford: *The Economic History of England 1760–1860*, esp. chapter IV, 'The Industrial Capitalists'.

C. Wilson: 'The Entrepreneur in the Industrial Revolution in Britain', *History* (June 1957).

L. Urwick: *A Short Survey of Industrial Management*, Occasional Papers, No. 1, B.I.M.

TOPICS FOR ESSAYS/DISCUSSIONS

1. The 'Domestic System'.
2. The Early Industrial Capitalists (see Flinn and Redford).
3. The Importance of Limited Liability.
4. Robert Owen as a pioneer of management.
5. Parliamentary intervention in industry in the 19th century.
6. The Entrepreneur in the Industrial Revolution.

[19] See G. C. Allen: *The Structure of British Industry*, London (1961). See also chapter Fourteen of the present book, 'Problems of Growth and Size'.

CHAPTER FOUR

THE DEVELOPMENT OF INDUSTRY AND MANAGEMENT—(II)

§ 1. Society and Management

It need hardly be stressed that no firm or organisation is an 'island' which exists in isolation from the society in which it has its being. But there are some less tangible social aspects, such as public opinion, attitudes towards nationalisation, competition, consumer protection and private enterprise—important aspects of the environment in which management operates, and which no management can ignore. In the final analysis the commercial success of a business will depend upon its public's image.[1]

Managers are influenced by the environment in which they operate. How they 'treat' their employees and each other, their attitude to their directors and customers, will depend partly on their personal character, but also on what is 'customary' at a given point in history, in the geographical location of their firms and the country they live in. "What managers strive for, and the rules they observe in doing so, will be influenced and often determined by the accepted goal and moves in their society".[2] The thought and behaviour of managers is also influenced by the managers' social and educational background, itself a product of the environment; their professional background will influence company policy.

Social concepts have influenced management throughout history, and the student should consider different stages of economic and social history from this point of view, with special attention to such matters as the stage of economic development, the general attitude to commerce and trade, the relationships between social classes, the strength of trade unionism and the prevalence or otherwise of governmental regulations.

It is not possible to trace a step-by-step development in management concepts, but the whole process seems to have been one of increasing social perception. The President of the American Management Association, Lawrence A. Appley, put it this way:

[1] See S. Hyman's article 'Society and Management' in *The Chartered Secretary* (May 1962).

[2] Rosemary Stewart: *The Reality of Management* (1963), chapter VIII, 'Management and Social Climate'.

SAVAGERY: The other fellow is my enemy and to be destroyed.

SLAVERY: the other fellow is to be conquered and put at my service.

SERVITUDE: The other fellow is to serve me for a consideration and ask no more.

WELFARE: The other fellow should be helped up when down, without too much concern for what gets him down.

PATERNALISM: The other fellow should be cared for, and I will decide to what extent.

PARTICIPATION: The other fellow has something to contribute to my efforts and can help me.

TRUSTEESHIP: That for which I am responsible is not mine. I am developing and administering it for the benefit of others.

STATESMANSHIP: The other fellow is capable of being far more than he is, and it is my responsibility to help him develop to his fullest potential.

The question of the social responsibility of management relates mainly to its attitude to labour. In the past, when much of labour was viewed as a directly variable cost, workers were employed on a short-term contract, and were dismissable as soon as there was insufficient work. The development of collective bargaining meant more security for the worker, for it may take the form of a contract with a longer term of notice, or a dismissal compensation clause. Such 'concessions' may be regarded as gains wrested from a reluctant management by the pressure of full employment. On the other hand, they can be attributed to the growing enlightenment of modern management who are facing their social responsibilities. The truth, presumably, lies somewhere between these two possibilities."[3]

In the period before the rise of modern industry, when craft organisation predominated, labour was regarded simply as something to be used and exploited. The early phase of the Industrial Revolution deprived the craftsman of his craft and destroyed the small measure of liberty and self-reliance he had formerly possessed. A new servitude and misery was inflicted on the worker; it reflected the disdain and distrust of the artisan, a determination to keep him 'in his place', which had been common throughout history. Although the machine had changed, the

[3] Noel Branton: *Introduction to the Theory and Practice of Management*, chapter 11, 'Social Responsibilities of Management'.

basic conditions of human industry, it did not immediately alter this ancient human relationship.

During the craft ages the needs and rights of workers were largely conditioned by external factors, but when industry in the machine age became emancipated from these influences and its problems became internal, the human problem in industry also became internal. "Only one solution is possible, namely the recognition by industry of the common interest of every member of the organisation on the success of the organisation itself."[4] At the end of the craft age, the doctrine of *laisser-faire* appeared; it was interpreted by the new capitalists as giving them full permission to exploit the industrial worker, without interference from the government or society. The *laisser-faire* doctrine worked only in the interest of the employers; the workers could not even legally organise themselves to protect their own interests (*Combination Act,* 1799), and it was not until 1865 that trade unionism was fully legalised in Britain. Employer's liability was utterly unknown, and the workers did not secure adequate protection until the Employer's Liability Act of 1880, and the Workmen's Compensation Act of 1906. Yet, as Mooney and Reiley insisted, in considering all the injustices of the Industrial Revolution and its 'crowning infamy', the industrial slavery of children, it would not be fair to place the blame wholly and exclusively on the manufacturer." Economic theory and public opinion had joined hands to justify profit at whatever human cost; even a philanthropist such as Wilberforce could favour the tyrranical Combination Act, and a philosopher such as John Locke, or leaders such as Pitt and Bentham, could condone child labour.

The main problem of industry in the 19th century was the breakdown of traditional communities and their slow re-grouping into new forms. The gilds had passed away, but in 1815 the trade unions were only in an embryonic state of development. The English people were slowly re-grouping themselves into Disraeli's 'two nations', the rich and the poor. The Factory Act of 1833, following tentative Acts of 1801 and 1819, was the first effective attempt at Government control, and the later Acts (1844, 1847, 1850, 1853, 1856, 1867, 1878, etc.) were concerned with gaining a piecemeal control over different types of factories and workshops.

[4] Mooney and Reilly: *Onward Industry!*, p. 409.

The birth of the trade unions in the 18th century is obscure, but it is interesting to note that early trade unionism was not a proletarian movement arising as a protest against intolerable conditions, nor did it arise among the lowest classes, but where apprenticeship and something of the old gild machinery still remained. There are several fairly clearly distinguishable phases in trade union history:

1799–1824: all 'combinations' were illegal;
1824: Combination Laws were repealed;
1825: an Act expressly permitted trade unions;
1834: the Grand National Consolidated Trade Union (attempt to set up a single all-comprehensive union);
1867: Reform Act, and the enfranchisement of the urban male workers;
1871: beginning of a period of legislation: Criminal Law Amendment Act, 1871; Trade Union Act, 1871; Conspiracy and Protection of Property Act, 1875. These Acts gave the Unions definite legal establishment;
1900: after this date began a period of acute trade union activity and litigation marked by the Taff Vale Case 1901 and the Osborne Judgment 1910;
1913: Trade Union Act which practically reversed the Osborne Judgment;
1926: the General Strike, declared to be illegal;
1927: Trade Union Act and Trade Disputes Act;
1946: Repeal of former.

It was not until after 1890 that the trade unions began to have an effect on the wage structure of industry, especially by their preference for day-rates over piece-rates and their development of conventional practices and written agreements. Employers, politicians and men of law regarded the trade unions with suspicion, but the trade union leaders mistrusted the industrial, political and legal world.

The attitude of management to labour has changed greatly in the past half-century. A safe generalisation seems to be that the authority of management declines with increasing industrialisation and the increase in the standard of living. The growth of government regulations and trade union power have also narrowed the range of managerial authority. As Rosemary Stewart[5] has remarked: "Even the differences in some companies between pre- and post-war are marked. What would be considered normal practice then would be looked on as inhuman today".

Skilful pursuit of social responsibilities has to start at the top, at the level of policy.[6] Personnel techniques are not enough: what is required is "the blending into a contented, co-operative team of many persons and groups of persons". Another important test of social skill in management practice is the leadership of men through *change:* management has to attain change in face of a strong inherent resistance among those individuals through whom alone change can be made effective.

§ 2. Human Relations in Industry: the Historical Perspective[7]

The problem of human relations in industry must be viewed in its historical setting, because industry is not merely an *economic* institution, but consists of *social* units and relationships which affect both the manner of living and the standard of living of workers; further, *attitudes* within industry and the structure of industry itself are greatly influenced by general social characteristics outside the industrial world, *e.g.* the educational system.

The industrial structure of Britain before 1900 was characterised by three main features: the rise of the *factory system*; the development inside industry of organised *industrial relations*; and the rise of *political democracy* which affected the environment in which industry operated.

(i) *The Factory System* was, at the beginning of the 19th century, still a revolutionary system, but it is wrong to suppose that it marked the end of a golden age in human relations, or that the domestic system gave far more worker satisfaction, or that there was no rift between capital and labour. Even so, the rise of the factory system did involve sharp breaks with the past which led to individual frustration and social strain; it called for a *new rhythm of work*, with all the attendant stresses and strains; it also demanded a *new discipline.* The early factory system brought forth

[5] Rosemary Stewart: *The Reality of Management*, p. 139.

[6] E. F. L. Brech (Ed.): *Principles and Practice of Management*, p. 862.

[7] The author expresses his indebtedness to Prof. Asa Briggs for permission to draw on a lecture in this section.

both good and bad bosses, the latter being interested only in how much money they could make or plough back. Hence, in 1833, *factory inspectors* made their first appearance in the industrial scene—a first attempt by the community as a whole to regulate conditions in the new factories. From 1833 onwards a whole code of factory legislation developed, reaching its climax in the great Factory Act of 1901; by then the emphasis was on controlling not the hours of work or conditions of adult male workers, but the conditions of work of women and children. Thus, at the beginning of the 20th century, the state was actively intervening to regulate certain industrial conditions.

(ii) *The Growth of Informal Industrial Relations*, as a consequence of collective agreement. Trade unions first developed in the skilled trades. The Birmingham wire-workers, for instance, wrote in their manifesto: "*The trade by which we live is our property, bought by years of servitude which gives us a vested right, and we have an exclusive claim on it. . . .*". A much more famous union, The Amalgamated Society of Engineers, said: "*We claim the same control over that in which we have a vested interest as the physician who holds his diploma or as the author who is protected by his copyright*". At first, then, the concept of the union was that of a *device* to protect the interests of its members, to enforce their solidarity, and to provide a guarantee that in negotiations and dealings with the employers the interests of the *workers as a whole* would be properly safeguarded. The Acts of 1871 and 1875 gave recognition to the trade unions as bargaining bodies. The 'new model' unions of the mid-19th century had a view of human relations which was one of amity and understanding between labour and capital. The Secretary of the Consolidated Society of Bookbinders wrote: "*The true state of employer and employed is that of amity; each should consider this state their true relation, and consider its interruption as the greatest of calamities*". Pioneers such as Mundella, Dale and Kettle exerted themselves to get simple forms of *joint* consultation working in their factories. The emphasis from the start was on *conciliation*, not arbitration, and by 1900 the tradition of voluntary discussion between trade unionists and employers had established itself as part of the English system of industrial relations. In 1891 the Royal Commission on Labour gave its blessing to this system of voluntary agreement, and the Conciliation Act of 1896 carried the process a little further. The Board of Trade had developed its power in industrial relations in the period 1880–1900; it had the right to interfere in industrial disputes, but only if both participants agreed that they wanted it to interfere.

(iii) *The Rise of Political Democracy.* In 1867, a most important date in British history, the working man in the towns obtained the vote, and it is no coincidence that the Act of 1867 was followed almost automatically by the trade union legislation of 1871 and 1875. Unskilled workers who were not organised in trade unions in the 1860s and 1870s began to look to the State for protection—to legislation instead of bargaining-power. Legislation was needed for the demands for a 'living wage', an eight-hour day for miners, improvements for workers in the 'sweated' trades and trades where the workers had no effective bargaining power. Hence new forces began to be felt at the end of the 19th century: the demand for a separate Labour representation, the demand for labour legislation, for practical action on the Government's part, including nationalisation.

§ 3. The Twentieth Century

It is convenient to focus attention on six main features:

(i) The continual growth of the power and status of the unskilled[8] labourers' unions or composite unions, including both skilled and unskilled workers. World War I gave a great impetus to this movement, and the three great 'giants' emerged: the Transport and General Workers' Union (1921), the National Union of Distributive and Allied Workers (1921), and the National Union of General and Distributive Workers (1924). There was simultaneously a narrowing of the differentials between the wages of the skilled and unskilled; this has created various

[8] For proportions of skilled, semi-skilled and unskilled workers see Georges Friedmann: *The Anatomy of Work,* London (1961), Statistical Appendix, pp. 160–183.

human relations problems in industry, as well as inter-union problems involving questions of status as much as questions of economics. There has also been a tendency to transfer much collective bargaining from the local to the *national* level.[9]

(ii) *The Growth of Trade Unionism in General.* One of the big 'revolutionary' changes of the 20th century is the change from trade unionists as agitators, as they were often regarded in 1900, to industrial statesmen at present. Parallel with this change was the development of *joint consultation* at the highest level between the T.U.C., the employers and the Government, which began after the General Strike and was sanctified by World War II. The T.U.C. itself is a creation of this period, its permanent body or General Council not being founded until 1921. Trade unionism became very important in the conduct of the State and development of the economy, and problems of human relations emerged with the trade union movement *e.g.* the question of the relationship between top trade union officials and the middle ranks of trade unions, or between the leaders and the rank-and-file. These problems have revealed serious flaws in communication.[10]

(iii) *The Growth of Joint Consultation* through bodies like works councils, the short-lived Joint Production Committees during World War II, and works committees of various kinds. Joint consultation has not been a panacea in industrial relations; there has been a tendency to segregate matters which are thought to fall within the ambit of joint consultation and other matters which are thought more

[9] The student interested in the question of the wages of unskilled, semi-skilled and skilled labour will find ample detail in K. G. J. C. Knowles *et al*: 'Difference between the Wages of Skilled and Unskilled Workers, 1880–1950', *Oxford University Institute of Statistics Bulletin* (1951); 'Dockworkers' Earnings', *Oxford University Institute of Statistics Bulletin* (1952); 'The Structure of Engineering Earnings', *Oxford University Institute of Statistics Bulletin* (1954); H. A. Turner: 'Trade Unions, Differentials and the Levelling of Wages', *Manchester School of Economics and Social Studies* (1952); S. H. Slichter, J. J. Healy and E. R. Livernash: *The Impact of Collective Bargaining on Management.*

[10] See E. H. Phelps Brown: *The Growth of British Industrial Relations*; S. and B. Webb: *Industrial Democracy*; A. Flanders and H. Clegg (Eds.): *The System of Industrial Relations in Great Britain*; A. Flanders: *Trade Unions*; E. L. Wigham: *Trade Unions*; T.U.C. Report: *Trade Union Structure and Closer Unity* (1944).

germane to collective bargaining, and the two developments have not been fused.[11]

(iv) *The Development of the Welfare State.* To understand this one must go back to the Liberal Governments of the years 1906–14, and appreciate the pressure of the growing Labour Party in the 20th century. Had there not been two World Wars, the movement towards 'welfare' would have been much slower. Three points must be stressed here: the welfare state has changed the concept of citizenship; it has made for much greater educational mobility; and it has caused bargaining power to tilt in favour of labour.[12] The era of social reform began with the social legislation of Lloyd George (1906–11); then came the National Insurance Act of 1911; in 1915 the Rent Restrictions Act was passed; in 1920 the Unemployment Insurance Act greatly extended the benefits of insurance.

(v) *The Development of a 'Managerial Society'.* One need not subscribe to the theory of the 'managerial revolution' to state that there is much more of the 'managerial society' than in 1900. There are many reasons for this development: the growing size and complexity of industrial production, limited liability, separation of ownership from control and the growing need for specialists, which have changed the context of industrial relations.

(vi) *The Technical Changes of the 20th Century, i.e.* mass production, flow production, the development of automation. Automation is not an easy word to define,[13] but it seems to cover the following: *transfer processing* (linking of fabrication operations, usually performed individually and in sequence, into a continuous process of an automatic character; *automatic assembly*; control engineering (automatic control of self-regulating processes by devices such

11 On joint consultation and collective bargaining see, for example, Sir Charles Renold: *Joint Consultation over Thirty Years* (1951); H. A. Clegg: *A New Approach to Industrial Democracy*; P. S. Florence: *Labour*; P. Ford: *The Economics of Collective Bargaining.*

12 See Hobman: *The Welfare State*; Wickwar: *The Social Services*; Lafitte: 'Social Aims of the Contemporary State' in *A New Outline of Modern Knowledge*, London (1958); a good summary of the beginnings of the Welfare State is given by A. Pollard: *The Development of the British Economy 1914–1950*, London (1962), pp. 34–41.

13 See Lord Halsbury: 'Automation—Verbal Fiction, Psychological Reality', *Impact* (December 1956), distributed through H.M.S.O.

as thermostats, automatic pilots); *communication engineering* (or that part of it relating to data processing, accountancy and mathematical operations conducted with electrical computers, and the linkage of computers to physical or chemical processes). These changes have had important effects upon the worker as worker; they have also changed his position as consumer since he has come to expect mass-production goods turned out in large quantities; his standard of living and level of aspiration have equally changed.

The current dangers, says Lord Halsbury, "lie in the division of society into two hostile sub-groups, a managerial group which is relatively free and a workers' group relatively unfree". There is still an economic class-distinction, but poverty in the old sense of the word has been largely eliminated. "The current issue, barely acknowledged to be so, is more freedom in relation to work". Automation is both a material and a psychological reality, at once a source of wealth and a source of fear.

§ 4. The Development of Personnel Administration

This is "one of the areas of management that is and has been critically important in economic expansion, for it has to do with the most effective utilisation of the manpower available to business units and to governments."[14] Some of the current problems of personnel administration are those of (i) *employment practices* which differ widely in European countries; the use of modern personnel methods may be complicated in many areas by family or political pressures; (ii) *industrial education and training*; (iii) *supervisory training*; this is nothing new, one firm being known to have begun it in 1878; the three major T.W.I. programmes of World War II (Job Instruction, Job Relations and Job Methods) were introduced in Britain by the Ministry of Labour in 1944; the concept of foremanship is being re-examined and the foreman is regarded as a true representative of management;[15] (iv) *internal and external training*; (v) *wage administration*; both in Europe and

[14] See F. T. Malm: 'The Development of Personnel Administration in Western Europe', *Personnel Management* (June 1961); also G. R. Moxon: 'The Growth of Personnel Management in Great Britain during the War', *International Labour Review* (1944).

[15] The autobiography of A. Williams: *Life in a Railway Factory* (1915) seems to show that the foreman, powerful as he was, inhabited a no-man's land, 'belonging' neither to 'management' nor to the workers.

the United States wage levels and wage structures are affected by economic and political influences.

In Britain, where it has reached a high stage of professional development, personnel administration evolved from an essentially 'welfare' origin during World War I. The Institute of of Personnel Management (previously the Institute of Labour Management) was founded in 1913 and incorporated in 1924 as the voluntary association of personnel specialists.

§ 5. The Development of Management Thought

Works dealing with industrial organisation began to appear in the early days of industrialism, *e.g.* Babbage's *On the Economy of Machinery and Manufacture* (1832), Gaskell's *Artisans and Machiners* (1836), Robert Owen's autobiography *Life of Robert Owen by Himself* (1857), as well as interesting commentaries of observers of the new scene, such as Cooke's *Notes of a Tour in the Manufacturing Districts of Lancashire* (1842), Gaskell's 'The Manufacturing Population of England' (1833). Later in the century appeared such works as Smith's *Workshop Management* (?1884), Rae's *Eight Hours Work* (1894), Jones's *Co-operative Production* (1894).

Management theory is, however, largely a product of the 20th century; a handful of writers have exerted such a seminal influence that they have become known as the 'classics' of management. They will be mentioned but briefly here, as they figure in other parts of this book.[16] (See Appendix to this chapter, pp. 64-7.)

§ 6. Essential Conditions for Satisfactory Human Relations in Industry

There seem to be three essential conditions:

(i) The individual must be treated as an end in himself, and not as a means to an end;

(ii) the individual must be provided with the basis of a good life;

(iii) the individual must understand that he cannot realise himself satisfactorily unless he is a member of a community.

[16] For summaries see E. F. L. Brech: *Organisation: the Framework of Management*, Appendix 1, 'An Outline History of Thought on Organisation', pp. 363–96; also Brech (Ed.): *Principles and Practice of Management*, Part I, Appendix 1, 'An Outline History of Management Thought'.

One of the first objectives today must be to create the right attitude to work. As Sir George Schuster[17] pointed out, a major consequence of the 'Industrial Revolution' was the identification of work with factory work, excessive hours and bad conditions—as a thing inherently bad, to be reduced as far as possible. But work should be regarded as the foundation of a man's happiness and satisfaction.

An important current problem for management is how to change the dominant outlook and create the right attitude to work. One barrier is the 'class' barrier, the idea that if a wage-earner works hard he is working essentially to swell the profits of a different class, that of the shareholders. Another influence affecting the attitude to work is the possibility of conflicting loyalties. Elton Mayo[18] stressed the need for 'Group Co-operation', but for this to be satisfactory each group must have its links with other groups and all together must blend in a single unit of industrial enterprise. "If that works well, the individual can feel a loyalty to his firm based upon his feeling that he is a partner in its enterprise, and he can get the satisfaction of comradeship in that way". The question of trade unions arises here, but it does not seem that the two loyalties are incompatible. Michael Shanks[19] has emphasised the sense of inequality which still exists among British workers, the antithesis of 'We' and 'They', which is one of the main deterrents to a dynamic and efficient industrial system. It is not merely a question of inequality of income: more important is inequality in *status*, *power* and *opportunity*, which perpetuates the old class antagonisms and the perennial suspicion of the managers. "It prevents the worker from feeling any responsibility for the workings of his industry—even if that industry is a nationalised one—and of any desire to co-operate in making it more efficient. It nourishes old grievances, and makes the worker ready to down tools and come out on strike when an occasion requires. It limits the worker's horizons to the standards of his own community and class, and acts as a main bulwark to the social barrier which lies behind so many of our current difficulties."

Several writers have suggested that the problem is not merely one between 'management' and 'workers', but also between

[17] Sir George Schuster: 'Human Relations and Production', in *Question*, Vol. 3, No. 2 (Spring 1951).

[18] Elton Mayo: *The Social Problems of an Industrial Civilisation.*

[19] M. Shanks: *The Stagnant Society*, p. 155.

'manual' and 'black-coated' workers. Snobbishness and class-distinctions permeate every organisation and exert a considerable influence on people's attitudes. There has been a carry-over from the early period of industrialisation, with its rigid distinction between 'master' and 'men', and the intermediate class of 'black-coated' or 'white-collar' workers has a vested interest in keeping the distinction alive. It would not be difficult, thinks Shanks, to extend most of the privileges now enjoyed by white-collar workers to industrial workers, thus destroying the system of industrial discrimination. How can this be done? Partly by national legislation, partly by management and the trade unions ensuring better amenities for the workers, through financial 'fringe benefits'[20] profit sharing, company functions, social and sports clubs. Yet the latter cannot be an effective substitute for sound management practice and personnel policies, and on their own will never ensure industrial peace.[21] 'Extravagant paternalism' will not create a better atmosphere between management and men; a basis of democracy rather than paternalism, is required. Workers' representatives must be consulted as much as possible "if only to get them to feel a greater sense of involvement in the affairs of the firm, and a greater sense of responsibility for its success. There is no greater morale-booster for a worker than the feeling that he, too, is consulted on policy questions and plays his part in influencing managerial decisions" (Shanks). But the ultimate control over policy must remain in management's hands, since decision-making is often a highly technical matter.

§ 7. Management and Incentives

Co-operation between management and workers is essential if efficiency and the standard of living are to be increased. The first step towards co-operation is to make sure that men on the production line understand that a firm must be progressive if it is to survive—it must make a better product at a lower price. In the final analysis it is perhaps true that self-respect and the respect of others are more important than financial incentives. In the period

[20] For a thorough discussion of fringe-benefits see A. Rubner: *Fringe Benefits* (London, 1963).

[21] K. Roberts: 'Workers' Fringe Benefits', *Business* (April 1963) (examines three companies); see also R. O. Clarke: 'The Social Aspects of Industrial Employment', chapter 6 of *Industrial Relations, Contemporary Problems and Perspectives* (ed. B. C. Roberts). On profit-sharing see R. Stewart: *The Reality of Management*, pp. 96–99.

since F. W. Taylor's first experiments in time study there have been great social, economic and technical changes in industry, and links can be established between these changes (*e.g.* depressions) and changes in incentive payment. It was not until after World War I that *non-financial* factors were systematically investigated, and studies were carried out showing the importance for morale and productivity of good relations in the factory. The results of research indicated that good relations, together with good working conditions and security, were often more important than high wages.[22]

It seems that a mixture of financial and non-financial incentives and deterrents operates constantly and at all levels in industry, the proportions varying according to external economic and social conditions. Wilfred Brown,[23] chairman of Glacier Metal Co. Ltd., believes that payment of workers according to their *all-round worth* as judged by their 'superiors' is both fairer and more dignified and more likely to bring out the best in both managers and managed.

APPENDIX TO CHAPTER FOUR

Three Pioneers of Management Thought

(i) F. W. TAYLOR (1856–1917)[24] began his experiments at the Midvale Steel Company in the early 1880s. He had passed the entrance examination to Harvard but in 1874 decided to become a pattern-maker and machinist in the shop of a small Philadelphia pump manufacturer. In 1878 he went to work at the Midvale company where, in six years, he rose from gang-boss to foreman of the machine shop, then to master mechanic, chief draughtsman and finally to chief engineer. In 1898 he was hired by the Bethlehem Steel Company where he carried out a series of experiments for finding the best method of handling pig iron, an account of which he gave in his book, *The Principles of Scientific Management*. He also conducted experiments in shovelling and metal-cutting, and developed a differential piecework plan based upon

22 See James F. Lincoln's account of the Lincoln Electric Company in *The Manager* (July 1954).

23 Wilfred Brown: *Piecework Abandoned*, London (1963).

24 F. W. Taylor: 'Shop Management', *Transactions of the American Society of Mechanical Engineers*, Vol. 24 (June 1903); 'On the Art of Cutting Metals', *Transactions of the American Society of Mechanical Engineers*, Vol. 28 (1907); *The Principles of Scientific Management* (New York, 1915). His biography is by F. B. Copley: *Frederick W. Taylor: Father of Scientific Management*, New York (1923).

standards developed through *time-study*. Other names important in the development of 'Scientific Management' were Henry L. Gantt[25] and Frank Gilbreth and his wife Lillian. Cooke[26] was particularly concerned with adapting the principles of scientific management to the problems of University and municipal administration.

Taylor believed that 'the Art of Management' rested upon four principles: a '*large daily task*' (*i.e.* an amount of work laid down by management after a detailed investigation); '*work done under standard conditions*' (*i.e.* freedom of the worker to get on with his job without having to obtain his material or parts, or to waste time by transporting the finished work); *high rates of pay*, based upon *objective selection* of the worker; *punishment of the worker*—loss of income—if he failed to reach the target set.

Taylor also referred to 'four great principles of management'—the development of a *true science* (of the job), the *scientific selection of the workers*, the *scientific education and development* of the workers, and *friendly co-operation* between management and labour. He regarded science as the *recording and objective measurement of facts relating to the worker and his job*, his main interest being in scientific study of work. He was thus a pioneer of work study.

On the organisational side he opposed the traditional system of military organisation, and wished it to be replaced by *functional management*,[27] a term almost synonymous with specialisation—"so dividing the work that each man from the assistant superintendent downwards should have as few functions as possible to perform". The typical workshop foreman had far too many functions and workers should be supervised by four people concerned with 'mental' work (route clerk, instruction card clerk, cost clerk, time clerk) and four concerned with 'manual' tasks (gang boss, speed boss, repair boss and disciplinarian).

Taylor was the first to formulate the '*exception principle*' in management. The manager should receive only condensed, summarised and invariably comparative reports which covered all management elements; he should have pointed out to him

[25] H. L. Gantt: *Field System*, New York (1908). Biography by L. P. Alford: *Henry Lawrence Gantt*, American Society of Mechanical Engineers (1934); see also A. W. Rathe: *Gantt on Management*, London (1962).

[26] M. L. Cooke: *Academic and Industrial Efficiency*, New York (1910).

[27] For a discussion of this term see Brech: *Organisation: the Framework of Management*.

exceptions to past averages or standards, both the *especially good* and *especially bad* exceptions, "thus giving him in a few minutes a full view of progress which is being made or the reverse, and leaving him free to consider the *broader lines of policy* and to *study the character, and fitness* of the *important men* under him".

(ii) MARY PARKER FOLLETT (1868–1933)[28] was concerned more with the study of the universality of organisational principles and human relationships than with administrative techniques or business policies. She was a great believer in the all-embracing principles of *co-ordination* and *integration.* Her dominant attitude was that business was a great institution, and the sociological system of individual co-operation was of great importance for management. She was born of a good Boston family, and graduated at Radcliffe College; she spent six years as a university student, including one at Cambridge (England). Thereafter she devoted thirty years to voluntary social work. She met many people, and had "a genius for friendship, for human contact . . . a combination of sympathy and detachment, a meeting of the intensely individual and the universal. . . . A profoundly philosophical and scientific mind, she enlisted countless other minds, which were neither, as willing, warm and enthusiastic collaborators."[29]

The essence of Mary Follett's contribution was the great emphasis she gave to the four 'principles of co-ordination':

(i) Co-ordination by *direct contact* of the people concerned;
(ii) Co-ordination in the *early* stages;
(iii) Co-ordination as the *reciprocal relating* of *all factors in a situation*;
(iv) Co-ordination as a *continuing process.*

In addition to this central philosophy of co-ordination, Mary Follett was mainly interested in such psychological and sociological issues as *conflict, consent engineering, power, control* and *authority.*

Conflict. She suggested three main ways of dealing with conflict: by *domination, compromise* and *integration.* The social problems

[28] See H. C. Metcalf and L. Urwick (Eds.): *Dynamic Administration. The Collected Papers of Mary Parker Follett,* London (1941); also L. Urwick (Ed.): *Freedom and Co-ordination. Lectures in Business Organisation* by Mary Parker Follett, London (1949), a later arrangement of lectures on business administration including her last published work.

[29] A useful analysis of Miss Follett's thought is N. K. Sethi's article, 'Mary Parker Follett: Pioneer in Management Theory', *Journal of the Academy of Management,* Vol. 5, No. 3 (Dec. 1962).

arising from conflict are disharmony in the organisation, ill-defined communication, disintegration of the flow of information.

Consent. The phrase 'consent engineering' occurs frequently in her writings. She distinguishes between consent as an *inactive* attitude, and *participation* which is "relating the parts so that you have a working unit".

Power. She regarded power as "simply the ability to make things happen, to be causal agent, to initiate change", and distinguishes between *power* and *strength*: power as a functional concept is not relative to or dependent on one's strong points or position.

Control and Authority. She rejects the notion of a *supreme control* or final authority and pins her faith in *functional* authority where each individual has "final authority for his own allotted task". Hence she suggested that the phrase *delegation of authority* should cease to be used: she wanted a functional breakdown of authority whereby each person doing a particular task would have full authority over each phase of it.

Leadership. She defined a leader as "the man who can show that the order is integral to the situation". She emphasised the *law of the situation*, making leadership a functional concept and not an authoritative dogma. She distinguished clearly between the *leadership of function*, the *leadership of personality*, and the *leadership of position*, and also drew attention to 'multiple leadership' or the role of lesser leaders. The idea of the 'common purpose' is integral to her conception of leadership.

(iii) HENRI FAYOL (1841–1925) received a good technical education and qualified as a mining engineer. At an early age he joined the French Comambault organisation, where he stayed until his retirment in 1918, having been managing director for thirty years. His famous book, *General and Industrial Management*, appeared in French in 1916, and an English translation in 1929.

Fayol began with an attempt to define management and to decide what personal qualities a manager needs for success. He divided all business activities into six categories: *technical, commercial, financial, security* (protection of persons and property), *accounting* and *managerial.* His particular concern was with the last-mentioned. He wrote: "To manage is to *forecast* and *plan*, to *organise*, to *command*, to *co-ordinate* and to *control*".

(*a*) Foreseeing and providing (*prévoyance*) meant "examining the future and drawing up the plan of action".

(*b*) Organising meant "building up the dual structure, material and human, of the undertaking".

(*c*) Commanding[30] meant "maintaining activity among the personnel".

(*d*) Co-ordinating meant "binding together, unifying and harmonising all activity and effort".

(*e*) Controlling meant "seeing that everything occurs in conformity with established rule and expressed command".

The most important personal qualities and kinds of knowledge are discussed under the headings *physical, mental, moral, general education, special knowledge* and *experience*.

Fayol was one of the first practising managers to try to draw up a list of 'principles' of management.[31] Three of these 'principles' are very important from the point of view of delegation and co-ordination. The 'scalar chain' is the chain of superiors from the top to the bottom of an enterprise, and constitutes the proper channels through which orders and requests should travel. Since this may be a lengthy line of communication, Fayol suggested that if two people equal in status, but on two different 'chains', wish to communicate directly (*i.e.* instead of going up one side of a triangle and down the other) they should be allowed to do so, provided that each has obtained general permission from his superior and that the latter is kept 'in the picture'. Fayol also stressed the principle of *unity of command*: "for any action whatsoever, an employee should receive orders from one superior only"; and *unity of direction*, the pre-condition of unified effort and co-ordination "one head and one plan for a group of activities having the same objective".

Fayol made the very important point, one that has been reiterated by many modern writers on management, that technical

[30] Prof. R. W. Revans has suggested that today we should use the word *inspire*, in spite of its rather sanctimonious overtones.

[31] There was a quarrel about the translation of Fayol's French word *administration* as 'management', which nearly led to a court case. (See Brech (Ed.): *Principles and Practice of Management*, 2nd ed. (1963), p. 23). It may be noted here that in modern French writings 'management' is *administration des enterprises*, or *direction des enterprises*, and 'management sciences' is *sciences de gestion.*

knowledge alone is insufficient for a person in a managerial position. Some would go even further today and say that a person in any position of *general* (not *line*) management should forget any expertise he may possess, since he has subordinate experts to advise him.[32]

The title of Fayol's book is *General* and *Industrial Administration*; his thesis was that his principles were of *universal* application, that they were not restricted to the industrial context.[33] He was at pains to point out that they apply in his view, equally well to political, religious, philanthropic and other human undertakings. (On Fayol see also pp. 141-2, 149, 150, 176.)

NOTE

It has not been possible in the space available to indicate more than a few of the more important aspects of economic and social history. Students are advised to look up particular points in the books indicated. Useful introductions (all published by James Brodie Ltd., Brodie House, Queen Square, Bath, Somerset) are:

J. S. Dugdale: *English Economic History.*

Collins: *English Social Conditions in the Second Half of the 18th Century.*

Reeder: *The Age of the Chartists.*

Dugdale and Reeder: *English Social Conditions in the Second Half of the 19th Century.*

See also:

J. S. Dugdale: *Economic and Social History* (English Universities Press, 1962).

ADDITIONAL READING ASSIGNMENTS

1. E. F. L. Brech (Ed.): *The Principles and Practice of Management*, Part V, chapter II, 'Social Skills and Responsibilities'.
2. Noel Branton: *Introduction to the Theory and Practice of Management*, chapter 11, 'Social Responsibilities of Management'.
3. Rosemary Stewart: *The Reality of Management*, chapter VIII, 'Management and Social Climate'.

32 The Right Hon. the Viscount Chandos chose the subject 'General Management in a Specialist's World', reproduced in *The Manager* (Dec. 1963) for the Ninth Elbourne Memorial Lecture (1963).

33 See Fayol's paper on 'The Administrative Theory of the State', in *Papers on the Science of Administration*, New York (1937); for some modern developments and views see R. N. McKean: *Efficiency in Government through Systems Analysis*; and G. Prys Williams: *The Limits of Business Administration and Responsibility* (1963). The last mentioned author compares authority and power in a business organisation with their parallel forms in civil and military government.

4. James D. Mooney and Alan C. Reiley: *Onward Industry!* chapters 25–30.
5. E. F. L. Brech (Ed.): *Principles and Practice of Management*, 'An Outline History of Management Literature', 2nd edition, pp. 83–93.
6. R. O. Clarke: 'The Social Aspects of Industrial Employment', chapter 6 of *Industrial Relations: Contemporary Problems and Perspectives* (ed. B. C. Roberts), London (1962).
7. William Pickles: 'Trade Unions in the Political Climate', chapter I of *Industrial Relations: Contemporary Problems and Perspectives* (ed. B. C. Roberts), London (1962).
8. Rosemary Stewart: *The Reality of Management*, London (1963), chapters VI and VIII.
9. Henri Fayol: *General and Industrial Management.*
10. L. Urwick and E. F. L. Brech: *The Making of Scientific Management*, Vol. I, Thirteen Pioneers.
11. Mary Parker Follett: *Freedom and Co-ordination: Lectures in Business Organisation* (ed. Urwick), London (1949).
12. E. F. L. Brech: *Organisation: The Framework of Management*, Appendix I, 'An Outline History of Thought on Organisation'.
13. Flanders and Clegg: *The System of Industrial Relations in Britain*, Oxford (1956), I: 'Social Background', by Asa Briggs, pp. 1–41.
14. L. Urwick (Ed.): *The Golden Book of Management. A Historical Record of the Life and Work of Seventy Pioneers*, London (1956).
15. Reinhard Bendix: *Work and Authority in Industry*, chapter 2, 'Entrepreneurial Ideologies in the Early Phase of Industrialisation: the Case of England', pp. 22–116. (The student should not be deterred by the title and length of this chapter; it well repays study); also chapter 5c and 5e (F. W. Taylor and Elton Mayo).
16. Sir William Robson Brown: *Management and Society* (1961), esp. chapts. I and VI.
17. M. B. Brodie: 'Henri Fayol: Administration industrielle et générale—a reinterpretation', *Public Administration*, Vol. 40 (Autumn 1962), pp. 311–17.

TOPICS FOR ESSAYS/DISCUSSIONS

1. Discuss, giving broad historical examples, the extent to which social concepts have influenced management theories.
2. What do you understand by the "social responsbilities" of management?
3. To what extent did 'traditional communities' break down as a consequence of the 'Industrial Revolution'?

4. In what ways has the attitude of management to labour changed in the present century?
5. Is there more of a 'management society' now than in 1900?
6. "In the average factory there are all sorts of subtle class distinctions which emphasise the inferiority of the industrial worker . . ." (See Shanks, *The Stagnant Society*, 'Democracy on the Factory Floor', pp. 155–61).
7. In the early days of industry: (*a*) employers were not expected to offer continuous employment; (*b*) workpeople were expected to make provision for their old age as best they could; (*c*) illness was a personal hazard; (*d*) the foreman exercised great, and often arbitrary and capricious, authority. Compare the situation with that of today.
8. Has the relative importance of direct financial incentives declined?
9. Has the Labour Party become less necessary to the trade unions?
10. "Failure to recognise the non-financial factors motivating man will result in disincentives which will reduce the level of productivity by lowering the employee's morale". (J. P. Lesperance).
11. " . . . it is no longer possible to distinguish in practice between Production Technology and Production Management, and in practice it would be unwise to do so".
12. In which matters should a personnel manager be regarded as expert? (See Brech, *Principles and Practice of Management*, Appendix pp. 624–9; M. P. Forman: *The Personnel Function of Management*, and Guy Hunter: *The Role of the Personnel Officer* (Occasional Papers Nos. 9 and 12, Institute of Personnel Management).
13. 'The Worker's Responsibility to Society'—What is it? (see, for example, Sir William Robson Brown: *Management and Society*, chapter VI).

CHAPTER FIVE

'SCIENTIFIC MANAGEMENT'

§ 1. Introduction

The term 'Scientific Management' did not become current in Britain until about 1910. The use of it was due to the work of the 'efficiency engineers' of the U.S.A. who had, in the preceding twenty years, been proclaiming that management was a distinct function with its own scientific approach and methods. The main aspects of the approach were:

(i) The critical analysis of *plant lay-out*[1] in order to *eliminate wasteful movement and effort.*

(ii) The study of jigs, fixtures and tools with the object of *economising skill and effort.*

(iii) The *planning of operations.*

(iv) The *planning of production* and its *recording and control.*

(v) The design of *organisation charts* which initiated the argument of *functional* as against *line-and-staff* organisation.

(vi) The detailed *study of jobs* by *recording* them and *dividing* them into elements, in order to eliminate unnecessary movements and attain the maximum economy. Any elements of a skilled man's work which could be regarded as essentially unskilled were passed over to unskilled workers. The skilled jobs of setting or maintaining machines were given to *specialists.* This was the division of labour pushed to its logical extreme.

(vii) The encouragement of *enhanced performance* through *time-study* and *incentive methods* of wage-payment.

At first scientific management subscribed to the old view that there was an optimum labour effort, and it was that management's task was to prevent labour from falling below the optimum. Later, however, when old customs and traditions had been modified or eliminated, it was discovered that the optimum level was considerably higher than hitherto believed; scientific management

[1] The modern development of lay-out study in the U.S.A. may be seen at its best in Richard Mather's excellent study *Lay-out Planning*, published in Britain by Industrial Education International, London (1961).

thus became in practice a set of methods not so much for maintaining effort as for enhancing it. The upshot was the development of new forms of *payment by results* and *costing systems*: in Britain the real pioneers of scientific management were, indeed, two young accountants, Fells and Garcke, who in 1887 published a book entitled *Factory Accounts*.

Scientific Management in its prime sense of rationalisation based upon time and motion study was, however, virtually unknown before 1914 and outside the U.S.A., but, as Hobsbawm[2] has shown, scientific management was implicit in mass-production, by specialised machines, on processes which began to develop rapidly towards the end of the nineteenth century. Thus, the Bristol boot-and-shoe employees who, in 1890, devised the team-system, applied Taylor's principles by *sub-dividing* the process and ensuring that the team was never kept waiting.

It was time-study which brought the stop-watch and job-study into the factory. In some of the most strongly unionised industries of late nineteenth century Britain, such as cotton, shipbuilding, the boot and shoe industry, piece-rates were the predominant method of payment, but payment by results now began to take more complicated forms—"a host of variations from proportionality were devised, and sometimes like sauces were known by the names of the chefs who concocted them". British workmen "loathed and dreaded" job study. "To the craftsman it brought loss of self-respect and loss of job control. Where he had been master, setting about the problem in his own way and time, he became a subordinate who had to do what he was told. The pressure for output, meant scamped work instead of true craftsmanship . . ."

Few men, craftsmen or not, but disliked the stop-watch. Further, the new method necessarily brought in wage-differentials, which "awoke jealousies".

§ 2. 'Scientific Management': F. W. Taylor (1856–1915)

The credit of starting the movement known as 'scientific' management is generally attributed to Frederick W. Taylor, but many modern management techniques were anticipated by M. R. Bolton and James Watt, Junior, in their Soho Foundry, *e.g.* a

[2] See E. J. Hobsbawm: 'Custom, Wages and Work-Load in Industry', in *Essays in Labour History*, ed. Briggs and Saville (1960).

crude system of work study, a system of payment by results, the pre-planning of operations, an embryonic costing procedure, as well as a sickness benefit fund run by a committee of employees. Taylor had other forerunners in the persons of Charles Babbage and the Frenchman Perronet.

Taylor underwent an apprenticeship in 1878 and joined the Midvale Steel Works (Philadelphia) as a labourer in the machine-shop. He subsequently gained very varied experience as shop clerk, machinist, gang-boss, foreman, maintenance foreman, head of the drawing office and chief engineer. Taylor's rather austere outlook was mainly limited to production and machine-shop practices. His best-known work is *The Principles of Scientific Management* (1911). Although Taylor seemed concerned with the discovery and elucidation of principles applicable to *general* management, his chief concern was with the efficiency of human beings as measured and controlled by *time and motion study*. Even so, he was at pains to point out at the beginning of his paper that it had been stimulated by the following three considerations:

(i) " . . . the great loss which the whole country is suffering through inefficiency in almost all our daily acts."

(ii) " . . . the remedy for this inefficiency lies in systematic management, rather than in searching for some unusual or extraordinary man."

(iii) " . . . the best management is a true science, resting upon clearly defined laws, rules and principles as a foundation . . . the fundamental rules of scientific management are applicable to all kinds of human activities, from our simplest individual acts to the work of our great corporations . . ."

Taylor pointed out that the sub-division of work, the selection of workers, and the methods of doing the job itself in the older forms of management were the result of tradition and prejudice. The object of the scientific manager was to replace traditional knowledge and methods by methods devised by people with a scientific or analytical bent, who subjected each operation to rigorous efficiency tests. Examples of the results achieved through finding what Taylor called "the one best* way" (itself a somewhat unscientific attitude) were: reducing to one-third the time spent in fetching and carrying trays in a sweet factory; reducing the

* 'best' in the sense of producing the greatest result with the least expenditure of time and energy.

number of separate movements in folding cotton from 29–30 to an average of 10–12 movements; reducing a foundry's working-hours from 10 to 8¾ by means of motion study, but simultaneously increasing its output from 48 to 147 items of a given kind of output.

By 'scientific' Taylor meant the substitution of logical study and measurement for haphazard, rule-or-thumb methods. Each *element of work*, he stressed, must be *scientifically determined*; the *training and selection* of workers must be along scientific lines; management and labour must *co-operate* in accordance with *scientific method*; and, finally, there must be a *more equal division of responsibility* between managers and workers, with the former assuming responsibility for the planning and organisation of work. Such attitudes involved removing the initiative from the operative to the office, the operative receiving detailed instructions on a card which had to be carried out to the letter. Hence, re-organisation necessitated an increase in the number of office-workers.

The old-type foreman had a plethora of duties—he had to be organiser, disciplinarian, 'Dutch uncle', technical expert all in one. He was, therefore, to be replaced by 'functional' foremen: one to interpret drawings and instructions, another to look after the setting up of the work, a third to deal with the speed of the machines, and so on. The new system involved the use of fresh methods of wage payment to secure the attainment of the detailed operations and the maintenance of the level of output. Operations had to be carefully timed, all operatives being kept within a reasonable range of the time taken by a "good, active" workman.

The importance of Taylor lies in the fact that he endeavoured to remove the obstacles to efficient work which arose because of faulty arrangements for which the worker himself was not responsible. Scientific management, as Taylor saw it, was an attempt to approach problems in an "engineering spirit"—to carry out *repeated, precise observations* in a spirit of objective enquiry, to reach *generalisations* on the basis of wide-ranging experimentation. The procedures which had proved so successful in science and technology were to be brought into management.

There is no intention here to minimise Taylor's contribution, but this does not mean that his larger claims, and those of his fellow enthusiasts, must be uncritically accepted. They claimed that all matters, including wage settlement, are based upon "natural laws" and that, once these are laid bare, they are unchallengeable. But even, to take an example, the conclusions of motion study are obviously influenced by the way in which workers selected for tests are chosen, and their speed of work relative to that of others; further, the attitude of the investigator himself to the workers may affect his conclusions. The workers may be influenced by the physical environment, the time and date, and their physical and psychological condition when tested. There were cases when 'scientific management' was invoked to justify every wage-change introduced. Some of the early investigators were good engineers, but perhaps deficient in their knowledge and appreciation of the human factor. Three important criticisms are:

(i) A new motion made up of the 'best' elements of the motions of individual workers is not necessarily the best, for some apparently wasteful motions are introduced to give rest to the muscles and introduce rhythm.

(ii) If a uniform output is demanded, psychological investigations have shown that there is a preliminary settlement period before output begins to rise to a maximum; this is followed by a period of fatigue and a sudden spurt at the close of the shift.

(iii) Both the aims and methods of scientific management were likely to cause friction with organised labour and to deny need or usefulness of collective bargaining.

The earlier systems of scientific management were gradually modified and developed in various ways, some of which proved disastrous and were abandoned. Far greater attention had to be paid to increasing workers' *welfare* and enlisting workers' support. The importance of Taylor as a pioneer was that he demonstrated the need for tackling industrial problems by *rational* methods.

§ 3. Functional Foremanship

Taylor's system was based upon the primary functional distinction between *planning* and *performing*—the determinative executive functions under different names:

Planning Department Foreman: Order-of-work man, Instruction Card Man, Cost-and-Time Clerk.

Performing Department Foreman: Gang-Boss, Speed Boss, Repair Boss, Inspector.

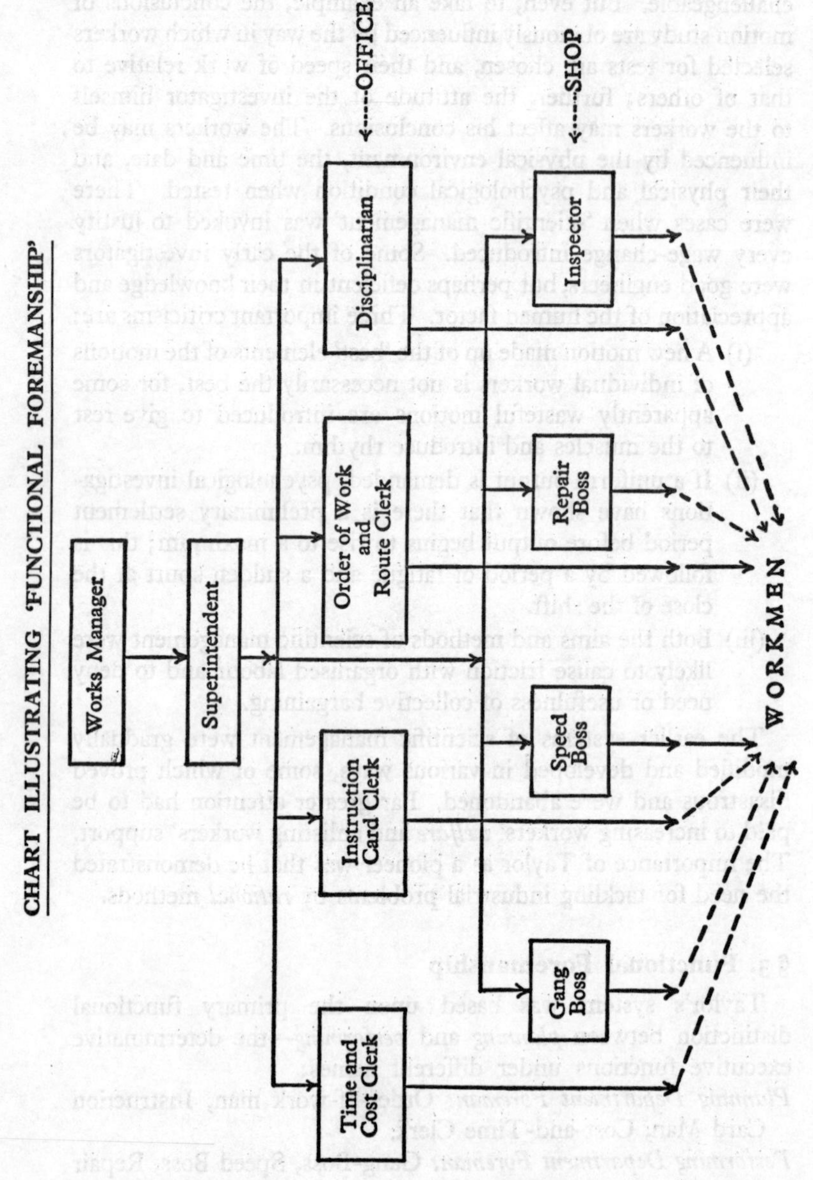

CHART ILLUSTRATING 'FUNCTIONAL FOREMANSHIP'

There was also an eighth functional boss, the disciplinarian, whose job was to settle disputes and adjust grievances, and represented the *judicial* functions. In every organisation there are three functions, the *determinative*, the *applicative* and the *interpretative* (*e.g.* in government, these are represented by the legislative, executive and judicial functions). Taylor applied these three primary principles of functionalism to his own technical problems and correlated them in relation to the work to be done.[3]

§ 4. Scientific Management: H. L. Gantt (1861–1919) and F. B. Gilbreth (1868–1924)

The two other leading figures in the introduction of scientific management in the U.S.A. were Gantt and Gilbreth, both of whom (as well as Taylor) became consultants—a relatively new profession.[4] Gantt was a prolific writer[5] on many aspects of management, though most people know him for the "Gantt chart". His attitude is revealed in the following quotation:

> "Improving the system of management means the elimination of elements of chance or accident and the accomplishment of all the ends desired, in accordance with the knowledge derived from a scientific investigation of everything down to the smallest detail of labour, for all misdirected effort is simply loss and must be borne by the employer or the employee."

Gantt was interested in the wider aspects of management and society and wrote on such matters as leadership, democracy and service to the community. He is, however, rightly famous for his charts and recording systems: bonus records, graphical records of work, task performances and wages, man record charts, machine record charts, idleness expense charts and the 'straight line' or 'Gantt chart', which enable several comparisons to be made at once. He realised that his graphical devices could easily degenerate into gimmicks. "The man who undertakes to introduce scientific management and pins his faith to rules and the use of forms and blanks without thoroughly comprehending the principles upon

[3] See James D. Mooney and Alan C. Reilly: *Onward Industry!* (1931), chapter Five.

[4] There were consultants (University professors) in the British chemical industry in the later 19th century: see L. F. Haber: *The Chemical Industry* (1960), chapt. 11, 'Owners and Managers'.

[5] An excellent selection of his writings is *Gantt on Management* (Ed.: Alex W. Rathe), American Management Association (1962) (London agents: Bailey Bros. and Swinfen Ltd.).

which it is based, will fail. Forms and blanks are simply the means to an end."

THE MAJOR LEVELS OF MANAGEMENT

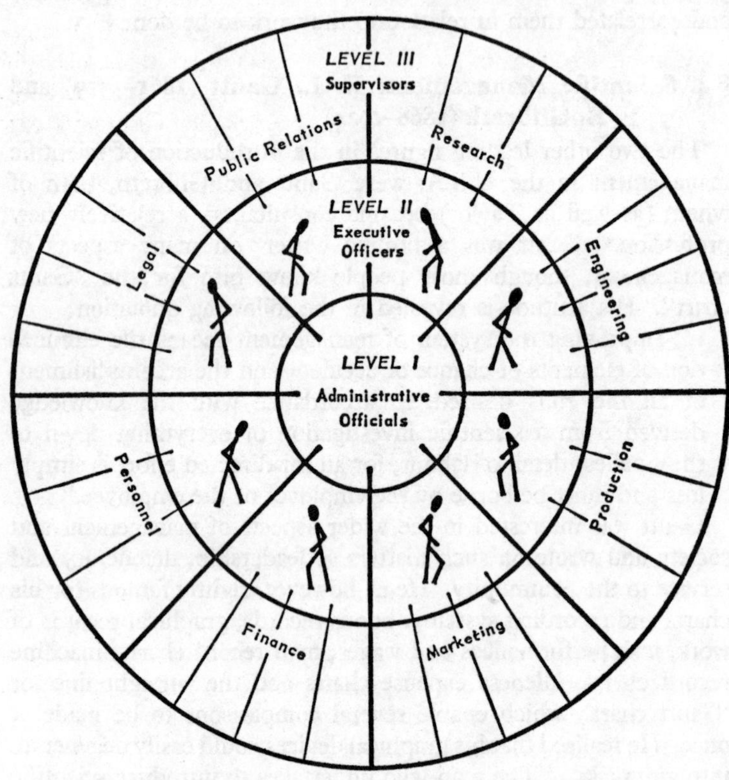

Level	*Designation*		*Accountable for*
I.	Administrative Officials	-	Directing Major Functions
II.	Executive Officers	-	Directing Supervision of Activities
III.	Supervisors and Foremen	-	Supervising Performance of Operations
••	Non-supervisory personnel perform specific tasks as directed		

Chart for illustrative purposes only; every structure must be designed to fit the needs of the individual enterprise which is affected.

Frank Bunker Gilbreth is the third of the 'Scientific Management' trinity, and was animated, like Taylor, by the idea of the 'one best way' to work; this meant physiological and psychological investigations of the worker's make-up and capacities, which led into the social sciences. By the age of 27 Gilbreth was chief superintendent of a company, but eventually set up his own contracting business in Boston. His major interest was *motion study*. In his study, *Bricklaying System*, he paid particular attention to the motions to be adopted, but also stressed the need for careful selection of workers, equipment, material and methods, and the establishment of a costing department. Gilbreth's wife did more than interpret her husband's work to others; she contributed in many ways to the original work of their partnership.[6]

§ 5. Methods Engineering

Gilbreth and Taylor were the first to develop motion study to the stage where it was meaningful and applicable to industry. Gilbreth devised the name '*therbligs*' (Gilbreth reversed) for seventeen fundamental motions covering such elements as *search, find, select, grasp, transport loaded, transport empty, position, assemble* . . ., which have developed into the modern methods engineer's eight rules of *motion economy*.[7]

It is useful at this stage to mention the aims and scope of modern *methods engineering*. The word was first coined by Maynard of the Methods Engineering Council of Pittsburg, Pennsylvania, "to cover an organised and scientific approach to the creating of effective working methods." The term is, as Avery states, an unfortunate one, since methods engineering is applicable not only to engineering but has a universal application. The objects of study of methods engineering are:[8]

(i) To conserve *operator effort*.
(ii) To conserve *material*.
(iii) To secure a *properly balanced labour force*.
(iv) To secure *maximum advantage from all mechanical aids* to production.
(v) To improve *quality*.

[6] Anne G. Shaw: 'Dr. Lillian Gilbreth', *Work Study and Industrial Engineering* (May 1962).
[7] See Michael Avery: *Methods Engineering*, London (1962).
[8] *ibid*, chapter 2, 'Methods Engineering'. This is a good survey for the non-specialist.

(vi) To make the *maximum use* of *individual skills.*

(vii) To simplify further manufacture by *simplification* and *standardisation.*

(viii) To set up *standards* for *control, costing* and *incentives.*

§ 6. The Hawthorne Experiments[9]

The Hawthorne Experiments were carried out at the Hawthorne works of the General Electric Company, Chicago, in the years 1924–27. It was a firm with 30,000 employees and, although a very progressive firm (pension schemes, sickness benefit, etc.) there was considerable dissatisfaction among the employees. The assumptions behind the experiments were those of the industrial psychology founded by Taylor and Gilbreth, *i.e.* it was assumed that the worker must be studied as an *isolated unit*, that from some points of view he resembled a machine, the *efficiency* of which could be scientifically estimated. It was assumed that the main factors affecting his efficiency were:

(i) *Wasteful or ineffectual movements* when carrying out a task.

(ii) *Fatigue*, regarded as a physico-chemical bodily condition due to accumulated waste products.

(iii) *Defects in the physical environment*—poor lighting, inadequate ventilation, excessive humidity.

The experiments have been regarded as a most striking example of 'serendipity'—the faculty of making unexpected discoveries *by accident*. Mayo and his assistants wished to measure the effect of changes in working conditions on the productivity of workers. Hence, they changed conditions of lighting, noise and so on, but with indifferent results. They discovered, however, that the most significant factors were the *social relationships* among the workers, and the workers' willingness to co-operate with the management. In one group the workers' co-operativeness led to increased output, at least temporarily, every time a change was introduced, even when working conditions deteriorated from the change; in another group working relationships were closely related to the different relationships betwen operators and supervisors. After long study it was realised that unknown and un-

[9] Useful introductions are: Brown: *The Social Psychology of Industry*, chapter 3, 'The Work of Elton Mayo'; Bendix: *Work and Authority in Industry*, pp. 308–40; for full accounts: Urwick and Brech, *The Making of Scientific Management*, Vol. III, and Roethlisberger and Dickson: *Management and the Worker*; see also H. A. Landsberger: *Hawthorne Revisited.*

suspected factors were upsetting the results of carefully planned, 'scientific' experiments. By the very act of setting up experimental situations the researchers had created social groups whose attitude had undergone unnoticed changes: the group of girls had become objects of attention, their morale had been boosted, their work had become much more interesting and significant to them.

The Hawthorne Experiments were the first intensive study of human behaviour in an industrial situation. 'Scientific Management' was rooted in the logic of engineering, but the Hawthorne study applied socio-psychological techniques to management problems, and aided the development of a theory of behaviour in human organisations; it also stressed the importance of social factors. "In the process of setting the conditions for the test, they (the researchers) had altered completely the *social situation* of the operators and their *customary attitudes* and *inter-personal relations*" (Roethlisberger and Dickson).

§ 7. Management as Art and Science

It seems a somewhat barren and pedantic activity to argue whether management should be regarded as a science or an art. It is, like medicine or engineering, a compound of both. Those who stress the 'art' at the expense of the 'science' are convinced that there is obviously a great deal of *personal skill* in the practice of management, skill centred on human judgment and human considerations of *co-operation* and *morale*. The scientific approach, however, stresses the need to obtain the relevant *facts* of a situation as the basis of thought and decision: the procedure of the manager should be to collect the facts and data, study and analyse them, draw conclusions, check their validity, make the final decision and again check its outcome. As Brech says, the choice of the label 'Scientific Management' was, perhaps, an unfortunate one, but "human aspects and situations were always among the facts to be studied and considered".[10]

Undoubtedly there is a *systematic body of knowledge* underlying competent management practice, and many of the individual fields of knowledge constitute academic disciplines. It is wrong to suppose, however, that these disciplines collectively form a new science of management. "Scientific management is the result of applying scientific knowledge and the scientific method to the

[10] See Brech (Ed.), *Principles and Practice of Management*, 2nd ed., pp. 25–27.

various aspects of management and the problems that arise from them. . . . The tools it brings to the job are the scientific methods of exact measurement, analysis and experiment, the conditions of which are so controlled as to be capable of being repeated independently and thus the findings cross-checked."[11] "Management as an art starts where science leaves off. Science deals with the measurable, the calculable, the predictable. But when management extends outside this field, which it does at numberless points in any business every day, science is powerless. . . . Art . . . is above all the ability to 'sense' a situation: that is to respond to its nature and demands in terms of the inner or intuitive senses . . ."[12] 'Scientific Management' therefore means that managers should use scientific procedures; it does not mean that there is a science of management.

When the respective roles of science and art in social problems are discussed, a distinction is being made between those problems which are *potentially answerable* and those to which, by their very nature, *no final answer* can be found. The main difference between the social sciences and the natural sciences is that in the former there are more variable factors, and these are less subject to measurement or control than in the physical sciences. Simon[13] found the main difference to lie in the fact that the social sciences "deal with conscious human beings whose behaviour is influenced by knowledge, memory and expectation". "Further, there seems to be no prospect that the social sciences will develop far enough for human behaviour to become remotely as predictable as the behaviour of matter."[14] Yet the physical and the social sciences are alike in that they must both be founded on accurate *observation* and *description*: once the facts have been ordered and classified they may serve as a basis for *explanations*. Explanations may take the form of *parallels*, *analogies*, *hypotheses*, and their plausibility may be tested from different angles. After such preliminary work has been carried out it may be possible to move into the practical field of *prescription*.

§ 8. Scientific Method and Management

The scientific approach to management problems implies

[11] Hooper: *Management Survey*, pp. 25–6.
[12] *ibid.*, p. 68.
[13] Simon: *Administrative Behaviour*, p. 251.
[14] D. E. Butler: *The Study of Political Behaviour*, London (1959), p. 21.

careful analysis of the facts relating to a particular problem and the devising of a course of action based upon the findings. A simple, everyday example of the scientific approach is the 4-Stage Process recommended by the T.W.I. Scheme.[15]

1. GET THE FACTS
   (i) Review the record.
   (ii) Find out what rules and customs apply.
   (iii) Talk with the individuals concerned.
   (iv) Get opinions and feelings.

   BE SURE YOU HAVE THE WHOLE STORY

2. WEIGH AND DECIDE
   (i) Fit the facts together.
   (ii) Consider their bearing on one another.
   (iii) What possible actions are there?
   (iv) Check practices and policies.
   (v) Consider the objective and effect on individual, group and production.

   DON'T JUMP TO CONCLUSIONS

3. CHECK RESULTS
   (i) How soon will you follow up?
   (ii) How often will you need to check?
   (iii) Watch for changes in output, attitudes and relationships.

   DID YOUR ACTION ACHIEVE YOUR OBJECTIVE?

ADDITIONAL READING ASSIGNMENTS

1. E. J. Hobsbawm: 'Custom, Wages and Work-Load in Nineteenth-Century Industry', in *Essays in Labour History*, edited by Asa Briggs and J. Saville, London (1960).
2. E. H. Phelps-Brown: *The Growth of British Industrial Relations*, London (1959), chapter II, 'The Conditions of Work'.
3. L. Urwick and E. F. L. Brech: *The Growth of Scientific Management.* For a fuller account of Scientific Management see Vol. I; also Vol. II, chapters III, VII and IX.
4. H. B. Drury: *Scientific Management*, Columbia (1918).
5. R. F. Hoxie: *Scientific Management and Labor*, New York (1915).
6. Alex W. Rathe: *Gantt on Management: Guidelines for Today's Executive*, London (1962).

[15] Quoted in Light: *The Nature of Management.*

7. Michael Avery: *Methods Engineering: An Introduction for Works and General Management*, London (1962), especially chapters 1, 2, 3, 4, 5, 6, 10, 13, 16.
8. Henry A. Albers: *Organised Executive Action*, chapter 11, 'Towards Scientific Management'.
9. William S. Beck: *Modern Science and the Nature of Life* (1961), chapter 10, 'Explanation in Science'.
10. Stanley D. Beck: *The Simplicity of Science* (1962), chapters 2, 'What is an Experiment?', and 3, 'What is a Theory?'.
11. Hugh G. J. Aitken: *Taylorism at Watertown Arsenal: Scientific Management in Action*, Harvard University Press; London, O.U.P. (1960).
12. R. Bendix: *Work and Authority in Industry*, New York and London (1956), Part 3, 5c.
13. E. H. Anderson: 'The Meaning of Scientific Management', *Harvard Business Review* (Nov. 1949).

TOPICS FOR DISCUSSION OR ESSAYS

1. In the early days of scientific management, emphasis was laid mainly on improving the foreman's performance, but modern management is concerned with the planning, co-ordination and control of every function of business. Discuss.
2. Discuss the method engineer's technique of analysis—What? Why? How? Who? Where? When? (see Avery, chapter 3).
3. "... the establishment of time values or standards as a measurement of human effort is at best a compromise". Why?
4. Write a critical evaluation of the work of Taylor, Gilbreth and Gantt.
5. Taylor's book (*The Principles of Scientific Management*) "represented too much an engineer's view". Do you agree?
6. Give a critical account of the Hawthorne Investigations.

CHAPTER SIX

MANAGEMENT SCIENCES—(I)
AIDS TO DECISION-MAKING AND CONTROL

1. Introduction: 'Management Sciences'
2. Rationalisation
3. Standardisation and Simplification
4. Operational Research (O.R.)
5. The Techniques of O.R.: Linear Programming; Queueing Theory, Monte Carlo Methods
6. Factorial Research
7. Work Study
8. Stock Control
9. Management, Measurement and Man

§ 1. Introduction: Management Sciences

When Taylor used the word *scientific* he was contrasting methods of measurement and control with the rule-of-thumb practices that had hitherto been customary. With all its scientific attitude, however, industrial engineering remained more of an art than a science, and it is only in the last twenty years or so that there has been a rapid change in views and outlook.

Since Taylor was a pioneer he had to suffer both "the jealousy of smaller rivals and the too great orthodoxy of his disciples".[1] Scientific management at first meant the rigid application of the methods which Taylor had adopted, rather than a new approach to industrial questions. World War I, with its need of greatly increased production and loosening of traditions, led to the application of devices which would increase output, and the beginnings of cost accountancy, planning and certain aspects of personnel management were seen in the better-managed concerns.

Official and voluntary bodies, which Taylor would not have found alien to his way of thinking, came into existence in England, such as the Department of Industrial and Scientific Research, the Industrial Fatigue Research Board, the National Institute of Industrial Psychology, the Industrial Welfare Society and the Institute of Cost and Works Accountants. During the depressed

[1] L. Urwick: *The Meaning of Rationalisation*, London (1929), chapter V, 'Scientific Management'.

period of 1922–26, however, many of the new 'experiments' were abandoned and there was a tendency to look back on the pre-1914 days as a standard. Nevertheless, much of the "changed mental attitude", as Urwick says, survived. In 1929 Urwick could write with justification: "It is . . . being recognised more clearly year by year, not only in the United States but in almost every industrial country, that whatever the value attaching to Taylor's particular systems and devices, permanent administration can only be achieved by using the scientific approach, the method of thinking, which he was the first to apply in this particular field".

Early 'scientific management' was largely concerned with such matters as the situation and layout of the workshop, type and arrangement of machinery, and materials, the most effective productive processes, the selection and training of 'first-class men' (as Taylor called his experts), and the 'best' methods of payment. Later developments have emphasised the importance of market research, sales forecasting and planned production to meet the forecasts. Hence, during the last two or three decades, there have developed various 'tools' or 'management sciences' which aid the manager to make decisions which are more likely to be correct than those based upon the indefinable qualities of 'flair' or 'intuition'.[2]

The sciences (or scientific approaches) which have developed are market analysis, budgetary control, stock control, planning and scheduling, quality control, labour incentives and control, maintenance control, ergonomics, cybernetics, operational research and management accounting. All the foregoing have become, or are rapidly becoming, technical specialisms, but the manager must appreciate what their experts are about, and the scope and limitations of their activities. The management sciences are concerned with management decision-making. It is obvious that the greatest advance has taken place in the last two decades in the realm of technology and the application of human effort in industry, but scientific principles can only be used by management to the extent that people are willing to use them. This was

[2] It is interesting to note that in the latest (1962) edition of the *Encyclopaedia Britannica* there is a new article by C. W. Churchman on 'Management Sciences', dealing with scientific disciplines which have been applied largely since 1945, including logic, mathematics (inventory theory, waiting line theory, linear programming, theory of games), mathematical statistics, engineering sciences, biology, psychology, economics, business administration, organisation theory.

pointed out by a British 'pioneer', Oliver Sheldon[3] in 1925. He believed there could be no 'science of co-operation'. What is now needed is usable hypotheses of how human beings behave and why they behave as they do.

§ 2. Rationalisation

The 1920s and 1930s were a period of excess productive capacity, and the 'rationalisation movement' in Britain was the attempt to copy with excess capacity in certain sections of the economy, notably the export industries; hence, it was also an attempt to deal with the unemployment problem. *Rationalisation* is a term which has had various definitions[4], *e.g.* industrial combination in place of the jungle of unregulated competition, the extension of mechanisation and the further development of 'scientific management' and efficiency methods. In its original German use rationalisation meant using every available means to improve the general economic situation through technical improvements and systematic organisation. The aim in Germany was to restrict the output of certain large industrial firms in order to keep it *within the limits of current market demands*, and of simultaneously bringing about a *reduction in costs*. The term came to have a wider meaning and was defined at the Economic Conference in Geneva (1927) as follows: "The methods of technique and organisation designed to secure the minimum waste of either effort or material", and including "the scientific organisation of labour, standardisation both of material and products, simplification of processes, and improvements in the system of transport and marketing". The Resolution adopted by the Committee on Industry at the Geneva Conference stated that rationalisation aimed simultaneously at:

(i) Securing the maximum efficiency of labour with the minimum effort;

(ii) Facilitating by a reduction in the variety of different patterns (where such variety has no obvious advantage) research into methods of manufacture, the use and replacement of standardising parts;

(iii) Eliminating waste of raw materials and power;

[3] Oliver Sheldon: *The Philosophy of Management*, London (1924).

[4] See L. Urwick: *The Meaning of Rationalisation*, London (1929); and W. Meakin: *The New Industrial Revolution*, London (1928).

(iv) Simplifying the distribution of commodities by

(v) Eliminating unnecessary transport, excessive financial burdens and the useless multiplication of middlemen.

The chief protagonist of rationalisation in Britain was Lord Melchett, who saw in it four advantages:

(i) It allowed the scientific allocation of capital expenditure and the financing of new plant and up-to-date equipment;

(ii) It encouraged specialisation, the closing down of inefficient firms, the concentration of management and commercial propaganda, selling and other expenses;

(iii) It prevented waste and overlapping—duplication of stocks, unnecessary varieties in the size and form of commodities, or overlapping of research;

(iv) It provided insurance against the fluctuation of markets and prices, and by promoting an orderly system of purchasing raw materials and marketing commodities, facilitated a world review of economic needs and supplies.

In France "Taylorism" had been enthusiastically taken up by a group of French engineers, among them Henri le Chatelier[5] and Charles de Fréminville, who used the expression "*l'organisation scientifique du travail*". But a reaction set in, focusing on the word scientific, and the phrase was modified into "*l'organisation rationnelle du travail*".

§ 3. Standardisation and Simplification[6]

The method of reducing manufacturing and commercial costs and of eliminating waste-effort implied by the terms rationalisation and simplification was important in Britain, not only in the heavy industries, but in those smaller miscellaneous industries which did not lend themselves to large-scale combination. Although there was no movement in Britain comparable to the American achievement in simplified practice, Britain was the pioneer: work was started in the 1890s with the object of promoting standardisation in engineering practice.

[5] Short studies of these men are to be found in Urwick and Brech: *The Making of Scientific Management*, Vol. 1.

[6] See Meakin, *op. cit.*, chapter VII; for further details, *Production Handbook*, New York (1958), Section 4; Brech (Ed.): *Principles and Practice of Management*, pp. 266–8; D. Woodward: 'International Standards for British Industry', *The Manager* (July 1963).

Standardisation is the process of devising standard specifications for all kinds of engineering materials and products.
Simplification is the effort to eliminate all unnecessary variations in products.

There is, as Meakin said, a "fine technical distinction between the two". Standardisation is now taken for granted; its advantages to the producer include bigger productive batches, the possibility of sub-dividing operations, reduction on idle plant, stocks, overhead staff costs, and, to the user, lower prices, inter-changeability and improved stocks and supplies. The disadvantages of standardisation are that it may sterilise design and leave the adoption of desirable or worth-while changes too late. In Britain standardisation has been developed by the British Standards Institution, which issues British Standard Specifications in four divisions.

§ 4. Operational Research

Operational research is the introduction of the scientific method for deciding on the best way of doing a given job; it is the application of scientific method to man-machine systems in order to solve problems of managerial policy.[7] The mode of procedure is as follows:

(i) An analysis is made of the system and a *model* (mathematical, probabilistic, analogic) is constructed.
(ii) A suitable system of *measurement* is devised and applied.
(iii) The model is then manipulated by a digital computer, in consultation with the managers concerned, to find a *solution* or forecast.
(iv) The *results* are then presented.

Operational research (O.R.) first developed during World War II, when the military authorities invoked the aid of scientists and mathematicians to help them on problems of strategic and operational decisions. It uses such techniques as Linear Programming, Non-linear and Dynamic Programming, Queueing

[7] See, for example, F. Brambilla: 'Operations Research as a Management Science', *Management International*, No. 4 (1961); two articles by Stafford Beer: 'Organisation of Operational Research', *Research* (May 1956); 'The Scope for Operational Research in Industry', *The Institute of Production Engineers' Journal* (May 1957); also 'Introduction to Operational Research', *Work Study and Industrial Engineering* (May 1962).
There are fuller accounts in Section 18, 'Operations Research' of the *Production Handbook* (New York 1958); and chapters 5 and 6 of D. E. Greene: *Production Technology: Some Recent Developments*, London (1962).

Theory, the Monte Carlo Method and the Theory of Games. An O.R. team consists of specialists (mathematician, computer, programmer, industrial engineer, statisticians and experts in the various fields—nuclear physics, biology, metallurgy, etc.) whose job it is to advise line management, and so enable it to base its decisions on a scientific analysis of a problem rather than on individual judgment or intuition. Even the individual is not usually a physical model, but *mathematical*, *i.e.* a set of equations which relates significant variables; or it is a *punched-card* model, where components of the operations are represented by individual punched cards, *e.g.* in a sales distribution problem each customer is represented by a punched card giving information about his location, type of business, frequency of purchase. A model may be either *exact* or *probabilistic*: exact if, in the operations or processes, *chance* plays a small part; probabilistic, if elements of *uncertainty* are explicitly recognised, *e.g.* advertising problems.

The primary task of the O.R. scientist is to construct a model or faithful representation of the operation. A mathematical model is one which expresses the factors of the system and their relationships in numbers and symbols, or in equations. A new tool of management is the *electronic digital computer*, which can perform the most tedious and complex calculations in a few minutes.[8] One way of solving operational problems is by the use of *simulation*: it studies systems by imitating or 'simulating' their behaviour,[9] *e.g.* models in wind-tunnels, flight simulators for training airline pilots, and the mechanical tortoises used to illustrate the nervous system of a mammal.[10]

A detailed example (National Coal Board).[11] The task was to assess the relative merits and economics of the different forms of transport systems used underground. There are three main systems, namely, rope haulages, belt conveyors and transport by locomotives, with variations of each of these (for example, the locomotives may be diesel-driven or battery-driven).

[8] A lucid introduction, which the layman can follow, of how a computer works is chapter 5, 'Digital Computers: Principles', of D. E. Greene: *Production Technology: Some Recent Developments*, London (1962).

[9] See A. Battersby's two articles: 'Simulation: a new weapon?', *The Manager* (February and March 1963).

[10] See the example of the first fully automatic car park ('Zidpark') given in Greene, *op. cit.*, pp. 193–4.

[11] Quoted in *Work Study and Industrial Engineering* (April 1958).

The first task was to assemble the *cost data* for all the systems under varying conditions, classifying the information of certain well-defined components, such as capital depreciation and interest, operating labour, maintenance cost and energy cost. The next step was to establish the relationships of each of these with length of haul, gradient and tonnage carried. Fairly accurate relationships were established, from which it was possible to calculate the running costs of each of these systems for a particular set of conditions. In this way it was possible to determine the cheapest system for any given set of conditions. The confidence limits of the calculated costs were established when the calculated differences were significant.

It was found that in many circumstances the calculated running costs of the different systems were not greatly different, although for level roads with high tonnages, the locomotive haulages were generally the most economical. This study led to the interesting conclusion that in the over-all consideration of underground haulage costs under many present-day conditions, the management's task at many existing collieries was to concentrate mainly on improving the efficiency of existing systems and to consider embarking on a programme of replacing one system by another only when substantial reorganisation for other reasons was necessary.

There were many valuable incidental conclusions from this investigation. For example, it was shown that one of the major cost components in conveying systems was that attributable to belt replacement, and the life of conveyor belting was therefore critical. This directed attention to the factors which determine belt life.

This example has been treated at some length to illustrate that a project which started with the fairly simple objective of comparing the merits of different types of equipment went on to a more detailed examination of maintenance and operating factors, and ultimately to the basic specifications of the equipment in question.

Both O.R. and work study are concerned with operational problems, and both are scientific procedures; both provide management with information for sounder decision-making. Work study is concerned mainly with the investigation and improvement of processes and operations which are self-contained, the variables of which are more easily isolable, measurable and controllable. O.R. has as its primary aim the provision of a system of mathematical statistical techniques which can be used to *predict* the relative desirability of *alternative* solutions for complex operational systems, the variables of which can be neither easily isolated nor measured, and in which there is often a high degree of interdependence and interaction between variables. Hence, it may be said, O.R. is the logical extension of work study.

Members of the team itself will be unable to understand the *whole* system being investigated, and team-work is thus essential. The line-manager must at least appreciate what the team is trying to do, and how it sets about its tasks.

Examples of the application of O.R. to industrial problems are:

(i) The minimisation of *delivery costs.*

(ii) Improved *rate of flow of materials* through the manufacturing unit, resulting in minimisation of capital invested in work-in-progress.

(iii) Improved means for predicting *minimum stock levels.*

(iv) *More effective machine-loading* when there is a diversity of products.

(v) Certain limited uses in the *marketing and sales* fields.

(vi) Improved methods of formulating *planned maintenance systems.*

What is a Model? A model involves the use of assumptions to simplify a complex situation. The individual uses models in everyday life, *e.g.* he may decide to go to the seaside on Sunday *assuming* four things work out the way he expects: the weather is fine; the car is in working order; his wife also wants to go; he does not have any urgent work to do. There may be other assumptions which he does not incorporate in his model because they appear less probable or important. A model builder must explain both his conclusions and his assumptions. Other types of model include the *engineering model* (*e.g.* model of an aircraft used in a wind-tunnel) and the *accounting model* (representing the flow of goods and services through an enterprise).

The danger in using models as aids to thinking is that some important conditions may be omitted or a simplified model may be inappropriately applied to a complex situation. How often one hears the exclamation: "It is all right in theory, but won't work in practice"! Yet, if a theory is logically constructed and is applied where the model fits, it will work in practice. (As an economist has pointed out,[12] it is precisely those people untrained in economic theory who tend to construct a *very partial* theory which blinds them to some of its possibilities).

§ 5. The Techniques of O.R.

It is impossible here to deal with these even in outline, but the techniques of Linear Programming, the Theory of Queues and the Monte Carlo Method may be briefly mentioned.

Linear programming[13] as its name implies assumes that there is a linear relationship between variables, and that the limits of the variation can be fairly well established. The objective and the limitations are stated as linear functions of the variables to be determined. Linear programming has been used to decide which plants should serve which markets, subject to the limitations of the plant capacities and specifications of market requirements. It has also been used to establish minimum distribution costs from factory to warehouse, better utilisation of production facilities, and provision of better methods for sales planning.

(Mathematical programming has now progressed far beyond simple linear techniques).

Queueing Theory.[14] Everyone has experience of queues, both in daily life and in industry. In a factory there may be more jobs than there are facilities to deal with them, or several jobs may simultaneously require the same machine. Similarly, if a manager has more than one job to do, or several subordinates waiting to see him, he may become a 'bottleneck' and cause waiting. Queues will form if jobs arrive at a machine at variable or random time intervals, or if a machine takes irregular periods to do the jobs, or if there is a combination of variable times and irregular arrivals.

[12] I.D.M. Little: 'The Economist in Whitehall', *Lloyds Bank Review* (April 1957).

[13] A lucid introduction for the layman is A. Henderson and R. Schlasfer: 'Mathematical Programming', chapter 2 of *New Decision-Making Tools for Managers* (ed. Bursk and Chapman), Harvard University Press (1963), pp. 30–94.

[14] A most readable and thorough discussion is provided in five articles by Kenneth Shone: 'The Queueing Theory', *Time and Motion Study* (September, October, December 1960; and March, April 1961).

Queueing Theory is, therefore, important for managers and senior work study officers; they should try to discover the causes of queue formation and the amount of time so wasted.

Queueing theory is a branch of probability theory; it can be used in such situations as serving customers in a cafeteria, handling calls on a telephone exchange, serving customers in retail stores or libraries, servicing semi-automatic equipment, setting up a balanced assembly line where the output rates of individual stations are subject to fluctuation. Queueing theory originated in Denmark, where the problem of congestion on telephone lines and exchanges was studied. For several years no further use could be made of the specialised statistical technique, but recently it has been successfully applied to such problems as the flow of work through a factory with the aim of minimising work-in-progress, the loading and unloading ships in port, and road, rail and air traffic problems.

A single example[15] will show how *random observation studies* (or 'ratio delay' studies) can measure the probability of people or things queueing:

> An overhead travelling crane served various machines in a bay 575 feet long, with 13 sections or departments. Sometimes the crane was required for more than one job; consequently so much labour time was lost that the management thought it would be economical to instal a second crane to run on the same rails; (a re-conditioned one costing £8,000).
>
> Random observations were made by three men over a 3-day period to collect data for the calculation of savings that an additional crane might give. The data is summarised in the following Table:

[15] Example given by Shone, *op. cit.* (article of September 1960), and reproduced by kind permission of the author and *Time and Motion Study*.

RANDOM OBSERVATIONS ON CRANE

(The workshop was observed on 92 occasions)

Section	*A* *Occasions crane seen working the Section*	*B* *Occasions persons waiting in Section*	*C* *Occasions jobs waiting in Section*
1	3	5	2
2	5	0	0
3	6	10	4
4	14	41	10
5	3	24	7
6	3	0	0
7	1	12	2
8	9	77	17
9	15	152	32
10	3	26	7
11	—	19	8
12	4	24	3
13	14	20	5
Totals	80	410	97

The following calculations are then made:

1. *From Column A*

   Proportion of occasions when crane was in use $= \frac{80}{92} = 0.87$.

   Hence, proportion of time crane was in use during shift = 0.87. This also gives the *load on crane*, = 0.87, and the proportion of time the crane was available but not used = 0.13.

2. *From Column B*

   Average number of workers waiting for crane =

   $\frac{410}{92} = 4.45$ workers per observation.

   Therefore, expected working time lost per 8-hour shift = 8×4.45 hours = 35.6 hours per observation.

   Cost of this waiting at 5s. 0d. per hour for 300 shifts in the year = 35.6 hour/shift × 300 shift/year × £¼ = £2,672 per annum.

3. *From Column C*

   Average time lost by loads waiting for crane =

   $\frac{97}{92} = 1.05$ hours/hour of time = 8.4 hours per 8-hour shift.

It must be remembered that the waiting-time in calculation 2 is only the time which was *observed* to have been lost, and is probably less than the actual time lost. The number of observations does not warrant firm conclusions, yet it is obvious that the case for an additional crane may be confirmed by further observations.

Monte Carlo Methods (Models of Queueing Situations). A method of finding the time spent in a queue is to set up a 'numerical model' of the situation and hence determine what would happen in the real situation. The main problem is how to select random times. The name Monte Carlo was adopted for this method, since card drawing, dice throwing and the spinning of roulette wheels have been used to achieve randomness. When events are unrelated to one another they are said to occur at random, *e.g.* arrival of aircraft at an airport, ships at a busy oil-refinery, ambulances at a hospital. If one is able to observe, however, by observation or experiment, what particular pattern or degree of variation the events appear to follow, this can be accepted as an *observed fact of the situation.*[16] In recent times scientific methods have evolved for analysing uncertainty and, at times, for assigning its causes; "even in cases where causes are still untraceable, the effects of uncertainty can be allowed for in setting up the best managerial system, just as the engineer can allow in designing and applying a machine for the possible failure of one of its parts. Perhaps the use of *quantitative methods* most profitable to management will be in the understanding, design and control of continuous processes that remain subject to breakdowns, delays, interruptions and other real faults and variations *beyond the power of management wholly to cure*". The general name given to this quantitative method is simulation.[17]

The following example of simulation (Monte Carlo Methods)[18] will illustrate the type of problem and approach:

An Example of Simulation: Monte Carlo Methods

Consider the following situation: It is observed that the number of tankers waiting in the river outside a refinery varies from zero

[16] R. W. Revans: 'Science and the Manager', *Management International* (1960–1).

[17] See the two articles by A. Battersby: 'Simulation: A New Weapon', *The Manager* (February and March 1963); also H. N. Shycon and R. B. Maffer: 'Simulation: Tool for Better Distribution', in Bursk and Chapman (Eds.): *New Decision-Making Tools for Managers*, Harvard University Press (1963). pp. 224–46.

[18] From an article in *Management International* (1961), reproduced by kind permission of the author, Prof. R. W. Revans.

up to ten. Averaged over all kinds of tankers, the cost of waiting time is £1,000 per day per tanker. Quantitative information can be found upon the following:

(*a*) distribution of tankers by type (crude-oil in, ballast out; refined product in, different refined product out; ballast in, refined out; etc.);

(*b*) distribution of tankers by time alongside jetties discharging or loading cargo, washing tanks, etc.;

(*c*) number of jetties and availability for particular needs, *e.g.* discharging ballast;

(*d*) distribution of tankers by depth of draught, and hence, by ability to berth at different levels of tide;

(*e*) fluctuations in hours of darkness during which certain types of tanker are unable to move in river;

(*f*) forecast of throughput of refinery and of future fleet capacity so as to estimate average arrival rate of tankers;

(*g*) costs of building extra jetties, installing discharge plant of increased capacity, deepening river, lighting fairway for movement during darkness, etc.

Under present conditions the average waiting time per tanker is 34 hours and 800 tankers use the refinery every year. Hence the annual cost of waiting time is more than one million pounds. What, if any, is the maximum economy to be achieved, what changes in operating conditions are needed to achieve it and what will the cost of those changes amount to? Such changes of operating conditions include:

(i) the building of one or more additional jetties;

(ii) the provision of ballast discharging mains or other services at jetties now lacking them;

(iii) the systematic reduction, either by work study, the re-equipment of existing jetties, or the re-development of the labour force, of the average times alongside of all tankers;

(iv) a reduction of the total throughput of the refinery by deflecting elsewhere tankers likely to need to wait more than a given length of time;

(v) the exclusion from the jetties of all tankers appearing to use them uneconomically (*e.g.* to effect repairs, to wash tanks or to take on or discharge small quantities of cargo only);

(vi) the illumination of the fairway, the use of radar and so forth, to make possible the movement of tankers during darkness;

(vii) the dredging of the river to make possible the passage of tankers at any state of the tide;

(viii) or any combination of these.

Some of these elements admit of more than one level of change; the average length of time alongside, for example, at present about 50 hours, could be reduced at various costs in wages or equipment, by 10 per cent, 20 per cent or even 30 per cent. But there is no virtue in reducing this beyond the point at which it costs more to do so than the saving in cost of waiting time achieved; nor is it economic to spend money on reducing time alongside if the same sum spent on the capital cost of a new jetty, or of dredging the river, or of lighting the fairway, would reduce the average waiting time by a greater amount than would the same amount of money spent on reducing time alongside. The interrelations between the various possibilities open to the owners of the refinery are of indescribable complexity, and yet, by the use of a particular branch of simulation, known as the Monte Carlo method, a practical answer to the problem as stated was found by a team of four workers within one month. The value of the incidental information alone (such as the likelihood of four or more ships wishing simultaneously to pump ballast into a common ring main) thrown up during the study far exceeded the cost of the exercise. Without the use of quantitative information and methods to handle it, this problem, like most others involving sequences of random events, could have been treated by intuition alone; and, if practical experience in management teaches us anything, it is the treachery of intuition when dealing with queueing situations.

§ 6. Factorial Research

Recent developments in O.R. have made it possible to determine some of the factors affecting success in business. Factorial research (F.R.) tries to disentangle significant factors from the insignificant and show management how profits can be increased. F.R. builds up analogue models, concentrating on the relationships of variable factors, and increases the effectiveness of managerial control. An actual case from a consultant will be useful.[18]

[18] John Montague: 'Success factors in business', *Work Study and Industrial Engineering* (May 1958).

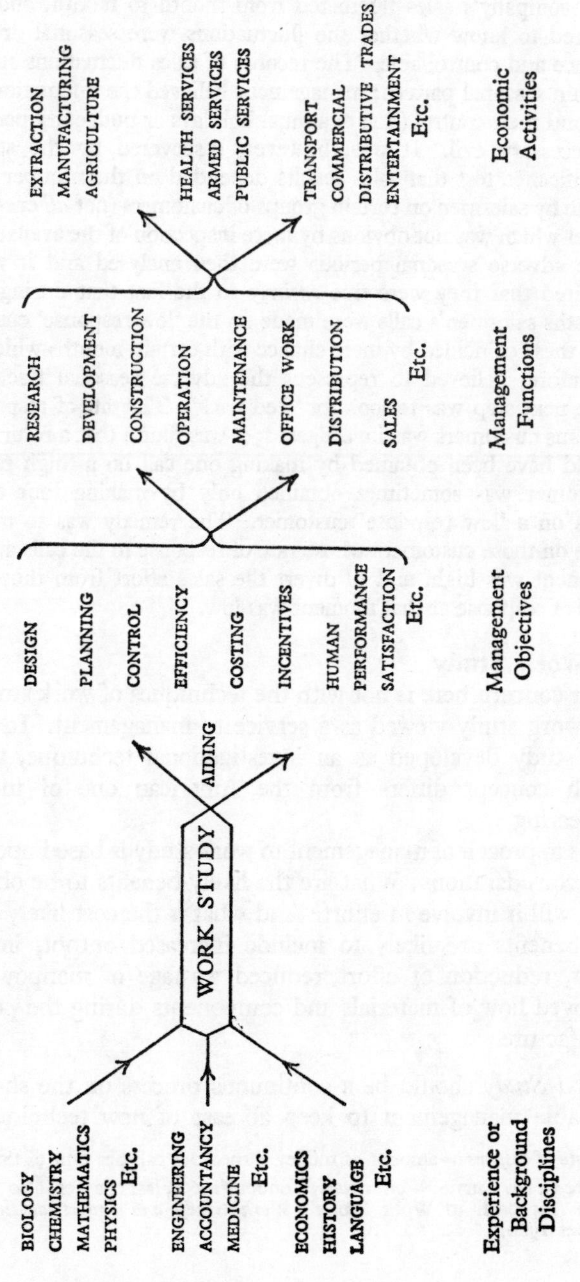

(after Currie)

A company's sales fluctuated from month to month, and it was desired to know whether the fluctuations were seasonal or due to chance and controllable. The records of sales fluctuations showed a certain seasonal pattern; management believed the fluctuations to be beyond their control (due to annual holidays or budgetary periods)—a necessary evil. It was, however, discovered by the statistical significance test that sales results depended on the number of calls made by salesmen on certain groups of customers (not *all* customers), a fact which was not obvious by mere inspection of the available data. The adverse seasonal periods were then analysed and it was discovered that they were due *entirely* to the fact that during certain months salesmen's calls were made on the 'low response' customers, and these coincided by mere chance with certain months which were, therefore, believed to represent the adverse seasonal fluctuations. The next step was to look for 'feed back'. The rate of response* of various customers was investigated; it was found that a return which could have been obtained by making one call on a 'high response' customer was sometimes obtained only by making four or more calls on a 'low response' customer. The remedy was to maximise calls on those customers whose rate of response to the calls at a given moment was high, and to divert the sales effort from those whose rate of response at that moment was low.

§ 7. Work Study

Our concern here is not with the techniques of work study, but with work study viewed as a service to management. In Britain work study developed as an investigational technique, and the British concept differs from the American one of industrial engineering.

The approach of management to work study is based upon three main considerations: What are the likely benefits to be obtained? What will it involve in effort? And what is the cost likely to be?[19] The benefits are likely to include increased output, improved layout, reduction of effort, reduced wastage of manpower, and improved flow of materials and components during the period of manufacture.

Method Study should be a continuous process on the shop floor to enable management to keep abreast of new techniques and

* *Rate of response*=amount of money earned per call per unit of time.

19 See R. M. Currie: *Work Study*, London (1960), last chapter: also 'Management's Approach to Work Study', *Work Study and Industrial Engineering* (October 1960).

equipment. Method study should be largely a co-operative effort, and not wholly a management function. The skilled tradesman's contribution should be encouraged and backed by a good suggestions scheme.

Work Measurement is the application of techniques designed to establish the time for a qualified worker to carry out a specific job at a defined level of performance (B.S. 3138). The basic principle of work measurement is *standard performance*—a rate of output at which productivity is at its maximum and labour costs at their lowest. The main techniques used are time study, analytical estimating, activity sampling, camera methods and predetermined times. The first step is to decide on the proper method for the occasion; the complete job is then broken down into a number of elemental movements or operations, which are then timed separately several times by a stop-watch and the times recorded. A *rating factor* is simultaneously recorded alongside: it is the work study man's assessment of the speed and effectiveness of the operator relative to the 100-figure of standard performance (*standard rating*). Next comes the process of 'extension', calculated as follows:

$$\text{Basic Time} = \frac{\text{Observed Time} \times \text{Observed Rating}}{\text{Standard Rating } (i.e.\ 100)}$$

Basic time is the time which any element would take if carried out at standard performance. A 'relaxation allowance' (anything from 10–50 per cent) is then added to each basic time. Lastly, the basic times are added together to give the 'standard time' for the job.

It is often said that the objectives of work measurement are to provide data for more effective planning and manning, performance indices, labour control and incentive schemes, but the basic purpose is to establish the proper times for a job. When these times have been established the conditions are propitious for the exercise of management control to achieve high output and optimum shop performance.[20]

O and M has been described as "work study in the office"[21] but there is no uniform opinion on the scope and responsibilities of an O and M Department. Definitions of Organisation and Methods

[20] Victor Smith, 'Work Study Measurement', *Time and Motion Study* (July 1962).

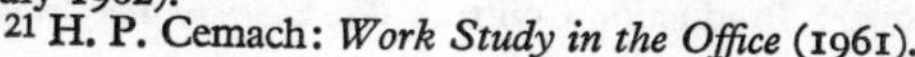
[21] H. P. Cemach: *Work Study in the Office* (1961).

have therefore varied between the fairly comprehensive to the relatively restricted. Mr. N. C. Pollock has suggested that O and M is: "An enquiry into the general effectiveness of the executive machinery and, secondly, an examination and design of clerical organisation, methods procedures and related activities".[22] Such a definition is neither too wide nor too narrow (as is, for instance, 'clerical work study').

A growth in the size and complexity of a business will create a need for impartial enquiry into the general executive machinery, *i.e.* the structure and framework of the business, the balance and grouping of responsibilities must be modified to meet the changing conditions brought about by growth.

The aim of O and M is to make office workers more productive by eliminating waste and simplifying the procedures of the *basic clerical operations*; communicating information; sorting and distributing; writing and recording original information; copying; checking; calculating; filing.

It need not be emphasised that the *form* is a basic weapon in the simplification of several of these procedures; form design occupies a central position in O and M work.[23]

Clerical work is one of the most expensive services to industry, and waste occurs when there is no co-ordination of clerical services through one body, and where *method study* principles in their most elementary form have not been applied.

§ 8. Production Control: Stock Control

Production control is "the control of the movements of materials, men, machines and money, so that the right quantities of the right materials are moved to the right places at the right times for the right cost".[24] Production control is essentially a physical function dependent upon the clerical provision of facts about *movement*—the rate, cost, direction and method of movement.

Only a few words can be said here about stock control. The importance of good stock control, both from the point of view of

[22] N. C. Pollock: 'What is O and M?'; *Work Study and Industrial Engineering* (Oct. 1957).

[23] See, for example, J. Dotan: 'The Form and its Function in Management', *Work Study and Industrial Engineering* (April 1960), and E. G. Robinson, 'A Pattern of Forms', *The Manager* (April 1959).

[24] Definition by E. W. Roper: 'Production Control', *Work Study and Industrial Engineering* (January 1958).

the individual firm and that of the national economy cannot be too strongly emphasised.[25] In 1960 the total stocks of material in Great Britain were worth £9,000 million, about half of which was held in manufacturing industry. Excessive stocks both immobilise our capital resources and give rise to the so-called 'inventory recession'.[26] The early part of Battersby's book shows that stock control can be reduced to a set of rules, once general policy decisions have been made. The rules can be applied by junior staff who are the instruments of *management by exception*, and bring only exceptional cases to the personal attention of the Materials Controller.[27] The student is particularly advised to study the argument relating to 'economic job lots' in Battersby's book.

§ 9. Conclusion: Management, Measurement and Man

Even the ancient world had measurement, but this was not *scientific*. As Revans has stressed, it is not sufficient to observe and measure: there must be an effort to establish *relationships* among the facts observed and measured if we wish to be scientific or help in the establishment of a science. Intuition will always be of great value to managers, but they must also be able to grasp the *underlying structure* of the situations they encounter.

It seems barren and pedantic to discuss whether or not management is a science or an art;[28] it is obviously both, like medicine, or engineering or architecture. It is, however, worth while noting that among the numerous meanings attaching to the word 'art', there are *human skill as opposed to nature* and the *practical application of any science*. "Those who maintain that management is an art stress the large element of *personal skill* involved; those who come down on the side of science stress that the basis of decision-making must be *measured fact*. The true view of management regards it as "a skilled process entailing human considerations, requiring maturity of judgment, a systematic approach, a wide range of knowledge".[29]

[25] See A. Battersby: *A Guide to Stock Control*, London (1963).

[26] *ibid.*, p. vii.

[27] *ibid.*, p. 95. On 'management by exception' see next chapter, VII of the present book.

[28] The student is nevertheless recommended to read the discussion in Frederic Hooper: *Management Survey*, chapter 2, 'Scientific Management', and chapter 3, 'Management as an Art'.

[29] E. F. L. Brech (Ed.): *Principles and Practice of Management*, Second edition, p. 27.

It seems in view of recent sociological research in the management field that it is more profitable to discuss the difference between the natural and the social sciences. There seems no prospect of the social sciences developing enough for human behaviour to become even remotely as predictable as the behaviour of matter;[30] this is the crux of the 'management problem'—the manager has to deal with men as well as matter. Management is a highly personal process, concerned ultimately with the management of people.

NOTE: SCIENTIFIC PROCEDURE

Since this term is encountered so frequently in modern management literature, it is useful to state briefly what it involves. Seven stages can be distinguished:

(i) State the problem;
(ii) Observe and collect the relevant data;
(iii) Classify the data;
(iv) Derive a theory and construct a 'model' on the basis of the known information, in order to represent the problem under consideration;
(v) Test the theory and the solution derived from it, so that exceptions may be identified;
(vi) Formulate a final theory with the controls and forecast results;
(vii) Test the solution.

Seldom can any of these steps be omitted, and it is dangerous to attempt short cuts.

ADDITIONAL READING ASSIGNMENTS

1. C. W. Churchman: Article 'Management Sciences', *Encyclopaedia Britannica* (1962).
2. L. Urwick: *The Meaning of Rationalisation*, London (1929).
3. W. Meakin: *The New Industrial Revolution*, London (1928).
4. S. Beer: 'The Scope for Operational Research in Industry'. The 1956 Georgy Bray Memorial Lecture, reprinted in *The Institution of Production Engineers' Journal* (May 1957).
5. Sir Charles Goodeve: 'Operational Research as an Aid to Management', *The Manager* (January 1960).
6. C. C. Hermann and J. F. Magee: 'Operations Research for Management', in *New Decision-Making Tools for Managers* (ed. Bursk and Chapman), Harvard University Press (1963), chapter 1.

[30] D. E. Butler: *The Study of Political Behaviour*, London (1959), p. 21; see also Simon: *Administrative Behaviour*, p. 251.

7. G. B. Carson (Ed.): *Production Handbook*, Section 18, 'Operations Research'.
8. D. E. Greene: *Production Technology: Some Recent Developments*, London (1962), chapts. 5 and 6.
9. R. M. Currie: *Work Study*, London (1961).
10. H. P. Cemach: *Work Study in the Office*, London (1961).
11. A. Battersby: *A Guide to Stock Control*, London (1963).
12. F. Hooper: *Management Survey*, chapters 2 and 3.
13. E. G. Bennion: 'Economics for Management', *Harvard Business Review* (March–April 1961).

Case Studies

1. 'Oxley Mills' (published by the Institution of Works Managers). 2 parts.
2. 'The Case of Pakitt Ltd.' (obtainable from the Human Sciences Unit, Warren Springs Laboratory, Gunnels Wood Road, Stevenage, Herts.)

TOPICS FOR ESSAYS/DISCUSSION

1. Discuss the general meaning of the term Rationalisation. Do you agree that in many cases it was used to camouflage dubious practices —combination (for price-maintenance), underselling (to drive weaker competitors from the field), manipulation of shares (to control markets)?
2. Discuss the advantages of standardisation: (*a*) to the producer; (*b*) to the consumer.
3. Illustrate the effective use of standardisation in the following fields: (*a*) Nomenclature; (*b*) Dimensions; (*c*) Quality; (*d*) Tools; (*e*) Performances; (*f*) Processes. (See Brech (Ed.) *Principles and Practice of Management*, Second Edition, pp. 269–70).
4. Discuss the scope and importance of Work Study as a management technique. What factors influence its application?
5. What do you understand by 'the human implications of Work Study'?

   (Students are recommended to study the Case of Pakitt Ltd.—S. Dalziel and L. Klein: *The Human Implications of Work Study* (1960).)
6. "Operational Research has an approach to offer management of every kind, and a set of powerful tools which are *universally* applicable" (S. Beer).
7. Discuss the usefulness of Simulation as a managerial tool.

8. What are the 'managerial aspects of quality control'? (See, for example, Manning in *Production Technology: Some Modern Developments*, pp. 239–45).
9. "Management as an art starts where science leaves off. . . . Art, in the context of management, is above all the ability to 'sense' a situation". (Hooper).
10. It has been said that a great deal of what falls within the following fields partakes far more of art than of science: (i) The passing down of orders; (ii) The upward flow of information; (iii) The devolution of responsibility; (iv) Control and 'keeping touch'; (v) The projection of the centre to the periphery, so as to identify the whole concern with a single aim and policy. Discuss.
11. What do you understand by the 'management sciences'? What are their limitations?

CHAPTER SEVEN

MANAGEMENT SCIENCES—(II)

1. Management Accounting
2. Costing
3. Break-even Analysis
4. Management Ratios and Inter-firm Comparison
5. Statistical Methods in Industry; Quality Control; 'O and M'
6. Industrial Psychology and Sociology
7. Ergonomics
8. Conclusion: Decision-Making

§ 1. Management Accounting

The aim of management accounting is to communicate to management the results of its actions so as to assist in the framing of policy, and to co-ordinate the members of the whole team into 'profit engineering'.[1] By profit engineering is meant deciding what is a *satisfactory level* of profit and then planning the operations of the business to achieve it. After the budgeted profit must come the sales budgets, but before they are finally approved the management accountant will have a fairly good idea of the profit they will yield. If the profit is unacceptably low, the burden of deciding what to do will fall on the managing director. Once the output has been set each department must measure the input required to yield that output. Every manager must know as much of the overall plan as will enable him to make his contribution: the agreeing of budgets makes it possible to delegate authority. The accountant himself must report on the profit of events as they occur, so that management *by exception** can be practised. The

* *Management 'by exception'* (or *'control by exception'*). This means the measurement and evaluation of actual progress in comparison with the target figures. Decisions are required to be made by management *only* if the comparison shows actual or expected variation or *variance*. Hence control by exception requires: (i) comparison of actual performance with expected performance; (ii) comparison of actual costs with target costs, in such a manner that suitable corrective action can be taken if things go awry. The 'exception principle' is significant from the point of view of *delegation*: a superior may come to an agreement with a subordinate that the latter should come to him only when things are going as planned, but should not otherwise bother him.

[1] See D. A. Manser: 'What the Accountant can Provide for Top Management', *The Cost Accountant*, Vol. 38, No. 12 (December 1960).

accountant's function here is to provide good standard *costs* for each product under the headings *direct* materials, direct labour, variable overheads, fixed overheads. In addition to a *financial plan* a *profit plan* should be made.

Many people who have had no training in book-keeping and accounts tend to be afraid of management accounting. It must be realised that the whole purpose of such accounting is to give management information in such a form that it can be readily understood by the non-expert. The term covers "all those services which can assist top management and the other departments in the formulation of policy, the control of its execution and the appreciation of its effectiveness . . . the system of recording should be devised *predominantly with management's needs in mind*".[2] The accountant himself must get rid of the 'historical' attitude of mind, *i.e.* over-concern with past facts, and concentrate on the present and the future.

It must not be thought that management accountancy is only of use in a large business. In the small firm[3] also it is useful to have *control information* (*i.e.* to help in the day-to-day running of the business); and *trend information* (to help in policy-decisions for the future). The traditional accounts can be re-arranged so as to provide information for management. Periodical *trading* or *operating returns* should be made two or three times a year and profit and loss on each item determined.

Statistical data will also be useful: units produced and sold, staff employed, productive and unproductive machine-time, so that management has a readily-available fund of useful information for reference. Forecasting and budgeting will generally prove to be the most intractable tasks in a small firm. The chief 'tools' required here are *monthly cash forecasts* to show how much cash is needed to carry on the business, and a statement showing the sources and disposal of finance; break-even charts and moving annual totals (M.A.T.s.) will also be useful.

Budgeting. Financial budgets for controlling operations are a very old device, *e.g.* government budgets go back some two centuries.

[2] H. W. Broad and K. S. Carmichael: *A Guide to Management Accounting*, p. 3 (an excellent, readable introduction); another brief, simple introduction is T. G. Rose: *Top Management Accounting*, London (1957).

[3] N. R. Bellwood: 'Improving Accounting for Management in a Small Business', *Accountancy*, Vol. LXIII, No. 824 (May 1962).

Since the 1920s budgeting has become a fundamental tool of management,[4] and has forced businessmen to improve their planning: standards of performance cannot be prepared in advance unless the manager has made up his mind about such matters as objectives, working conditions. Such planning may be just as valuable as the later measurement and control; budgeting is also a useful *co-ordinative* device in the realm of such related activities as purchasing, production, storage and sales.

Budgetary planning begins with *output budgets* (sales and production) which indicate the *desired* targets; *departmental* budgets are then prepared, showing what each department is expected to attain and the resources to be used; finally, the detailed budgets are combined in an integrated global budget.

Budgetary control should not be regarded as a system of rigid control, but a method of attaining the overall objectives of growth. External conditions such as the level of demand may vary, and it is essential that the budgets lend themselves to *adjustment*. When it is impossible to make a firm forecast of the future, a *flexible* budget is prepared.[5] A flexible budget does not indicate that management has no clear policy, but there are certain circumstances beyond its control[6] *e.g.* in the case of new ventures, or where the business is subject to the vagaries of the weather, or where sales are unpredictable because of the nature of the business.

§ 2. Costing

(i) *Standard Costing*. It is not the job of the accountant to create policy, but to influence it, to supply management with prompt, accurate and effective information. Standard costs are similar to estimated costs in that both are determined *before* rather than after the period to which they relate but, unlike estimated costs, standard costs are built up 'brick by brick' from the various cost elements, and are directly linked with certain operational standards for control purposes. Each level of management must receive

[4] See H. E. Bethan, Part IV 'Control' of Brech (Ed.) *Principles and Practice of Management*; Broad and Carmichael, *op. cit.*, chapters III, 'The Sales Budget'; IV, 'The Production Budget'; V, 'The Capital Budgets'. A straightforward textbook is A. C. Edey: *Business Budgets and Accounts*.

[5] See D. Solomons: 'Flexible Budgets and the Analysis of Overhead Variances', *Management International* (1961/I).

[6] See Bethan, *op. cit.*, pp. 662–3 and 793–840 (Worked Examples) and, for examples, Broad and Carmichael, *op. cit.*, pp. 13–18.

the information most useful to it. Standard costing does not replace historical costing, but endeavours to determine what a product can *reasonably be expected* to cost. There are two important aspects of standard costing:

(*a*) The '*exception principle*': investigation and action are directed at the points where the *actual* expenditure deviates from the *planned* expenditure.

(*b*) *Actual costs* should be prepared for *departments* or *cost centres only*, and not for individual jobs or products. In this way the efficiency of each department can be checked by comparing the actual cost with the standard cost of the actual production achieved.

It is obvious that variable budgets are difficult to apply if a firm is handling different products; standard costs are a method of dealing with this problem. In a standard cost system the budgeted costs (for labour, materials, etc.) are computed per unit for *each* different product. Then, at the end of a given period, the number of units of different products that have been manufactured is multiplied by their respective costs. Thus several totals are obtained—for materials, labour, overheads, that together mirror the specific product-mix for the period. These totals constitute control standards that can be used to evaluate performance for the period.

The first stage in the introduction of standard costs is to set the standards, *i.e.* performance standards and costing-rates. Standard Specification Schedules must be prepared for each product, containing full details of it. Standard Costing Rates are prepared for materials, labour and overheads, and Standard Product Costs can then be compiled. The actual cost and the standard cost are then brought together and the variances determined and analysed—*i.e. total* variance, *uncontrollable* variance (due to external price movements or wage awards), *controllable* variance (due to factors within the organisation), *price* variance (due to using materials at a price different from the revised standard price), and *quantity* variance (due to using a different quantity of materials from that specified).

(ii) *Marginal Costing*. *Marginal cost* may be defined as the amount, at any *given volume* of production or output, by which *aggregate* costs are changed if the volume of production or output is increased by one unit.[7] More simply: if, starting from our present position, we produce one unit more of a certain product, the additional expenditure entailed is the marginal cost of that product.* *Marginal costing* is the ascertainment of marginal cost by differentiating between fixed and variable costs and the effect on profit of changes in volume or type of output.

Increasing use is now being made of the technique of marginal costing, but there is still a sharp division between those who favour the traditional approach, *i.e.* the allocation of *all* costs to products, and those 'marginalists' who wish to allocate only *variable* costs, and consider it illogical to include in product costs those costs which will be incurred whatever the level of output. Such costs, it is stated, should be regarded as 'the costs of being in business' and should be charged off to the Profit and Loss Account. Marginal costs provide important information for *profit planning*—they show the effect on profits of increasing or decreasing the volume of business and indicate by how much it is permissible to reduce selling prices and still obtain a contribution towards fixed overheads.[8]

It is convenient here to summarise recent thinking on the classification of costs. The traditional classification was into PRIME (or VARIABLE) COSTS, varying with output, *i.e.* labour, raw materials, power, heat and lighting; and FIXED (or SUPPLEMENTARY) COSTS, not varying with output, *i.e.* rent, capital charges, certain maintenance costs, marketing costs, managerial and certain staff costs. The latter have to be met whether production takes place or not. A more subtle analysis is as follows:

* The student should study that part of the economics syllabus dealing with costs at the same time.

7 See also definitions on p. 8 of *A Report on Marginal Costing* (Institute of Cost and Works Accountants), London (1961); see also 'Marginal Costing: A New Tool for Management' in *The Accountant* (June 25th 1955), and H. Hart: 'Some Aspects of Marginal Cost and Marginal Costing', *International Accountants' Journal* (June 1960).

8 For an interesting example of orthodox *versus* marginal costing see A. P. Cohen: 'Production Economics in the Confectionery Industry', *Work Study and Industrial Engineering* (May 1962).

Variable costs are divided into directly variable and semi-variable:

Directly Variable

Raw Materials; Packages; Process Fuel; Electricity; Carriage. (Vary in *direct proportion* to production.)

Semi-Variable

Labour; Materials (other than raw materials, packages and fuel) employed in process and maintenance departments, stores and warehouses.

(Also vary with production but *not* in direct proportion.)

Fixed Costs can also be divided into *Sectional* and *General*:

Sectional (relating to a particular section of the business; would cease to be incurred if that section were discontinued).

Note. A 'Section' may be either a product or group of products, or a market or group of markets.

General (relating to a business as a whole; will continue to be incurred at roughly the same level, whether or not any particular section of the business is discontinued).

§ 3. Break-Even Analysis

A break-even chart[9] is a graphic representation of a company's 'break-even point', *i.e.* the point at which it will neither make a profit nor suffer a loss from its operations. It may also be defined as that point where profits turn into losses or losses turn into profits. It is a systematic portrayal of past or projected costs and revenues in relation to volume. Break-even analysis is thus a subject in which the economist and the cost accountant meet.

Before the chart can be made it is necessary to segregate expenses into *fixed* expenses (those not affected by changes in the volume of sales); and *variable* expenses, which vary in direct proportion to sales. It must be stressed, however, that expenses cannot be *rigidly* grouped into fixed and variable, and that a major part of the classification will be based upon judgment.

'FIXED' EXPENSES may include: Rent, Taxes, Insurance, Indirect Labour, Heating and Lighting, Direct Labour, Supervision,

[9] See Appendix B, 'The Break-even Chart', in *A Report on Marginal Costing*, Institute of Cost and Works Accountants (1961); Brech (Ed.) *Principles and Practice of Management*, Part IV, chapter IV, 'Profit Planning and Break-even Analysis'.

Another lucid account is given in W. Rautenstrauch and R. Villiers: *The Economics of Industrial Management*, chapter V, New York (1957).

Administrative Expenses and certain Selling Costs. (Direct labour is generally taken as a variable expense).

'VARIABLE' EXPENSES are those which increase as production increases, and decrease as the volume of production dwindles. They may consist of: Depreciation (if based on production); Depreciation (if based on life in years); Power; Freight In; Freight on Sales.

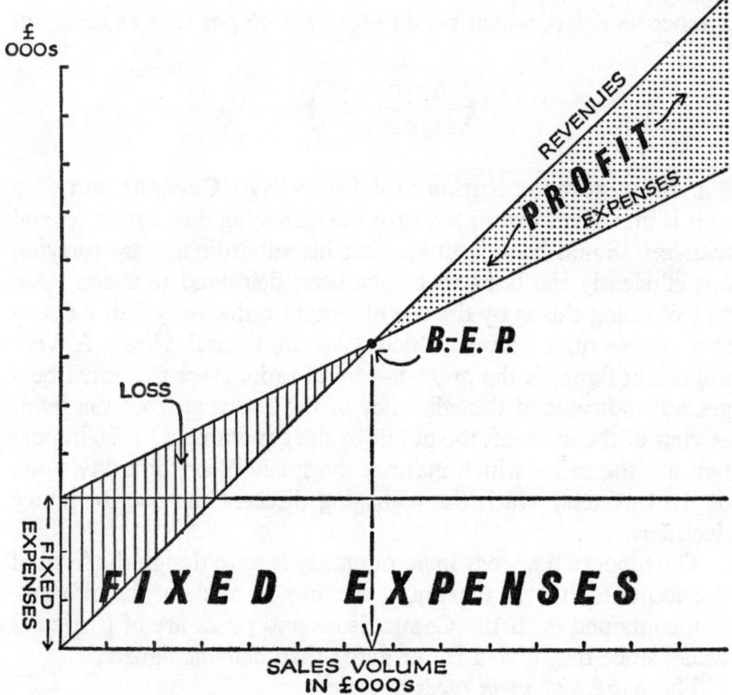

Example:

Suppose the practical capacity of a plant were 12,000 units a year with a selling price of £40 per unit. Suppose also that fixed expenses total £162,000 and variable expenses £16 per unit (=40 per cent of sales), the break-even point can be calculated as follows:

I

$$\text{B.E.P.} = \text{Fixed Expenses } \textit{divided by } 1 - \frac{\text{Variable Expenses}}{\text{Sales}}$$

$$= 162{,}000 \text{ divided by } 1 - \frac{192{,}000}{480{,}000}$$

$$= \frac{162{,}000}{1-0.40} = \frac{162{,}000}{0.60} = 270{,}000$$

Break-even Point in sales is, therefore, £270,000. Since the selling-price is £40 per unit, the total units at the B.E.P. would be $\frac{270{,}000}{40} = 6{,}750$, which would represent 56 per cent of capacity.

$$\left(\frac{6{,}750}{12{,}000} = 56\right).$$

§ 4. Management Ratios and Inter-firm Comparison

It is important that in any firm the managing director or general manager should be able to see that his subordinates are carrying out efficiently the tasks that have been delegated to them. One way of doing this is by the use of certain ratios—say half a dozen sets of essential figures which give an overall view. A very important figure is the *profit-to-capital* ratio, since this must be a general indicator of the efficiency of the business from the point of view of the investor, the public or the government. Also important are the ratios which indicate the financial or 'liquidity' state of the business, which the managing director can use for policy decisions.

The modern tendency in accountancy is so to design the form of the accounts that the maximum use may be made of the information contained in them. Comparisons and ratios are of particular value, since they give a better guide than *absolute* figures.

There are *four main types* of ratios:

(i) *Financial or balance-sheet ratios*, which show the relationship between one balance-sheet item and another.

(ii) *Operating ratios*, which are derived from the operating statement (Profit and Loss Account).

(iii) *Inter-related ratios*, which show the relationship between a balance-sheet item and an operating statement item (1 to 2 above).

(iv) *Other ratios* which relate a balance-sheet item or operating statement item to a *unit of time*.

The prosperity of a business depends largely on the recognition and application of a few principles. Thus investment in *fixed assets* must be held within reasonable limits, which will vary with the size of the firm, type and location; *liabilities*, both funded and current, must be kept within definable limits; *inventories* must be turned over a normal number of times a year; *receivables* must be kept liquid, and *net working capital* must be adequate.

The basic assumption of accounting ratios[10] is that *significant relationships* exist between various sets of figures and that by juxtaposing the figures for two activities their relative efficiency can be assessed. Ratios can be effectively used in *forecasting and planning*: past ratios are pointers to trends in costs, sales, profits.[11] They can also provide an additional *tool of control, i.e.* ratios can be used to 'signpost' plans, budgeted ratios being compared with the actual patios as calculated, so that they become an integral part of the budget system. They are also important tools for quickly assessing *solvency* or *profitability*, and for exposing over-trading.

Examples of Ratios

(i) *The 'Primary' Ratio* is the *return on capital employed*; it indicates the *efficiency of the use of capital*. 'Capital employed' includes fixed assets, plus stocks, stores and work-in-progress, *plus* other net current assets. A low return may indicate that capital is under-employed or it may indicate that capital is fully but inefficiently employed. (For this purpose return = profit *before* tax).

[10] The early work in Britain is in scattered articles, one of the first being E. H. Davison: 'Inter-firm Comparisons of Financial Ratios: their Value to Management', *The Manager* (Special B.I.M. Conference Issue, December 1956); only in the latest editions has the subject entered text-book literature, e.g. Carter's *Advanced Accounts* (new edit. by D. Garbutt); Brech (Ed.): *Principles and Practice of Management*, pp. 789–92 and 1005–10; and J. Batty: *Management Accounting*, London (1963).

[11] Profit is sometimes regarded as a 'dirty' word, but in any firm a surplus of income over actual expenditure is still needed to fund future developments. Profit measures the net effectiveness and soundness of an enterprise and, without it, talk about the loftier 'social responsibilities' of management is meaningless. See, for example, P. Drucker: *The Practice of Management*, pp. 65–9, *idem.*, 'Managing for Business Effectiveness', *Harvard Business Review* (June–July 1963).

The profitability concept measures not the *maximum* profit a business *can* produce, but the *minimum* it *must* produce.

(ii) *The 'Quick' or 'Liquidity' Ratio* is found by dividing liquid assets by current liabilities. *Liquid assets* are cash-in-hand, debts due to the company falling due within one month, and any encashable securities; *current liabilities* are all amounts due for payment in the near future.

$$\text{Quick Ratio} = \frac{\text{LIQUID ASSETS}}{\text{CURRENT LIABILITIES}}$$

It is difficult to generalise, but this ratio in many cases should be roughly 1:1, otherwise the company needs more liquid cash. In a business in which debtors habitually pay more slowly than creditors the rates may have to be as high as 2:1.

(iii) *'Current' Ratio*, found by dividing current assets by current liabilities. *Current assets* include liquid assets realisable within a month, and deferred assets such as material stocks, work-in-progress and finished goods. This ratio indicates how much *working capital* is available at any given moment. The ratio should be approximately 2:1 but this again depends on the nature of the firm.

(iv) *Sales Ratios.* There are three of these: Sales to Debtors, Sales to Fixed Assets, Sales over Working Capital.

Sales to Debtors: if the terms of payment were 1 month a usual ratio would be 12:1; any serious deviation from this would indicate that certain large customers were falling behind. This ratio spotlights the rate at which cash is received from credit sales.

Sales to Fixed Assets: is found by calculating how much sales revenue is obtained for every £ invested, the amount of revenue being a pointer to the efficiency with which assets are used.

Sales to Working Capital, which gives an indication when selling is excessive; the aim here should be not to over-tax working capital by accepting too many orders ahead of production.

(v) *Stock Ratios.* These are used to evaluate the efficiency, from the financial angle, of the company's policy with regard to raw material stock, work-in-progress and finished stock holdings.

Examples:

(*a*) $\dfrac{\text{Raw Material Stocks}}{\text{Total Sales Turnover}}$ and (*b*) $\dfrac{\text{Work-in-Progress}}{\text{Turnover}}$	These may indicate what occurs when sales fluctuate. If the company's policy is to maintain stock even when sales are falling the ratio will show any tendency to overloading.
(*c*) $\dfrac{\text{Raw Material Stocks}}{\text{Purchase}}$:	shows how many times a year the stock is 'turned over'. It is calculated by taking the total purchases for a *year* and dividing by the *average* stock figure for the *month.* This ratio may lead to investigation why certain stocks are sluggish.

(vi) *Cost Ratios.* Several ratios have been devised in this field, *e.g.:*

(*a*) $\dfrac{\text{Factory Costs}}{\text{Sales}}$ (*b*) $\dfrac{\text{Administrative Costs}}{\text{Sales}}$

(*c*) $\dfrac{\text{Selling Costs}}{\text{Sales}}$ (*d*) $\dfrac{\text{Distribution Costs}}{\text{Sales}}$

A much more elaborate list than the one above can be prepared: a recent one contains over 30 ratios, many of which would be of interest and value to one executive but not to another. The point is that if they are used intelligently they give management a useful tool for the *measurement* of relative efficiency: they are another example of the substitution of quantitative thinking for intuition.

Inter-firm Comparison. In 1956 the B.I.M. set up a Committee to examine the use of accounting ratios for the purpose of making comparisons between firms in the same industry* and of roughly the same size. In a large company comparisons can be made

* On the official meaning of the term 'industry' the student should study the section on 'Standard Industrial Classification' (S.I.C.) in Beacham and Williams: *Economics of Industrial Organisation.*

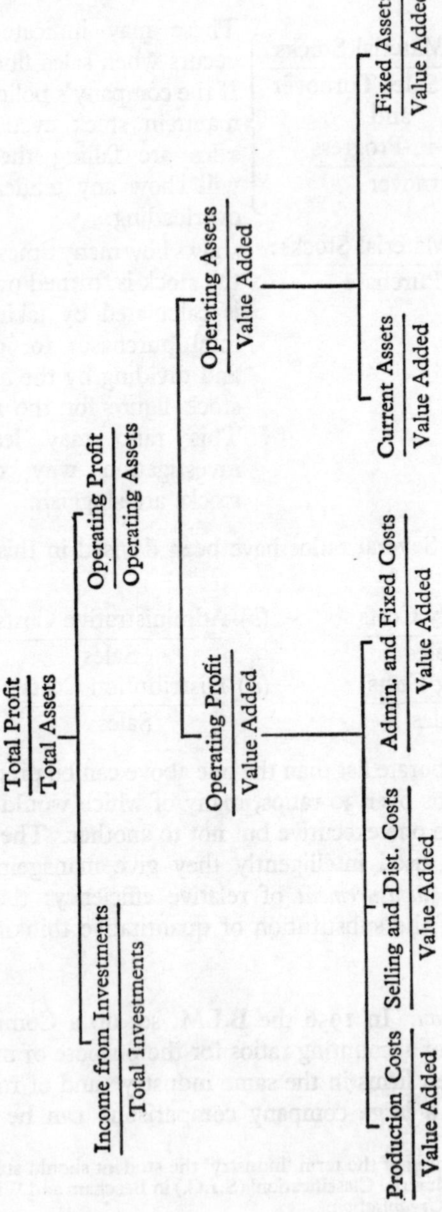

Note: 'Value added' = Sales *less* Raw Materials
or Conversion Cost + Profits

A Ratio-Comparison 'Pyramid'

between one factory or branch and another. Such comparisons may afford guides to investment policy, such as the *comparative profitability* and the *comparative efficiency* of different production methods, or of *comparative labour efficiencies*, or of the desirable level of stock. The medium-sized or small business lacks these advantages if it is content with information emanating solely from its own operations. It is obviously useful if, under the cover of anonymity, comparison of certain crucial ratios can be made with other firms of similar size in the same industry. It does not follow, because Firm X's figures deviate even considerably from the average of, say, twenty other similar firms, that there is cause either for exultation or despondency: the deviations do, however, suggest at what points an investigation might be carried out. Companies which join the I.F.C. Scheme are divided into 'activity groups' of like companies so that performances can be compared on an equitable basis: all information is given in confidence and the companies are provided with anonymous code numbers. The results of the comparison are available only to participating members; any firm with a balance-sheet and profit-and-loss account can join the scheme.[12]

§ 5. Statistics in Industry, Market Research, Quality Control

Statistical methods were not systematically introduced into industry until after World War I. The first publication was a French study dealing with artillery (1903), but after 1923 the engineers of the Bell Telephone Company applied the calculus of probability to the study of telephone material. In 1929 the Joint Committee for the Development of Statistical Applications in Engineering and Manufacturing was set up; a Committee for Statistical Studies was also set up by the British Standard Institution. During World War II a commission of the U.S. War Department issued such booklets as *Guide for Quality Control*, *Control Chart Method for Analyzing Data*, and *Control Chart Method for Controlling Quality during Production*. Similar publications appeared in Britain.

[12] For an example, see Brech (Ed.): *Principles and Practice of Management*, pp. 1008–10; see also the pamphlet *The Measurement of Efficiency in Large Organisations* (B.I.M. 1963).

This book cannot deal with statistical techniques[13] but only with the use and value of techniques for management, especially in connection with decision-making.[14] A few words on the pitfalls of statistics for the uninitiate may be mentioned here. Statistics is sometimes defined as the *science of averages*, *i.e.* it is concerned with averages or estimates based on the fundamental principle of the *constancy of large numbers*; it need not be stressed, however, that averages can be very misleading. Thus, for example, the *Retail Price Index*[15] is an average with all merits and weaknesses of an average: it is extremely valuable in providing a broad indication of the trend of prices, but it tells us nothing about any *particular* price or group of prices.

Another important statistical technique is that of *sampling*—'the art of fact-finding without getting all the facts'—which is essential when only a limited number of observations can be made. Market research, Gallup polls, retail price indices all make use of this technique. Although a case has been made out by Prof. Kendall[16] that sampling is an 'exact science', yet, however carefully the samples are taken, there is always the possibility that the result in any one sample may diverge widely from the true values in the aggregate. The number of samples, too, in relation to the whole, affects the accuracy of the inferences. The 'Ordinary Share Index' of *The Financial Times* is a good example of the value and limitations of sampling. Its purpose is to show the *general trend* of equity prices, but out of the thousands of individual stocks only thirty representative 'leaders' are selected. The index is geometric in order to soften the effect on the index of brusque movements in one or two prices. Even so, a sharp movement of only one price

[13] There are numerous introductory books on Statistical Method, of which the following may be mentioned: I. R. Vesselo: *How to Read Statistics*; W. J. Reichmann: *Use and Abuse of Statistics* (1961); Moroney: *Facts from Figures* (Penguin Books). See also M. B. Brodie: *On Thinking Statistically*, London (1963).

[14] See D. G. Moore: 'Better Management through Statistics', *The Manager* (February 1963). The author is Senior Statistician with the Reed Paper Group and deals with accident rates, checking the value of stores, production control and Monte Carlo techniques.

[15] See *Method of Construction and Calculation of the Index of Retail Prices* (H.M.S.O., 1956); and *Report on Revision of the Index of Retail Prices*, Cmnd. 1657 (1962).

On the use of statistics in a different context see M. G. Kendall: *Statistics and Personnel Management*.

[16] M. G. Kendall: 'Sampling as an Exact Science', in *Lloyds Bank Review* (1958).

has caused a major movement in the index. Its value is that it is a *general* indicator, particularly over a long period.

Percentages must be used with caution. The opponents of equal pay for equal work argued that sickness/absentee rates for women were 50 per cent higher than those for men, but the actual figures were 4½ days *per annum* as against 3 days for men. The *increase* in immigration from the West Indies to Britain in 1959–60 was 43 per cent: in popular journalism this became a 'flood', but it was only 0.1 per cent of the total population of this country.

The task of the statistician is to measure accurately, couch problems in quantitative terms and prepare the ground for a logical inference; his fact-finding, however, does not supersede judgment, it is complementary. The statistician studies a problem objectively, collects the necessary data, tabulates and summarises as accurately and as free from bias as possible. There his job ends: the managers who use his findings must exercise care and discretion, study the facts in their context in order to get them into an order which reveals the true relationships. "On the shop floor it is necessary to see the trees, and even, perhaps, the individual leaves. In the board room it is the woods and forests that must be seen . . ." (Moore).

Quality control[17] techniques can be applied to any element or aspect of manufacturing. There are two aims: to ensure that the result of one process is adequate as a basis for the next, and to ensure that the product is of sufficiently high quality to enhance the firm's reputation, satisfy the customer or avoid legal prosecution (*e.g.* drugs, rope, ammunition). Quality control uses statistical methods for measuring deviation from standard quality by recording sample tests on a chart; it is especially important in mass-production. Control can be based either on the quantity of defectives found in samples or on recorded measurements of the individual parts in the samples. Quality control can be practised in the office[18] as well as on the shop floor, but the idea of regular sampling of clerical work is still new to most office-managers.

17 For a useful brief survey see G. A. Garreau: 'Statistical Quality Control' in D. E. Greene: *Production Technology: Some Recent Developments* (London, 1962), pp. 216–45; also the tail-piece to this article by D. E. Manning: 'Managerial Aspects of Quality Control'; and T. H. Brown: 'Quality Control', chapter 17 of *New Decision-Making Tools for Managers* (ed. Bursk and Chapman), New York (1963). A fuller account is given in *The Production Handbook* (ed. Carson), New York (1958), Section 8, 'Quality Control'.

18 See P. N. Wallis: *Quality Control in the Office*, Current Affairs Ltd., London (1961).

Market research[19] (to be distinguished from market*ing* research, which is the systematic study of the factors relevant to selling and marketing), collects information about the market and customers and analyses its findings. The information may be collected by *personal observation* as to consumer habits and their trends, the use of *official* publications or by carrying out *sample surveys*, three methods which show an ascending degree of sophistication and technique. An important aim is to discover what 'image' the public has of a particular product and why it has this image. Hence, in addition, *motivational* research may be carried out.

§ 6. Industrial Psychology and Sociology

The term 'industrial psychology' must be used carefully and not equated with the philosophy of the human factor in industry, or the pseudo-science of industry, or a concern with the abnormal or pathological. It is "the scientific study of human behaviour and experience within the context of work".[20] Since psychology itself is by no means a unified science, industrial psychology also exhibits a diversity of approach and outlook. It has been said, however, that in all the areas in which industrial psychology has made headway and gained acceptance, the concept of *measurement* has been involved. Recent published work is concerned largely with *social* factors, such as *attitudes*, *leadership*, *motives* and *group influences*. Investigations are increasingly carried out by teams of scientists, including psychologists, economists, sociologists, anthropologists, physiologists, anatomists, specialists in industrial design, in industrial relations and in administration. In the past many have expressed a distrustful or sceptical attitude towards industrial psychology, but attitudes are becoming more favourable as it is realised that industrial psychologists are not cranks or witch-doctors. It seems possible that in the future psychological research will be gradually permeated by demands of an essentially practical nature.

19 For an introduction see Brech (Ed.): *Principles and Practice of Management*, Part 1, chapter 11, 'Market Research', by R. G. Lagden. Short books dealing with this subject are: A. H. R. Delens: *Principles of Market Research*, London (1950); Max K. Adler: *Modern Market Research*, London (1951); and L. Hardy: *Marketing for Profit*, London (1962).

20 An excellent summary of recent developments is given in two articles, 'Current Trends in Industrial Psychology', Part I and Part II, *Personnel Management* (September 1962 and December 1962).

The following is a list of the major fields in which investigation is proceeding at present:

(i) *Improvement of Individual Efficiency*

(*a*) *Selection of the right man for the job*—the area in which research has achieved the most impressive results.

(*b*) *Training: operator* training (the most efficient methods for the acquisition of skills); training of *supervisors* (designed to change the supervisor's attitudes or alter his behaviour vis-à-vis his staff); training of *technicians and scientific workers*; training in *specific subjects*—public speaking, report writing, rapid reading.

(*c*) *Work Study and 'Human Engineering'*, including job analysis, work measurement, wage incentives, work methods, the physical environment, safety.

(ii) *Enhancement of Individual Satisfaction*

(*a*) *Job Attitudes:* the study of the attitudes, morale and motivation is one of the leading topics in current investigations. Attitudes are usually measured by means of *standardised scales*, given by questionnaire or interview. A remarkable finding is the prevalence of *job* dissatisfaction.

(*b*) *Occupational Adjustment and Maladjustment.* It has been widely held that employees with emotional disturbances are more likely to be absent, alcoholic or sick, poor at his work, have poor relationships with his co-workers. Much of the work undertaken as counselling is non-scientific, but there is an increasing use of controlled observations and experiments. A recent report has analysed the reasons why some two million Americans were rejected or prematurely separated from service during World War II, on account of mental or emotional instability; some of the findings are undoubtedly of relevance to peacetime employment.[21]

[21] E. Ginzberg *et al.*: *The Ineffective Soldier: Lessons for Management and the Nation*, 3 vols., New York (1959).

(iii) *Achievement of 'Organisational Effectiveness'*

(*a*) Research is now being carried out into the *nature of the organisation*, and into determining the human implications of policies, practices and different types of organisation.

(*b*) *Management and Supervision.* Modern research aims at finding methods of describing *types of leadership* in terms of their most characteristic elements. Statistical analysis is used to determine the most important variables; it is then possible to investigate the extent to which the factors are associated with different types of organisation.

(*c*) *Relationships between Groups in the Organisation.* It is important that different groups and departments should work in harmony. The most important area for research is that of management-labour relations.

Some of the problems with which industrial psychologists were previously concerned, *e.g.* noise, lighting, monotony, are now less actively pursued, perhaps because their findings are now commonly accepted. In some instances, however, earlier conclusions are being modified or refined; thus, *fatigue* is a most important factor in work study problems, but hitherto the approach of management to fatigue had been entirely empirical; the 'co-efficients of fatigue' were purely arbitrary, lacking any scientific foundation.[22]

The experimental psychologist has an important contribution to the problem of fitting the job to the worker. Selection and training are processes of fitting the worker to the job, and it is only recently that scientists have come to realise the full possibilities of the complementary process of adapting work so as to *eliminate excessive demands*, thus minimising the need for selection and training. In recent years experimental psychologists, anatomists and physiologists have looked at practical problems in the light of their special problems of human ability and the human body.

[22] See, for example, two articles by Lucien Lauru, 'The Measurement of Fatigue', *The Manager* (May and June 1954); and K. F. H. Murrell: 'The Nature and Measurement of Industrial Fatigue', *Work Study and Industrial Engineering* (December 1960). E. G. Chambers: two articles on 'Industrial Fatigue', *Work Study and Industrial Engineering* (February and March 1962).

There is an obvious overlap between industrial psychology in its technical sense and social psychology, sociology and psychiatry. To take the latter field first: Elliott Jaques[23] pointed out that industrial life influences our 'emotional health' by "playing into already existing instability or neurosis in the individual, and allowing each one to act out the disturbed parts of his personality in his work". Again, the superior-subordinate relationship may cause conflict at the unconscious level. Jaques has frequently noticed, for example, "unconscious feelings of hostility and persecution such that . . . victimization and unfair practices are commonly anticipated to an extent which may be out of all proportion to the real situation".

The social psychology and sociology of industry have a long pedigree, though many developments have taken place in recent times, especially in the study of groups.[24] Among early contributions may be mentioned Ure's *Philosophy of Manufacturers* (1835), Marx, *Das Kapital* (1867–94), *Industrial Democracy* (1897) by the Webbs; and Durkheim's *The Division of Labour in Society.*

In the early part of this century there was Cole's *Chaos and Order in Industry* (1920), Rowntree's *The Human Factor in Business* (1925) and Cathcart's book (1928) of the same title. Some outstanding modern works are Roethlisberger's *Management and Morale* (Cambridge, Mass. 1943), Warner and Low's *The Social System of the Factory* (New Haven, 1947), Mayo's *The Human Problems of an Industrial Civilisation* and *The Social Problems of an Industrial Civilisation* (1948), Ferdinand Zweig's *Labour, Life and Poverty* (1948) and *The British Worker** (1952), E. Jaques's *The Changing Culture of a Factory* (1952), and monographs such as *The Dockers*, ed. Simey (1955) and Zweig's *Men in the Pits* (1948). So far work has concerned itself with such questions as the *social history* of industry, the industrial enterprise regarded as a *social institution,* the *formal* and *informal* organisation of industry and questions of *status* and *class,* sociological aspects of *industrial conflict* and *industrial relations,* and the wider questions of *industry and society* and the effects on the social structure of employment of technological changes.

* obtainable in a Pelican edition.

23 Elliott Jaques: 'Psycho-pathology in Industrial Life', *The Twentieth Century* (May 1956).

24 For an introduction see Brown: *The Social Psychology of Industry,* chapter 5 'The Informal Organisation of Industry', and W. H. J. Sprott: *Human Groups* (Penguin Books).

Before World War I the social structure of the firm was very simple; it consisted basically of the owner and, perhaps, his representatives, and the two main groups of 'staff' and 'manual' workers, the former being regarded as belonging to a higher social stratum than the latter. With the growing complexity and increase in size of factories the new element of 'works staff' was introduced, enjoying staff privileges but working the same hours as manual workers. Today the reward of such workers has declined so far that many semi-skilled workers earn more than they. Another change has been the growth in the number of semi-skilled operatives, and in the variety of jobs regarded as skilled. The future 'skill-mix' of industry will be very different from that of the present day. Further, owing to the increasing complexity of industrial production, higher educational standards will be required, quite apart from the social responsibility of higher education.[25]

As a result of these changes it seems as if the age-old demarcations of class will become increasingly blurred. The fundamental problem of industry and society, neglected in the past, will be how to find a place for man in an industrial order inescapably subject to technical requirements and natural forces. For man is in essence a social being. To regard him as an individual enjoying an independent existence who then enters into social relationships with his fellows seems to be a reversal of the true order of things. Man is also a responsible being, and if he cannot act responsibly he is deprived of something which belongs to his dignity; he loses his self-respect. It is important, now as never before, that people in industry should begin to realise the inescapable, creative dependence of men on one another: the four main partners—management, scientists, technicians and 'workers' must regard themselves not as in opposition but as fundamentally necessary to one another. An attempt by management to speak the last word in isolation leads to autocracy and dictatorship, against which human nature will revolt. If scientists and technicians have the last word life will become subjected to impersonal and technical considerations. If workers insist upon having the last word they will be left without the direction, leadership and expert knowledge essential to the achievement of their aims.

[25] R. O. Clarke: 'The Social Aspects of Industrial Employment', in *Industrial Relations, Contemporary Problems and Perspectives* (ed. B. C. Roberts).

§ 7. Ergonomics[26]

The word is derived from the Greek *ergon*, 'work' and *nomos*, 'law': ergonomics is the study of man in relation to his *working environment*, or of fitting the job to the man (or woman), or 'more work with less effort'. In the past working conditions were often influenced by the nature of the work itself, and the type of equipment used; the worker had to adapt himself to the conditions and get on with the job. It is now realised that work must be studied from the worker's point of view, with the object of improving conditions so that the worker can not only perform a task more speedily, more easily and more comfortably, but also more accurately. If the onset of fatigue and boredom can be staved off, then higher productivity will result.

Ergonomics, then, as the word implies, studies the laws governing the output of human energy; it is a multi-disciplinary study, based upon the researches and experiments of anatomists, physiologists, psychologists and design engineers. A typical problem in ergonomics can be seen in the considerations which go into the design of a cockpit—seating, thermal environment, position and design of levers and controls, position and design of the instrument panel, clothing and the aspects of endurance, fatigue and performance of the pilot. The phrase 'working environment' is thus taken to include tools and equipment, as well as the surrounding conditions—temperature, humidity, air movement, radiant heat, noise, lighting, colour, smells.[27]

In the industrial problems of enhancing the efficiency of the man-machine unit, ergonomics can help in two ways: at the initial *design* stage of a process or product, and in the modification of existing equipment. The effectiveness of a tool or machine depends not only upon its functional efficiency and reliability, but also upon the ability of the human operator to control it easily. This ability is greatly influenced by the design of the machine. In those firms which have an established work study department the ergonomist can supply a useful supplementary aid to production efficiency, by introducing modifications to existing machines and to the layout of shops, and to the control of the environment.

26 See W. T. Singleton: *The Industrial Use of Ergonomics*, D.S.I.R. (H.M.S.O.) Some books on the subject are listed at the end of this chapter.

27 See the articles by Alan Cross: 'Some Observations on Ergonomics', especially Part III, 'Environmental Conditions', *Time and Motion Study* (January 1961).

He uses the same procedures of task analysis to cover the *mental* as well as the physical aspects of the work.

At present there is a need for co-operation between engineers and biologists at the drawing-board stage;[28] this means that the engineer must have some training in the understanding of the human body. The same reasoning applies to management. But it is not sufficient to fit the *physical* conditions of work to man's capacities and limitations; it is also necessary to create a 'psychological climate' in which he will be both satisfied and effective.

§ 8. Conclusion: Decision-making

The last two chapters have introduced the student to some of the more recent 'tools' and techniques of measurement for control. All these techniques are increasingly in the hands of highly specialised personnel. It is the duty of the manager to know sufficient about their work, in general terms, to appreciate the possible significance of their results. The essential meaning of what operational researchers are trying to do can be imparted without the excessive use of mathematics; again, the basic notions of management accountancy can be explained to a person who has no special training in accountancy—otherwise, what use would it be, since its aim is to provide the non-specialist top manager with insights and pointers?

We have moved a long way in the past century from Scientific Management to Management Sciences. Take the case of work study. Some people still believe that work study consists only of those activities which derive from Taylor's 'time-study' or Gilbreth's 'motion-study', but work study includes numerous techniques for analysing and measuring what is being done, with the object of seeking improvement or providing management with better bases for decision and control. For example, although incentive schemes are not part of work study, yet work measurement is an essential preliminary to any just payment-by-results scheme.[29]

Most of the management sciences have evolved in the past decade or two, and new developments are constantly taking place. *Cybernetics*, for example, is a science which views industry as

[28] For some examples of 'ergonomic design' see Alan Cross's article in *Time and Motion Study* (December 1960).

[29] See R. M. Currie: *Financial Incentives Based on Work Measurement*, London (1963).

something 'living', or behaving as if it were alive; it is the 'science of communication and control', studying these mechanisms in both machines and animals, "since nothing is less static or more operational than a live process".[30] This new science was launched by Norbert Wiener in 1948;[31] he was concerned with communication difficulties in the central nervous system, computors, organisations and society.

No doubt numerous business decisions are made by that vague entity 'intuition', *i.e.* without resort to *conscious* or *rational* processes, and there is still room for imaginative and personal judgment of a situation. The tendency is, however, for intuition (or 'flair' or 'hunch') to be merged in a rational process. It seems safe to say that there can never be a science *of* management in the sense that all events in both the material and human field will be predictable: decisions always have to be made under conditions of imperfect knowledge of the future. The existence of *uncertainty*[32] as distinct from *risk* means that managers have to formulate hypotheses about the future; their 'expectation models' are largely subjective forecasts, but based on *objective* data increasingly supplied by the management sciences.

Four phases can be distinguished in rational decision-making: making a *diagnosis*; finding *alternative solutions*; *analysing and comparing alternatives*; and finally *selecting* which *plan* must be followed. The most difficult diagnosis is that of situations which involve many inter-related problems; any 'solution' proposed for one will affect what is feasible or necessary in other areas.

In every diagnosis a high degree of personal judgment is involved; the definition itself of a problem should not be regarded as fixed and unalterable. Even in the search for alternatives new evidence and new issues may be uncovered.[33]

30 See Brech (Ed.): *Principles and Practice of Management*, pp. 939–41.

31 N. Wiener: *Cybernetics, Control and Communication in the Animal and the Machine*, New York (1948); a co-founder was C. E. Shannon of the Bell Telephone Laboratories. For introductions to cybernetics see end of this chapter.

32 See G. S. Shackle: *Uncertainty in Economics*, chapts. 1 and 2; also M. H. Spencer: 'Uncertainty, Expectations and Foundations of the Theory of Planning', *Journal of the Academy of Management*, Vol. 5, No. 3 (December 1962).

33 See Newman and Sumner: *The Process of Management*, Part 3, 'Planning: Element of Decision-Making', also the case studies, pp. 342–56.

ADDITIONAL READING ASSIGNMENTS

The following lists are provided for students who wish to study any of the matters discussed in greater detail.

Management Accounting and Costing

H. W. Broad and K. S. Carmichael: *A Guide to Management Accounting* (1963).

J. Batty: *Management Accountancy* (1963).

A Report on Marginal Costing (Inst. of Cost and Works Accountants, 1962).

K. S. Most: *Standard Costs.*

Psychology and Sociology

H. J. Eysenck: *Uses and Abuses of Psychology* (Penguin Books).

H. J. Eysenck: *Sense and Nonsense in Psychology* (Penguin Books).

W. J. Sprott: *Human Groups* (Penguin Books).

M. S. Viteles: *Motivation and Morale in Industry.*

R. A. Brady: *Business as a System of Power.*

V. L. Allen: *Power in Trade Unions.*

H. Croome: *Human Problems of Innovations* (H.M.S.O. pamphlet).

J. Woodward: *Management and Technology* (H.M.S.O. pamphlet).

E. Jaques: *The Changing Culture of a Factory.*

W. E. Moore: *Industrial Relations and the Social Order.*

B. C. Roberts (Ed.): *Industrial Relations. Contemporary Problems and Perspectives.*

Ergonomics

E. J. McCormick: *Human Engineering.*

Ergonomics in Industry, Proceedings of D.S.I.R. Conference (H.M.S.O., 1960).

W. F. Floyd and A. T. Welford: *Human Factors in Equipment Design* (Ergonomics Research Society, 1954).

P. A. Verdier: *Basic Human Factors for Engineers.*

Adaptation du Travail à l'Homme. Session d'Etude sur L'Ergonomie pour les Ingénieurs (O.C.D.E., Paris).

W. F. Floyd and A. T. Welford (Eds.): *Fatigue* (Ergonomic Research Society, 1953).

Colour and Lighting in Factories (British Colour Council).

K. H. G. Murrell: *Ergonomics* (1964).

Management Ratios and Interfirm Comparison

J. Batty: *Management Accountancy.*
K. Pennycuick: *Industrial Diagnosis,* chapt. XIII.
Efficiency Comparisons within Large Organisations (B.I.M./I.F.C. 1962).

Statistics

C. Chivers: *Vital Statistics for Trade Unionists.*
C. A. Blyth: *The Use of Economic Statistics.*
M. B. Brodie: *On Thinking Statistically.*

O and M

H. P. Cemach: *Work Study in the Office.*
G. Mills and O. Standingford: *Office Administration.*
J. C. Denyer: *Office Management.*
E. V. Grills and C. J. Berg: *Work Measurement in the Office* (McGraw-Hill, 1959).
The Measuring of Work in the Office (B.I.M. 1956).
Work Study and O and M in Local Government (British Productivity Council).

Cybernetics

Norbert Wiener: *Cybernetics* (New York. 1948).
Norbert Wiener: *The Human Use of Human Beings* (New York, 1956).
W. R. Ashby: *An Introduction to Cybernetics.*
P. de Latil: *Thinking by Machine.*
G. M. T. Guilbaud: *What is Cybernetics?*
K. W. Deutsch: *The Nerves of Government* (the cybernetic approach to the study of political institutions).

TOPICS FOR DISCUSSIONS/ESSAYS

1. What is the value of properly conducted comparisons between the various operating units of a large organisation? (see *Efficiency Comparisons within Large Organisations,* B.I.M. 1962).
2. Draw a specimen Break-even Chart and discuss its use. (see, for example, Appendix B.1 to *A Report on Marginal Costing,* Inst. of Cost and Works Accountants, 1961).
3. "Management is continually having to make decisions for which financial and cost information provides the essential background." Discuss.

4. "Return on capital employed provides the overall yardstick by which the use of business resources may be measured". What points need to be taken into consideration when interpreting this figure? (see *Efficiency Comparisons within Large Organisations*, B.I.M., pp. 24–27).
5. The British Standard *Glossary of Terms in Work Study* (B.S. 3138: 1959) defines work study as "those techniques . . . used in the examination of human work in *all* its contexts". Is "Work Study applied to the Office" a satisfactory definition of O and M?
6. Clerical work is one of the most expensive services to industry. Discuss briefly inefficiencies in clerical work under the following headings: Delays; Loss; Errors; Duplications; Wasted Effort; Wasted Material; Low Output; Bad Service; Lack of Security; Unreasonable Idle Time.
7. Indicate briefly some recent investigations in ergonomics and cybernetics and their potential value to the manager.
8. Outline some of the research methods available to a manufacturer in his market investigations (see, for example, Brech (Ed.) *Principles and Practice of Management*, Second Edition, pp. 130–39).
9. Write short notes on: (*a*) Budgetary Planning; (*b*) Budgetary Control; and (*c*) Flexible Budgetary Control (see, for example, Brech (Ed.): *Principles and Practice of Management*, pp. 658–63).

PART THREE

MANAGEMENT PROCEDURES

PART THREE

MANAGEMENT PROCEDURES

CHAPTER EIGHT

'ADMINISTRATION', 'MANAGEMENT' AND 'ORGANISATION'

§ 1. What is Administration?

The dictionary (*Concise Oxford*) defines *administration* simply as *management*, substituting one word the meaning of which it is desired to elaborate for another: administration is 'management (of business)', or 'management of public affairs; government'. The administrator is defined as 'manager; one capable of organising; one who performs official duties (of religion, justice, etc.)'. Clearly such definitions, defining each word in terms of the others, do not get us very far.

Perhaps a good starting point is to say that any firm (business, concern) is established to do a certain job, and its organisation is the 'framework' of responsibilities through which it attains its ends. The main purpose of administration (from Latin *administrare* ='to serve') is to infuse life into the organisation, to make it function, by both positive and negative measures—negative, because there may be obstacles which have to be removed.

It is probably true that no discussion is more replete with clichés and platitudes than the discussion of what constitutes administration. Whatever it is, it is not something *static*; it is living and changing and cannot remain unchanged for very long; it will have to change as new methods are introduced, such as electronic computers, quicker communications.

In the past the word administration has been used in several different senses, *e.g.* top government ('the Eisenhower Administration'); administration of justice; and also in the sense of day-to-day running, as in the Services ('the admin. block'). On the other hand, it may refer to *policy-making and the execution of policy* as contrasted with management viewed as the *ordering and co-ordinating* of men, materials and machines. Another use is that of the direction of a group of people towards a common goal, but that is also a definition of management. The present writer prefers to think of administration as covering the *whole* organisation: the development of a flexible human machine for a given purpose or set of purposes, and the keeping of this constantly under review. Administration arose out of the need to *keep records* (clerks, scribes) and the need for having a centralised person to receive and disburse moneys (bursars).

It has been said that if good management is the "art of getting something done quickly, economically and efficiently", then "all administrators are, or should be, managers".[1] The general field of administrative functions has been summarised by Sir Frederic Hooper as follows:[2]

(i) The passing down of orders.
(ii) The upward flow of information.
(iii) The devolution of responsibility.
(iv) Control and 'keeping touch'.
(v) The projection of the centre to the periphery, so as to identify the whole concern with a single aim and policy.

The administrator, says Sir Edward Bridges, has two main questions to settle:[3]

(i) Whether the scheme of organisation is technically sound and economical;
(ii) How it will work given the personalities of the chief members of his staff.

He must, therefore, understand the main principles of organisation, the main ones being:

(i) To insist on a *clear demarcation of responsibility* between his sections;
(ii) To see that the *lines of responsibility* are so drawn that important issues of policy are *not divided* between *two or more* branches, but that each is the responsibility of one branch or individual;
(iii) To see that the '*span of control*' is not too wide;
(iv) To see that there are proper arrangements for *co-ordinating* sections whose work interlocks closely.
(v) To be satisfied that there is a *proper delegation of duties* so that the important, and *only* the important, things are submitted to higher authority, and that the Heads of Sections can run their show without too much interference.

[1] A. L. Banks and J. A. Hislop: *The Art of Administration*, p. 110.

[2] F. Hooper: *Management Survey*, Pelican ed., p. 65.

[3] Sir Edward Bridges: 'Administration: What is It?', in *The Making of an Administrator* (Ed. A. Dunsire).

(vi) To see that decisions are taken as *closely* as possible to the place where things happen.

If all these are but common sense, says Sir Edward, "they are based on a good deal of experience of the likely points of weakness in organisations, and of the fallibility of human beings, and of the best ways to combat them". Sir Edward believes that "no hard and fast lines" can be drawn between the specialised skills of organisation and management and the knowledge or capacity which the general administrator requires. You cannot say just where one begins and the other ends.

The *qualities of a good administrator are*:

(i) The power of *rapid analysis*—ability to grasp all the facts in a complicated situation, sort them out and perceive their inter-relationships.

(ii) The capacity to recognise the *essential points* in a situation.

(iii) The sense of *timing*.

(iv) The capacity to think much less in terms of things as they are today but in terms of *what is going to happen in the future* (3, 6, 12 months ahead).

(v) The capacity to *hold an even balance* between discrimination about the points he can concede and the points on which he must stand firm.

(vi) *Personal qualities;* imagination, perseverance, capacity to understand and lead people.

In the past administration has often been used to mean a superior process restricted to the *upper* executive structure, the highest planning function, the authority deciding on general policies.[4] There seems, however, no need to retain this usage today, and management is perhaps a better title for the process as a whole. As Simon[5] pointed out, decision-making does not finish when the *general purpose* of an organisation has been settled. On the contrary, "the task of 'deciding' pervades the entire administrative organisation quite as much as the task of 'doing'—indeed, it is integrally tied up with the latter."

If one is to follow popular usage, the main significance of administration seems to centre on the *procedures or routines of planning and control*—it is a useful label to apply to these aspects

[4] See for example, Mooney and Reiley: *Onward Industry!* pp. 487–8.

[5] H. A. Simon: *Administrative Behaviour*, p. 1.

of the total process.[6] The definition suggested by Brech is:

"ADMINISTRATION: That part of management which is concerned with the installation and carrying out of the procedures by which the programme is laid down and communicated, and the progress of activities is regulated and checked against plans."

§ 2. Management

There are similarly many definitions of management, the dictionary including such definitions as training horses and "trickery, deceitful connivance". Perhaps the best brief definition is "getting things done through others". Other definitions include "making co-operative endeavours function properly", or "converting disorganised resources of men, machines and money into a useful enterprise. '*The* management' would therefore include all persons in an enterprise who are officially vested with authority and accountability for those who actually get the work done. Managers are the activating element of an enterprise.

Management is a *social process*: it is social since managerial activity is mainly concerned with *relations between people*; it is a *process* because it comprises actions that lead to the accomplishment of objectives. A manager *co-ordinates* other people's activities rather than performs operations himself. Management is also a continuous process, since new situations are constantly arising and there is a ceaseless flow of problems. The total task of management may be highly complex, and it is then useful, for analytical purposes, to divide it up into PLANNING, ORGANISING, LEADING, CO-ORDINATING, CONTROLLING.

§ 3. The Fundamental Tasks of Management

(i) *Looking ahead:* trying to visualise the results desired, the needs and markets, significant trends.

(ii) *Establishing objectives*—policies, criteria and standards for performance; formulation of plans, budgets and management controls.

(iii) *Attaining results through others*—forming and maintaining a sound organisation.

(iv) *Searching for improvements*, including appraisal of results, decision-making, remedial action.

[6] Brech, in *Principles and Practice of Management*, 2nd ed., p. 23.

(v) *Helping subordinates*—inspiring confidence, motivating teamwork, maintaining respect and discipline; education and training.

Brech's definition is:

"MANAGEMENT—A social process entailing responsibility for the effective and economical planning and regulation of the operations of an enterprise, in fulfilment of a given purpose or task, such responsibility involving:

(*a*) judgment and decision in determining plans and in using data to control performance and progress against plans; and

(*b*) the guidance, integration, motivation and supervision of the personnel composing the enterprise and carrying out its operations."

§ 4. The Detailed Activities within the Five Major Functions[7]

I. PLANNING

1. Trends
2. Objectives
3. Policies
4. Programmes
5. Budgets
6. Work assignments
7. Schedules
8. Growth and Expansion
9. Controls and Reports
10. Improvements

II. ORGANISATION AND STAFFING

1. Organisation Charts
2. Functional Charts
3. Position Descriptions
4. Performance Standards
5. Job Evaluations
6. Qualifications Requirements
7. Compensation Programme
8. Staffing and Recruitment
9. Relationships
10. Personnel Utilisation

III. DIRECTION AND LEADERSHIP

1. Delegation
2. Interpretation
3. Understanding
4. Acceptance of accountability
5. Training and motivation
6. Discipline
7. Group Dynamics
8. Morale
9. Productivity
10. Job satisfaction

[7] After D. Carlson: *Modern Management, Principles and Practices*, O.E.C.D., Pairs, 1962, pp. 21–2.

IV. CO-ORDINATION

1. Co-ordination (up, down, across)	6. Between H.Q. and Field
2. Integration of all activities	7. With regulatory agencies
3. Within the organisation	8. With the industry
4. Within departments	9. With the community
5. Between departments	10. All other relationships

V. CONTROLS: RATIOS, STANDARDS

1. Criteria for measuring results	6. Performance appraisals
2. Project your desired results	7. Remedial action
3. Establish check-points	8. Work simplification
4. Schedules and time-tables	9. Audits and Reports
5. Sequence of importance	10. Board approvals

§ 5. What is Organisation?

Some definitions are given below for the student's critical consideration:

(i) " . . . the form of every human association for the attainment of a common purpose" (Mooney and Reiley: *Onward Industry*, p. 10).

(ii) " . . . the ordered structure created to accomplish a definite objective" (Whitehead: *How to Become a Successful Manager*, ch. 7).

(iii) " . . . the process of identifying and grouping activities for the most effective achievement of the policy of an undertaking" (Falk: *The Business of Management*, p. 51).

(iv) "The 'organisational' structure is the framework within which people act; the organisation of a business is the arrangement of people in it so that they act as one body. 'To organise' is to arrange the parts so that they shall act as one body" (Walter Puckey, *Management Principles*, p. 24).

(v) " . . . determining what activities are necessary to any purpose (or 'plan') and arranging them in groups which may be assigned to individuals" (Urwick: *The Elements of Administration*).

(vi) "A firm is in essence a living organism composed of the men who work for it" (K. Pennycuick: *Industrial Diagnosis*, p. 20).

The economist's definition of organisation is the arrangement and combination of resources (natural resources and capital goods and labour) to achieve an economic aim, either (i) with the resources *available* (the aim then being to achieve the maximum result); or (ii) to achieve a *given* objective with the *least* expenditure of effort. The task of organisation falls to the lot of the *entrepreneur*, the one who brings together the factors of production, undertakes *risks* and shoulders the *uncertainty* of the enterprise. It is, however, very rare that the entrepreneur is a single person, and organisation must be regarded as a complex structure at the apex of which is the Board of Directors.

One of the best discussions of the entrepreneur is also one of the earliest—that of J. B. Say in 1821:[8] "He is called upon to estimate, with tolerable accuracy, the importance of the specific product, the probable amount of the demand, and the means of its production".

§ 6. 'Principles' of Organisation

It has been frequently said that there are no principles in the scientific sense (explanatory principles) but only 'wrinkles' which have been put forward on the basis of practical experience. As Brech[9] has said, there is no suggestion of principles with the firm force of a law or the certitude of an axiom, but "something more like the directive character of a 'precept', whose primary purpose is to serve as a guide to the correct formulation of a sound framework of integrated executive action".[10] Herbert Simon goes so far as to say that 'principles' are essentially useless, but that his study provides "a framework for the analysis and description of administrative situations, and with a set of factors that must be weighed in arriving at any valid proposal for administrative organisation".

When we talk of the 'fundamentals' of management we imply that lessons can be learned from experience and transferred from one situation to another. If, in different circumstances, fundamentals can be recognised and resolved by resort to 'principles', then problems can be more effectively resolved and techniques

8 J. B. Say: *A Treatise on Political Economy*, London (1821), p. 104.

9 Brech: *Organisation, the Framework of Management*, p. 72.

10 H. Simon: *Administrative Behaviour*, p. xxxiv (Introduction).

more efficiently applied. It is highly doubtful whether such a complete body of principles will ever exist as to furnish guidance for the solution of all managerial problems. Yet the fact that management has been successful in business, government and other enterprises supports the view that a considerable body of principles (in the sense of provisional generalisations) does in fact exist, and that "it serves increasingly to crystallize the purpose of management and simplify the task of training managers".[11]

Only two examples of attempts to draw up principles will be given here, the so-called Ten Commandments prepared by the American Management Association in 1941, and Fayol's Principles. The student can himself study other examples, *e.g.* those of Brech.

Ten Commandments of Good Organisation

1. *Definite* and *clear-cut responsibilities* should be assigned to each executive.
2. *Responsibility* should always be coupled with corresponding *authority.*
3. *No change* should be made in the *scope or responsibilities of a position* without a definite understanding to that effect on the part of all persons concerned.
4. No executive or employee occupying a single position in the organisation should be subject to *definite orders* from *more than one source.*
5. Orders should never be given to subordinates *over the head* of a responsible executive. Rather than do this the officer in question should be supplanted.
6. *Criticisms of subordinates* should, whenever possible, be made *privately*, and in no case should a subordinate be criticised in the presence of executives or employees of *equal or lower rank.*
7. No *dispute or difference* between executives as to *authority* or *responsibilities* should be considered *too trivial* for *prompt and careful adjudication.*
8. *Promotions, wage changes* and *disciplinary action* should always be approved by the *executive immediately superior* to the one *directly* responsible.
9. No executive or employee should ever be required, or expected, to be *at the same time* an *assistant to*, and *critic of*, another.

[11] Koontz and O'Donnell: *Principles of Management*, p. 12.

10. Any executive whose work is subject to *regular inspection* should, whenever practicable, be given the *assistance and facilities* necessary to enable him to maintain an *independent check* on the *quality* of his work.

Fayol's Principles

1. *Division of Work*—the principle of specialisation in all kinds of work, both technical and managerial.
2. *Authority and Responsibility*—these are related, the latter being the corollary of the former and arising out of it.
3. *Discipline*—this requires good superiors at all levels, clear and fair agreements and judicious application of penalties.
4. *Unity of Command*—an employee should receive orders from one superior only.
5. *Unity of Direction*—the principle that each group of activities having the same objective must have one leader, and one plan. This principle relates to the functioning of the 'body corporate' whereas unity of command relates to the functioning of personnel.
6. *Subordination of Individual Interest to General Interest*—the interest of the group should supersede that of the individual; in the cases of differences reconciliation should come from management.
7. *Remuneration of Personnel*—Remuneration and methods of payment should be fair and afford the maximum satisfaction to employee and employer.
8. *Centralisation*—individual circumstances will influence the degree of centralisation in an enterprise, the object being 'the best over-all yield'.
9. *The Scalar Chain*—there should be clear levels of authority from the highest to the lowest ranks. The chain should be short-circuited only when scrupulous obedience to the principle would be detrimental.
10. *Order*—a place for everything or everyone, and everything or everyone in its or his place.
11. *Equity*—a combination of kindliness and justice in managers dealing with subordinates.
12. *Stability of Tenure of Personnel*—the dangers and cost of unnecessary turnover.

13. *Initiative*—superiors should 'sacrifice personal vanity' in order to permit subordinates to exercise their initiative.
14. '*Esprit de Corps*'—union is strength: an extension of the principle of unity of command. (Team-work and the importance of good communications.)

Fayol believed that his 'principles' were of universal application, applying equally well to business, government, religions or any other institutions, and Fayol himself assisted the French government in a re-organisation of the Post Office. In the field of government the American *Report of the President's Committee on Administrative Management*, is that of a public corporation, the Tennessee Valley Authority. Urwick[12] believes that the "alleged contrast between business and government is without foundation. To conduct a business undertaking is, in fact, to govern it; to govern a municipality or an empire is, in fact, to manage it. Both activities are directed to the same end, the arrangement of a human system of co-operation for certain purposes".

Urwick quotes with approval Mary Parker Follett's statement from her lecture on leadership[13]: "Whatever problems we solve in business management may help towards the solution of world problems, since the principles of organisation and administration which are discovered as best for business can be applied to government and international relations". On the whole, one cannot make exception to this attitude. It must be remembered, however, that the British Civil Service is politically neutral and that its main task is to support the Government of the time and keep it in power.[14]

This chapter has indicated some of the confusion that exists regarding the key-terms administration, management and organisation. Whether the analysis of these terms is merely an academic exercise the student should try to decide for himself.

15. "Brech tells us that the dynamic concept of organisation is outmoded, and that 'organisation as a term relates to structure'. More's the pity . . . if more people regarded organisation in the dynamic sense of continuous progress, its value would be greater" (Walter Puckey: *Management Principles*, p. 29).
16. Is there any difference between public administration and business administration?

[12] L. Urwick: *A Short Survey of Industrial Management*, p. 5.
[13] Rowntree Lecture Conference, Oxford (1928).
[14] See C. J. Sisson: *The Spirit of British Administration*, London (1950).

ADDITIONAL READING ASSIGNMENTS

1. A. L. Banks and J. A. Hislop: *The Art of Administration* (1961), chapter xii, 'Organisation and Management'.
2. Walter Puckey: *Management Principles* (1962), chapters 2, 3 and 9.
3. L. Urwick: *A Short Survey of Industrial Management*, B.I.M. Occasional Papers, No. 1.
4. A. Dunsire (Ed.): *The Making of an Administrator*—Sir Edward Bridges, 'Administration: What Is It? And How Can It be Learnt?'; Lt.-Col. L. F. Urwick, 'Management and the Administrator'; A. Dunsire, 'Comment'.
5. E. F. L. Brech: *Organisation, the Framework of Management.*
6. E. F. L. Brech (Ed.): *The Principles and Practice of Management*, Part I, 'Management in Principle', by Brech.
7. Ordway Tead: *The Art of Administration* (New York, 1951).
8. H. Fayol: *General and Industrial Administration.*

A NOTE ON ORGANISATION CHARTS AND MANUALS

(for examples of organisation charts see pp. 178–86)

Organisational charts are "two-dimensional pictures of three-dimensional relationships." Charts have been criticised in that:

(i) Human relationships cannot be adequately represented on paper.
(ii) Organisation charts are not kept up to date.
(iii) By excessive definition of responsibilities they may restrict communication as easily as encourage it.
(iv) The methods used in designing charts are often loose.

A chart should give at least three important pieces of information: the departmental, divisional or group breakdown of the company; the names and titles of people; the span of control of the key personnel. It is important to give *names* as well as titles, because if one individual is changed others may also have to be changed, as well as departmental relationships.[15]

Many organisations have discovered basic weaknesses as a result of attempting to draw up an organisation chart;[16] difficulties have arisen because of *overlapping functions*, *neglected functions* and *crossed lines of authority*. Unbiased study may reveal some of the following flaws:

[15] See W. Puckey: *Management Principles*, pp. 89–96.

[16] See M. Guigoz: 'Organisation Charts and People', *Management International* 1961/I: "... people end up by being so busy making the organisation chart work ... that no one has the time to think dynamically about the real problems of the firm."

L

(i) Neglect of important functions.
(ii) Overstressing of secondary functions.
(iii) Duplication of functions.
(iv) A function 'split' among two or more departments.
(v) Illogical arrangement of functions.
(vi) Unnecessary loading of executives.
(vii) Able personnel in subordinate positions.
(viii) Mediocre ability at important points.
(ix) Specialists engaged in functions out of their lines (*e.g.* production man handling factory costs).
(x) The same person engaged in several different functions.

Organisation Manuals supplement charts by giving the general policy, rules and regulations of the Company. Each executive and each employee should know the scope and function of his department, his own place in it, and his duties.

The advantages of using charts and manuals are: the fixing of responsibility and authority; the clear specifications of functions and tasks; easy assignment of titles; every employee has a clear conception of a company as a whole; they also help to grade and classify work and tasks.

* * * *

What is perhaps the first example of a modern organisation chart in British Literature (from J. S. Lewis's *The Commercial Organisation of Factories* (1896) is reproduced in Urwick and Brech: *The Making of Scientific Management*, Vol. II, opposite p. 81.

CHAPTER NINE

PLANNING, CONTROL AND LEADERSHIP

§ 1. Introduction: Decision-making

The purpose of decision-making is consciously to direct human behaviour towards some future goal. Planning implies the selection, from *alternatives*, of objectives, policies, procedures and programmes. Hence, the essence of planning is the making of decisions, the selection of future courses of action. If alternatives did not exist, there would obviously be no need for making decisions; on the other hand, all decisions must involve planning, since decisions lead inevitably to future courses of action. "It is no wonder then, that managers tend to see decision making as their central job. But it is not often recognised that decisions involve planning, even though they may be made quickly under emergency circumstances and with little thought, or may influence a course of action for only a few minutes".[1]

Decision-making involves a choice from two or more alternatives, and managerial decisions are always concerned with events which will occur in the future. The basic problem of any firm is a problem of economic choice, *i.e.* to obtain an allocation of its resources between alternative uses which, within its own scheme of risk preferences and social constraints, will best attain these objectives. Existing capital assets have to be allocated between alternative uses, and immediate and potential financial resources have to be allocated between alternative investment opportunities.[2]

Some decisional problems can be solved by statistical techniques (probability theory), *e.g.* the prediction of such events as the number of machine-breakdowns, the size of labour turnover, the proportion of quality rejects, and other matters for which there is enough statistical evidence to compute the chances that a given event will occur. Inferred probability means inferring from *limited* data the probability of a particular outcome. A more important tool, already briefly discussed in Part I of this book, is

[1] Koontz and O'Donnell: *Principles of Management*, p. 574.

[2] See A. J. Merrett and G. Bannock: *Business Economics and Statistics* (1962), 'Introduction'; also L. Robbins: *The Nature and Significance of Economic Science,* chapter I.

operational research, which goes to work by constructing models of the decisional problem under consideration. Operational research is especially important for management in the area of selection among alternatives. In model construction the objectives sought by management must be formulated and, wherever possible, expressed in *quantitative* terms, *e.g.* the increase of profits, the reduction of costs, the expansion of output. It is also important during model construction to try and determine the factors or variables which ought to influence the attainment of the objective, dividing them into those which can, and those which cannot, be controlled by management.

In spite of the use of scientific 'tools', however, much managerial decision-making involves *intuitive* processes. Little is known of the psychology of such processes, but, even if they are ill-understood, there is no doubt of their importance in solving decisional problems. Recently economists have paid attention to the development of theories of subjective decision-making, *e.g.* Shackle[3] believes that a manager can best solve the 'uncertainty problem' by evaluating alternatives until he arrives at a solution which offers a minimum of 'potential surprise', and the degree of error in any decision can be gauged by the degree of potential surprise. *Uncertainty* is immanent in business life; the future is uncertain because of new advances in science and technology, new legal developments, competition, weather, wars, changes in taste and fashion, and though the business-man must endeavour to predict what will happen, he can never fully foresee the future. Nevertheless, a manager must be ready to make a decision even when he is uncertain, and the great majority of decisions are necessarily based, to some extent, on evidence that is unreliable or fragmentary.

Drucker[4] has distinguished between 'tactical' and 'strategic' decisions. The former consist of relatively unimportant, routine decisions, in which the task is to choose between a few alternatives, the main criterion being usually one of economy: the problem is the most economical adaptation of known resources. But strategic decisions are much more important and involve "either finding out what the situation is, or changing it; either finding out what the resources are or what they should be". Strategic decisions are the

[3] G. L. S. Shackle: *Uncertainty in Economics* (1955).
[4] P. Drucker: *The Practice of Management*, chapter 18.

truly managerial decisions and include decisions on business objectives and the means to attain them, decisions affecting productivity, organisation decisions and operating decisions. Such decisions should never be taken through problem-solving, for "the important and difficult job is never to find the right answers, it is to find the right question".

Decision-making may be divided into five distinct processes:

(i) *Defining the problem.* A diagnosis of the situation must be made and a problem identified and clarified.

(ii) *Finding alternative solutions.* Alternatives may range from doing nothing at all, to finding a way of coping with the difficulty or removing it, or even modifying the objective.

(iii) *Analysing and comparing alternatives.* Facts and opinions are analysed and a list of pros and cons is drawn up for each alternative.

(iv) *Selecting the plan to be followed.* Here the manager often has to try to balance several different factors, such as cost, morale, public reaction, which are irreducible to a common denominator.

(v) *Making the decision effective.* A managerial decision is always a decision as to what other people should do.

The solution becomes a decision only when action is taken and this conversion of decision into action requires that people understand what change in behaviour is expected of them, and what change to expect in the behaviour of their colleagues and subordinates.

It is seldom that a manager can follow the above phases of decision-making in the neat order given: the phases do, however, provide a useful framework for introducing some order into his thoughts and planning efforts.

§ 2. Planning

By planning is meant establishing the objectives of the enterprise, anticipating possible 'snags' and problems, and preparing tentative solutions. It is first necessary for the managers of an enterprise to make up their minds what they want to accomplish, and then plot the use of time, resources and effort towards the realisation of their objectives. Management must decide *what* it hopes to do, *when* it expects to attain certain results, *who* is going to do *what*, and *how* it will be done. Objectives must not be couched in 'broad, windy phrases'[5] but must be both 'easy to assimilate' and 'reasonable of achievement'. As Falk points out, "The finest organisation brains and money can devise will never produce the desired result if the end is obscure. Pre-occupation with organisational problems has tended to bedevil many enterprises in which, had the *objectives*, the *ends* been crystal-clear, the means of achieving them would have fallen quickly and logically into place".[6]

Realistic planning must be based on an analysis of:

(i) the *resources* of the firm: what it has *now*.

(ii) the *past history* of the firm: how it has reached its present position.

(iii) the *present situation* as compared with the past.

(iv) the future objectives.

All levels of management and supervision must be concerned with planning, but the higher levels of management will necessarily be more concerned with *long-range* planning and strategy, with ratios and trends, with the formulation of general policy and objectives, with the adaptation of the organisation structure to changing conditions, and with finance. It is useful to distinguish three basic levels of planning:

TOP LEVEL PLANNING:	STRATEGY	(Administrators)
SECOND LEVEL PLANNING:	TACTICS	(Executives)
THIRD LEVEL PLANNING:	SUPERVISORS	(Departmental Operations)

To take the third level: planning will cover such matters as work layout, individual assignments, specific schedules and departmental facilities, instruction of employees, progress reports and remedial actions.

A distinction should be made between *organisational* and *administrative* planning: the former is concerned with such matters as objectives, scale of finance, methods and machinery, sequence of operations and processes, rules, regulations and standards. The latter is concerned with *how* the business is run, including management practices, personnel practices, union relations, and individual and group relations.[7]

[5] Roger Falk: *The Business of Management*, p. 53.

[6] *ibid.* Falk refers to the 'case-studies in failure' at the end of his book for illustrations of this point.

[7] For a detailed discussion see R. C. Sampson: *The Staff Role in Management. Its Creative Uses* (1955), Part Two, VI and VII.

§ 3. Forecasting

One of Henri Fayol's main 'principles' was that of *prévoyance*, or 'foresight'.* He went so far as to say that "if foresight is not the whole of management at least it is an essential part of it".[8] All business situations contain elements of uncertainty, but systematic forecasting can help the manager to appreciate the complexity of a given situation more clearly and prepare him for any eventualities which might arise.

Many of the most crucial management decisions are based upon forecasting. The best-made schemes of mice and men 'gang aft aglay', and the longer the period for which forecasts are made, the less secure the assumptions on which they are made, and the greater the elements of risk and uncertainty they contain. The length of the period of forecast varies greatly from industry to industry, in the field of ladies' fashions it might be only a few months or even weeks; in the case of such commodities as aircraft, oil and steel the difficulties of long-term forecasting of developments need not be emphasised. Indeed, in all industries based upon advanced scientific and technological research, the future is extremely hazardous. The corpus of scientific knowledge, it has been said, is now doubling every 10 years and radical innovations in materials and processes may be 'just around the corner'. In many cases, however, forecasts are made for fairly short periods, a year or two at the most. 'Long-range' planning would be interpreted by some industrialists as 3–5 years, but some firms try to think in terms of much longer periods.[9]

The *transformation period* is the time it takes to transform productive *resources* into products or services, and the full transformation of an industrial plant may take a decade or two. There is also the problem of time lags between cost *commitments* and *reserve*. Contracts or purchases made over a period of a few days only may take a period of years of sales to meet and the liquidity of the company is greatly reduced. Long-term planning is mainly concerned with capital expenditure projects, and such plans frequently provide the foundation for all other plans.

* *prévoyance* in French means 'foresight', 'fore-thought' or 'precaution' and *prévoyant* means 'far-sighted' (administration); 'forecasting', on the other hand, is *prévision*.

8 Fayol: *General and Industrial Management*, p. 43.

9 For a useful discussion on 'long-term', 'annual forecasting', 'short-term' profit planning and weekly or daily 'activity-planning', see Brech (Ed.): *Principles and Practice of Management*, Part IV chapter II, pp. 642–46.

A forecast may often be a 'shot in the dark', a 'hunch' or it may be made by a specialist staff. Fayol was in favour of annual forecasts and ten-yearly projections, the latter being revised every five years or even more frequently if the annual forecasts revealed unexpected trends. Apart from the fundamental value of forecasting as the prelude to the development of plans, this activity has the added importance of forcing key personnel to think creatively and keep in touch with new scientific and socio-economic developments. Forecasting may also focus attention upon weak decisional areas where control in inadequate or lacking. There can be no unity in developmental plans unless there is co-ordinated forecasting.

It must be recognised, however, that whatever scientific appurtenances and techniques are available, every forecast is subject to error, through lack of knowledge, through unfortunate guesswork, over-optimism or undue pessimism.

§ 4. Business Forecasting

There is not space here to go into the technicalities of forecasting. Demand forecasts have a triple use: to assist production planning, sales planning and the evaluation of investment.[10] As regards production planning, sales forecasts may assist the manager to avoid over-production, short-time working and excess stocks, and the high costs associated with meeting, or failing to meet, unforeseen increases in demand. Demand forecasts are used in sales planning by dividing the domestic market into zones and territories and placing a number of salesmen under each sales manager. The salesmen are allocated to the different territories and given some indication of the level of sales which they are expected to achieve.

Sales forecasting can be used in helping to determine the 'optimum size enterprise'.[11] Assuming that a company has decided to build at least a minimum-size plant and that it desires to provide production capacity to meet its sales requirements—which may or may not correspond with the sales forecast—then the problem is to decide how large the plant shall be. Suppose that the sales

[10] For a good, brief introduction see Merrett and Bannock: *Business Economics and Statistics*, 3, 'Business Forecasting'.

[11] See Robert M. Lawless and P. R. Haas, Jr.: 'How to Determine the Right-Size Plant', *Harvard Business Review* (May–June 1962).

forecast has been made for a six-year period beyond the time required for the construction of the plant. As Lawless and Haas point out, forecasts beyond six years are "usually of questionable accuracy". The question of plant size can be reduced to four possible courses of action:

Decision 1. Build to match the six-year forecast.

Decision 2. Build to match the three-year forecast, adding one increment of expansion during the third year to meet the sixth-year requirement *if needed.*

Decision 3. Build to match the two-year sales forecast, adding two increments to match the fourth- and sixth-year requirement *if needed.*

Decision 4. Build the minimum-size plant required for the first-year forecast and add an increment of expansion each year for five years if needed.

If it so happens that projected growth stops at some point during the six-year period, then Decisions 2, 3 and 4 permit flexibility and the cost of the anticipated expansions can be avoided if the sales do not match up to the forecasts. It is up to the manager to decide which method of evaluation is most appropriate to this kind of problem.

§ 5. Policies

By planning is meant the charting in advance of effects which it is believed will proceed from a given course of action, so that the particular course which is most productive can be chosen. Thus, for each course of action it is necessary to consider the advantages, the possible disadvantages, the attendant costs, and the expected gains. Planning has to be carried out in a highly complex context: there are first of all government policies to consider, as well as social factors; price policies must be worked out, advertising strategies, product innovations and developments in operational techniques.

Policies are the fundamental statements setting out the objectives of a business, and in addition to the general policy of a firm the following special aspects must be considered: Product, Production, Sales and Finance.

Product Policy. The question here is that of deciding what product or products to make in view of local, national and international demand, and the special conditions attaching to the market in these differing circumstances. It may be possible to use the by-products of the main occupation to produce apparently unrelated products, *e.g.* meat-canning and fertilisers. Market forecasting techniques include *trend-cycle analysis* (the projection of past behaviour), *correlation analysis* (finding the relationship between sales, material income, the weather, and so on) and *survey and interview techniques.* The difficulty in forecasting the demand for new products arises from the lack of *historical data.* A possible approach to this problem is to carry out research in a restricted area and use the results as indicators of the potential in a wider context. Alternatively the sales history of an item in the same category as the new product, *e.g.* a piece of household equipment, may be used as a rough guide to the sales potential of the new product. Again a 'new' product may be regarded as a substitute for an existing product.

A project initiated today cannot be left to the various departments of the firm to design, develop and produce without some kind of 'direction control' or co-ordination of their activities. As P. L. Johnson suggests, a closely controlled system of 'project authorisations' is the best insurance that an original idea will result in a successful finished product, and this calls for a full-time product planner. A 'project authorisation' is a collection of information which will enable those in control to decide whether or not to proceed with the project; it sets out the aims and objects of the project so that management can discuss them and sanction expenditure. As design and development proceed, several amendments may be made to the original authorisation and will be based on market research information, estimated works cost, estimated costs of tooling, and time factors influencing the programme. "If a project is handled in this way it can proceed, step by step, towards a product which is as close as possible to the ideal product it was originally intended to market".[12]

Production Policy. The main questions here are to decide on the layout of plant and machinery, and on the relative proportions of

[12] For an interesting development of this approach see P. L. Johnson: 'The Product Planner', *The Manager* (March 1961).

plant to be devoted to mass-production and job-order production, so that there can be accurate planning of scheduling and routing. Production planning and control are concerned mainly with the *routeing* of operations, with *scheduling* the time-sequences, and with *assigning* work to be done in such a way that men, machines, equipment and tools are used in the most efficient manner. Production planning is greatly aided by such devices as Gantt Chart[13] which shows the expected production results over a period of time, route-cards and operation sheets.

Sales Policy includes such matters as determining the distribution channels, the price structure of products, the volume and type of advertising, the territory and its subdivisions and the remuneration of sales policy.

Financial Policy and Budgets. A budget is a statement of anticipated income and/or expenditure for a given period; it is prepared in advance but based upon past experience, present conditions, and estimated future trends. A budget is the most important tool in financial planning and a leading factor in the development and implementation of policy. Budgets may be prepared for production, sales, materials, plant and equipment, manufacturing cost, labour and financial and capital requirements.

Other important aspects of policy are:

Purchasing Policy is concerned with such matters as the kind of firms from which the company will buy purchases, the extent to which it will use specifications, and alternative sources of supply.

Personnel Policy is concerned with training and education plans, pensions, incentive plans, vacations, age limitations, management development and succession plans, insurance, financial assistance and similar matters. Personnel policies help to determine the kind of persons employed and whether or not they are interested in staying with the firm.

Research and Development. It has been said that scientific knowledge and technology are now doubling every ten years, as

[13] Gantt devised many charts—see Alex W. Rathe (Ed.): *Gantt on Management*, American Management Association (1962); also Brech (Ed.): *Principles and Practice of Management*, pp. 356–7. People now refer to one chart in particular as *the* Gantt Chart.

a result of the vast amount of research which is being conducted. Research and development are of great importance, especially for large companies.

§ 5. Profit Planning

By profit planning is meant the devising of a continuous plan which will lead to the realisation of a defined profit.[14] The mere existence of such a plan will not, of course, guarantee that the figure will be reached, but the plan sets out details of the predetermined profit which, it is hoped, will be gained as a result of the year's operations, and also shows the contribution to the total made by the various sectors and activities of a company.

A profit plan should be so formulated as to take into account the payment of a reasonable dividend on the issued capital of the company; the payment of interest on any issued debentures; the allocation of a portion to reserve funds; and the setting aside of further reserves to enhance liquidity in case sales revenue should decline in the future. Profit in these days is sometimes regarded as a 'dirty word' but, as Peter Drucker recently put it, the manager's duty and responsibility is to strive for the best possible economic results from the resources currently employed or available, and "even such lofty management tasks" as "assessing corporate social responsibilities and cultural responsibilities" are firmly rooted in the economic soil.[15] Management has to earn a rate of profit which will *at least* cover its contractual and equity obligations and enable it to carry out its policy for allocation to reserves.

There are several causes of deviation from an expressed profitability, such as the volume and cost of production, the volume and composition of sales, the selling-prices of products, and the marketing of costs. If adverse variations occur as a result of inadequate or ineffective control, the result will often be reduced profit.

A profit plan cannot be realised unless budgeted sales are attained; in practice, therefore, it is necessary regularly to review actual sales realised against budgeted sales. In addition, the cost of manufacturing and marketing the product must not exceed the

[14] See, for example, eight articles on 'Profit Planning' by H. Dugdale, in *The Commercial Accountant*, Vol. XIV (1963-4).

[15] P. Drucker: 'Managing for Business Effectiveness', *Harvard Business Review* (May–June 1963).

predetermined standard costs. Short-term profit-and-loss accounts must be prepared showing: (i) the standard cost of goods manufactured; (ii) their actual cost; (iii) the total variation between standard and actual cost; (iv) the analysis of any variation under the sub-heads of material direct labour and overheads.

If the overall profit for manufacturing and marketing operations seems capable of achievement from the triple point of view of percentage profit on turnover, providing a satisfactory dividend for the payment of interest on loan capital, and providing a further surplus for allocation to reserve funds, it must be then broken down in terms of product profit contribution. To do this it is necessary to evaluate sales budget quantities at their respective product standard costs, which assumes that a mangement accounting scheme is in operation or in course of installation.

§ 6. Planning of Management Succession

A very important aspect of administrative planning is that of trying to ensure a steady supply of managers and supervisors of high calibre. The research carried out by the Acton Society Trust[16] dealt with the background of present managers in certain large companies and with the arrangements made by companies to provide for future managers. Some companies still think it safe to rely on the old methods and find managers from the shop floor; they tend to justify themselves by talking about the 'late developer'. Only one-third of the companies visited made any systematic attempt to discover the potential talent in their midst.

The planning of management succession implies a systematic policy based on the following points:

(i) Some method of estimating future management requirements.

(ii) Some method of talent-spotting.

(iii) Some method of selection other than *ad hoc* nomination.

(iv) Some method of individual development for those considered suitable for promotion to senior posts, *e.g.* job rotation.

(v) Some form of management education and training. (A distinction may be drawn between management *develop-*

16 See *Management Succession* (Acton Society Trust); also Rosemary Stewart 'Management Succession' in *The Year Book of the Coke Oven Managers Association*, 1959.

ment (mainly the responsibility of the individual firm); management *education* (a mind-stretching process, concerned with fostering the ability to think); and management *training* (dealing with practical techniques).

Rosemary Stewart suggests some questions which the departmental manager should ask himself if he is really interested in management development and not merely paying lip-service to it:

(i) What would you do if the most valuable member of your team were offered promotion?

(ii) Does every individual in your department really know how *you* think he is getting on?

(iii) Do you know the capabilities of everybody in your department?

(iv) What have you done to try and strengthen some of X's weak points?

(v) If you send your foreman on a Human Relations course, will he be able to regard you as the embodiment of what he has learnt there?

(vi) Do you know a 'good man' when you see one?

(vii) Do you ever say, "None of the people in my department is any good"?, or "I don't know what the young are coming to"? Yet, if your subordinates do not become better managers than you, you will have failed in an important part of your responsibilities as a manager.

The writers of the Acton report came to the conclusion that there should be a policy which ensures that the problem is appreciated even if it cannot be solved, *e.g.* management could compile figures of 'management wastage': they should know how many managers are likely to retire in the next five years and whether their successors are ready.

The works manager should be particularly concerned with the selection and training of foremen and charge-hands. Some of the main aims in training are:

(i) To impart technical knowledge.

(ii) To impart knowledge of workmen's conditions of employment and of each man's duties.

(iii) To develop leadership qualities and the ability to organise.

(iv) To encourage desirable attitudes towards the company and its policy.

(v) To give a broad view of the organisation and administration of the company as a whole.

(vi) In certain circumstances, to train every foreman to take over *any* foreman's job.

The problem is to identify the manager wherever he may be in the organisation and to ensure that he has the opportunity to learn and develop. It is probably wise, as Tyzack[17] has suggested, not to commit one's judgment more than one, or sometimes two, moves ahead.

§ 7. Analysing, Planning and Scheduling Large Complex Projects: CPM, PERT and RAMPS

The 'Critical Path Method' (CPM) is a new, fairly simple technique of determining which jobs or activities of the many comprising a project are 'critical' in their effect on the total project time; and of determining how best to schedule all jobs in the project in order to reach a target date at minimum cost. CPM can be applied to such projects as the construction of a building or a highway, planning and launching a new product, research and engineering of design projects and scheduling ship construction and repairs.[18] Such projects have certain characteristics that are essential for analysis:

(i) The projects consist of a well-defined collection of jobs or *activities* which, when completed, mark the end of the project;

(ii) the jobs may be started and stopped independently of one another;

(iii) the jobs are ordered, *i.e.* performed in technological sequence.

An everyday example is the building of a house (study the Project Graph in the *Harvard Business Review*). It is believed that CPM will be a powerful and effective tool for decision-making at all levels of management. Thus, a Project Graph will help the fore-

[17] J. E. V. Tyzack: 'Restlessness and Intellectual Under-employment in Management Trainees', *Time and Motion Study* (Jan. 1961).

[18] An introduction, with good diagrams, is given by Levy, Thompson and Wiest: 'The ABCs of the Critical Path Method', *Harvard Business Review* (Sept.–Oct. 1963); also Andrew Muir 'PERT? CPM? RAMPS?', *Time and Motion Study* (April 1963). See also K. M. Lockyer: *An Introduction to Critical Path Method* (1964) and G. N. Stillian and others: *PERT* (New York, 1962).

man to understand the sequencing of jobs and underline the necessity of 'pushing' those that are critical. The manager concerned with day-to-day operations in all departments can measure progress, or lack of it, against plans and take speedy action where required. For the top manager CPM may well prove to be an ideal tool, for it will enable him to focus attention on crucial areas of large projects and assist him greatly in overall planning and co-ordination.

PERT (Programme Evaluation and Research Technique) differs from CPM in that three estimates are made—an *optimistic*, a *most likely* and a *pessimistic* estimate. In this way the element of uncertainty is introduced and it is possible to calculate the probabilities of any stage of the operations being completed by a certain time.

RAMPS (Resource Allocation and Multi-Project Scheduling) allows various restrictions to be placed on resources and can cope with the planning of several projects that have to be carried out simultaneously.

These are three techniques of 'network analysis', which is one of the approaches of operational research.

§ 8. Control. By *control* is meant the general direction of an enterprise based upon facts which can be quantitatively expressed —facts which are obtained from accounting techniques, market research, work study and budgetary control. In recent times managements have come to rely more and more on well-defined systems of control in the spheres of production, sales and finance.

In any control process there are three essential steps:[19]

(i) *Standards must be set at strategic points.* The general objectives of an enterprise must be broken down into objectives for individual departments and section. Goals are then developed for output, cost and quality by the use of such techniques as standards, sales quotas, schedules and budgets.

(ii) *Control Standards are linked with individual responsibility.* It is essential to define clearly individual duties so that certain activities to be controlled can be readily identified

[19] For a fuller discussion see W. H. Newman: *Administrative Action*, chapt. 23, on which the above is based.

with individuals. There will be some objectives, however, which it is difficult to attach to any particular individual.

(iii) *Concentration is focussed on strategic control points.* Such control points must be "timely, economical, comprehensive and balanced".

Timely, so that significant deviations can be readily seen, indicating when control needs to be exercised.

Economical, in the sense that observation and control should not require elaborate organisation and apparatus, but there will be situations in which measurement of results will be so difficult or expensive that control is placed in the process itself.

Comprehensive, i.e. some of the control points should summarise several operations, *e.g.* overall expense figures.

Balanced, in the sense that no one aspect should be overstressed at the expense of others, *e.g.* volume of output at the expense of quality.

It is obvious that control processes cannot be set up overnight and, in a new and growing company, the gradual establishment of controls must be an important aspect of the initial planning, so that the individuals concerned can develop their techniques and the machinery for co-ordination.

In her lecture[20] of 'The Process of Control' Miss Follett stated that "control and fact-control are becoming synonymous", and that "control is coming more and more to mean fact-control rather than man-control", and *central* control is coming more and more to mean the co-relation of many controls rather than a super-imposed control". Later in her lecture Miss Follett reaffirms her point of view that control means in essence *co-ordination.*

§ 9. Production Planning and Control

Of particular interest to the works manager is production planning and control, the purpose of which is to organise the supply and movement of materials, labour and to organise machine utilisation so that the desired results in terms of *quantity, quality,*

[20] M. P. Follett: 'The Process of Control', chapter VI of *Freedom and Co-ordination,* London (1949); also printed in Gulick and Urwick: *Papers on the Science of Administration.*

time and *place* can be attained.[21] Organised production planning is increasingly necessary under modern conditions because of the complexity of production, the need for careful timing, the need to anticipate changes and the desire to combine resources in the most economical way.

By *routing* is meant the preparation of route-cards by *scheduling*, the phasing of specific jobs into a general timetable. The main objects of production planning are to control the flow of work, to achieve a balance between different departments, and to relate orders and delivery promises to the available capacity.

Production control has been simply defined as the control of *movement*[22] and must be based upon four essential factors:

(i) The *rate* of movement, *i.e.* the number of units which have to be moved in a given period;
(ii) The *cost* of movement, *i.e.* the amount of money a firm can afford to spend on the manufacturing process.
(iii) The *direction* of movement, *i.e.* the path which materials have to take during their complete progress through the factory.
(iv) The *method* of movement.

Hence, production control is essentially a *physical* function, but dependent upon the clerical provision of the above facts about movement. In addition, information about current shop load is necessary. In a small factory (say 50–200 employees) a great deal of *direct* control is necessary but manager and foremen must receive enough information to enable them to control without having to carry everything in their heads. The information includes cost estimates, outstanding quotations, firm orders received, stock position, factory load and work-in-progress.[23]

§ 10. Quality Control[24]

The aim here is, through the Inspection Department, to control

[21] A good introduction is Section 2, 'Production Planning and Control', of *Production Handbook* (ed. Maynard), New York (1959).

[22] See E. W. Roper: 'Production Control'. *Work Study and Industrial Engineering* (Jan. 1958).

[23] See *Production Control in A Small Factory* (B.I.M.)—especially the Order Flow Chart at the end of the book.

[24] On the inspection function see Brech (Ed.): *Principles and Practice of Management*, pp. 450–60; on quality control see Carson: *Production Handbook*, Section 8, 'Quality Control', and N. L. Enrick: *Quality Control*.

the standard and workmanship of the company's product, since "a high quality is the best form of advertising". Quality control ensures that the final product conforms to predetermined standards of size, shape, workmanship, performance, and physical or chemical composition. The setting-up of *standards* is thus the essence of quality control—standards which are first set by the degree of quality demanded by customers. Inspection must take place at all strategic points—in the goods-inward department, during machining and processing, and at the finished-goods stage. Especially important is the inspection of an item on which a cycle of operations has been completed. Inspection will often be carried out by *sampling* techniques, but in the case of critical parts in an assembly, inspection may be 'a hundred per cent'. By *total* quality control is meant quality determination throughout the entire production schedule from the initial conception and design to the shipping of the final product. "With such an approach to quality control, greater emphasis has tended to be placed on prevention of quality deviations than on inspection and appraisal"[25] Quality control should not be in the hands of anyone whose prime concern is for meeting production targets.

In the past the Inspection Department has often been regarded as a necessary evil, but it performs a vital service not only in ensuring that the design and quality of goods are satisfactory, but also in bringing to light and trying to cure many ills of which management may be unaware. Hence, the Chief Inspector is a very important figure; he should have a strong but understanding personality, be able to get on well with his colleagues and command their respect, and must have a vision wide enough to embrace the company and its products as a whole. He must be an independent authority, working under the Managing Director or the Board as a whole. It has been suggested[26] that the Chief Inspector should not be a man who has been promoted through various degrees of responsibility within the same firm but who should, at the time of his appointment, be a comparative stranger to the functional heads of other departments—a man who has moved about in industry.

It must be stressed that quality is not an "accident"; it must be designed and planned into the job at the outset. Mr. C. E. S.

[25] Koontz and O'Donnell: *Principles of Management*, p. 648.

[26] H. Henderson: 'Quality Control in Engineering', *Time and Motion Study* (Sept. 1958).

Burgess has explained[27] how at his firm a much closer link has been forged between Production and Design, by setting up a 'Manufacturing Development' department, one of the tasks of which is to keep designers fully informed of the production requirements which can be embodied in *initial* designs. He envisages another link in the future when Inspection will be able to have its say on "what inspection equipment will be required to comply with the new techniques we have to master. Technical development is so rapid that unless this particular point is covered in the *very early* stages, inspection equipment is obsolete before it is even utilised".

§ 11. Environmental Control[28]

A matter of especial interest and importance to the works manager is the control of the physical environment of the place of work. The main constituents of the physical environment are *light* (both natural and artificial), *thermal comfort* (in both summer and winter), *ventilation*, *colour*, *noise* and *dangerous or toxic substances*. In the future it will be necessary to provide an environment that is optimal rather than merely acceptable. Environmental planning is a complicated business involving knowledge of both building and processes; it tended in the past to go by default but is becoming increasingly important. It seems reasonable to expect that better work will be done in good rather than bad conditions. It is the task of top management to decide on the priorities for the particular situation, *e.g.* if close temperature control is required for the production process, daylight may have to be sacrificed because of the summer-heat gains through glass.

§ 12. Standards for Planning and Control[29]

Any system of planning and control implies the existence of criteria for the fixing of targets and for the assessment of achievement. Such standards include statistics, charts, management ratios and progress reports, which provide management with

[27] C. E. S. Burgess: 'Planned Organisation for Quality Production', *Inst. of Production Engineers' Journal* (Sept. 1959).

[28] See especially articles in *Better Factories* (an Institute of Directors' Publication), notably the articles by Professor J. K. Page, 'Environmental Control', and 'Noise in Factories', and H. L. Gloag, 'The Use of Colour in Factories'. A bibliography is given on pp. 278–9 of this book.

[29] T. G. Rose: *Higher Business Control*, 7th edition (1963).

various kinds of information and insights. The techniques of budgetary control and higher control are also used. Some of these matters have already been discussed in chapter VII of this book. It is not possible here to go into the technicalities of *charts*, the construction and uses of which can be quickly appreciated by glancing through special monographs[30] on the subject. A few words may be said here on *Higher Business Control*, a subject to which T. G. Rose has devoted his attention for the past thirty years.

Higher Business Control is defined as "the general management of a business on a planned basis, the adherence to the plan being watched by a monthly survey made from the Business, Technical, Trading and Financial viewpoints, which are known as the four 'Positions' " (Rose). Monthly Schedules (or Board Returns) are issued from the sources responsible for the relevant figures, and there is also a *Standard Check List* for each of the four positions, consisting of items which need a regular monthly check. By keeping a *Working Book* into which monthly working returns are copied, a permanent central statistical record is maintained. The Managing Director receives two Reports:

Part I (submitted in the first week of the month following the month under review), covering the Business and Technical Positions.

Part II (submitted in the third week) covering the Trading and Financial Positions.

As Rose stresses, no special staff or calculations are required: the method simply takes the ordinary figures which every accountant compiles and the ordinary sales statistics. The central principle is that of "finding out what the managing director ought to know month by month in the four sections, and presenting that knowledge to him in a simple manner".

Of the Four Positions the Business Position is perhaps the most important, and covers three groups of data: Orders Received, Invoices Issued, and Orders Outstanding.

§ 13. Leadership

It is convenient at this stage to discuss the question of industrial leadership. Before World War II, it is often said, managements were 'irresponsible' except to the shareholders, and the latter

[30] *e.g.* T. G. Rose: *Business Charts*; W. Clark: *The Gantt Chart.*

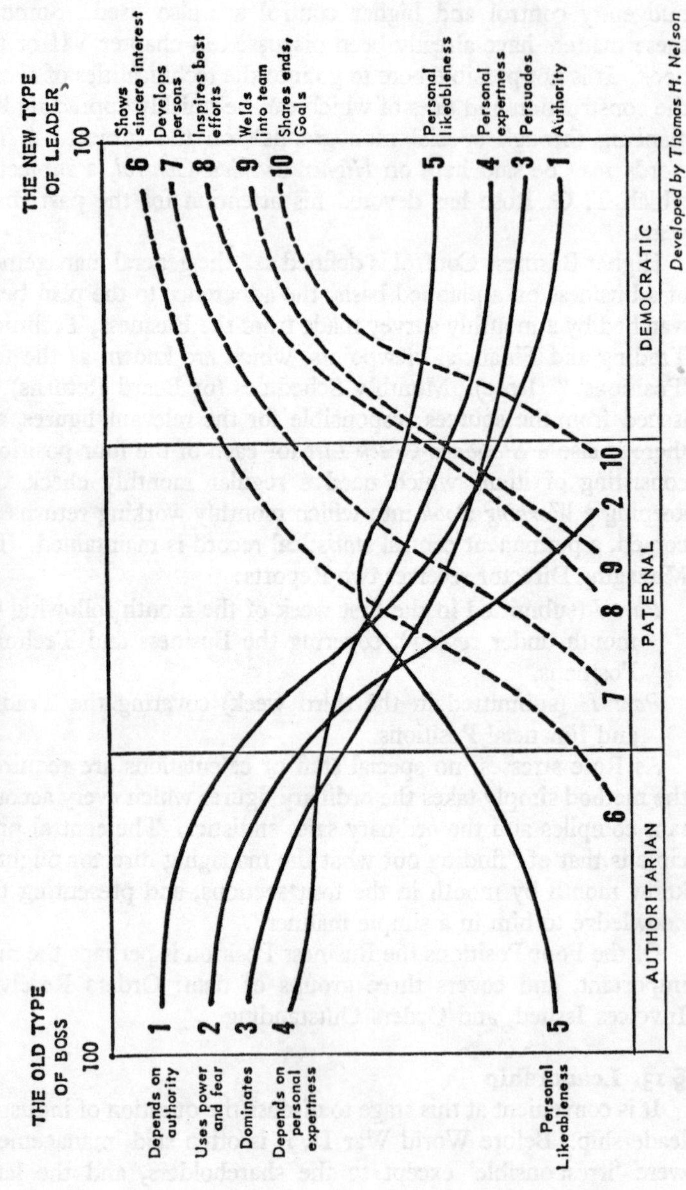
TEN CHARACTERISTICS OF LEADERSHIP
THE OLD TYPE OF BOSS
100
THE NEW TYPE OF LEADER
100
1 Depends on authority
2 Uses power and fear
3 Dominates
4 Depends on personal expertness
5 Personal Likeableness
6 Shows sincere interest
7 Develops persons
8 Inspires best efforts
9 Welds into team
10 Shares ends, Goals
5 Personal likeableness
4 Personal expertness
3 Persuades
1 Authority
6 7 8 9 2 10
AUTHORITARIAN
PATERNAL
DEMOCRATIC
Developed by Thomas H. Nelson

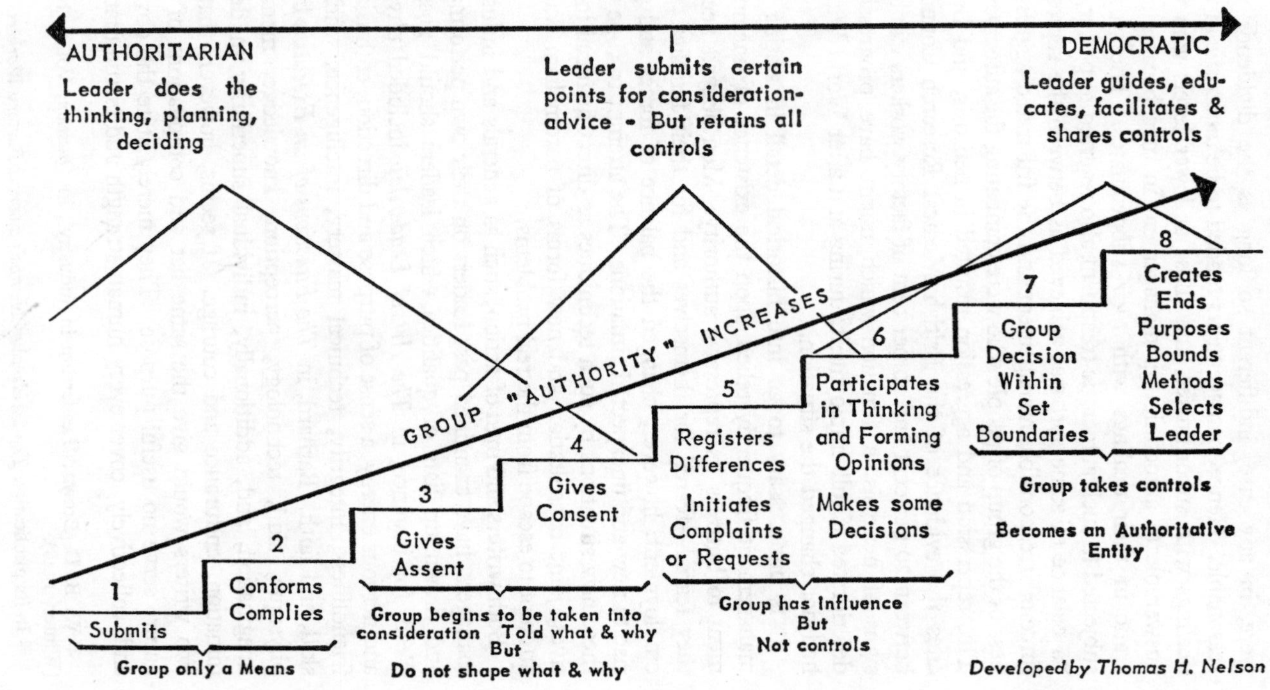
TYPES OF RESPONSES TO LEADERSHIP
AUTHORITARIAN
Leader does the thinking, planning, deciding
Leader submits certain points for consideration-advice - But retains all controls
DEMOCRATIC
Leader guides, educates, facilitates & shares controls
GROUP "AUTHORITY" INCREASES
1
Submits
2
Conforms
Complies
3
Gives
Assent
4
Gives
Consent
5
Registers
Differences
Initiates
Complaints
or Requests
6
Participates
in Thinking
and Forming
Opinions
Makes some
Decisions
7
Group
Decision
Within
Set
Boundaries
8
Creates
Ends
Purposes
Bounds
Methods
Selects
Leader
Group only a Means
Group begins to be taken into consideration Told what & why
But
Do not shape what & why
Group has Influence
But
Not controls
Group takes controls
Becomes an Authoritative Entity
Developed by Thomas H. Nelson

were, in any case, indifferent so long as the dividends were reasonable. Hence, managements tended to be *autocratic* in their dealings with subordinates, and those at lower levels who were answerable to autocratic top management in turn became autocratic in their dealings with *their* subordinates. The workers subjected to such autocratic treatment also resorted to power, and "a balance of some sort was achieved as between the repressive force of irresponsible management and the frustrated aggressiveness of the group of people who were combating the autocracy".[31] This repression and aggression resulted in neurosis, and Brown cites the evidence of the British Medical Research Council[32]: between 20 per cent and 30 per cent of factory workers exhibited signs of neurosis, a situation which might have progressively deteriorated if full employment, during and after World War II, had not changed the situation.

It is unnecessary to go into historical detail in stating that management frequently relied upon the existence of unemployment to buttress its repressive authority. Men obeyed because they feared—feared for themselves and for their families. Full employment, however, changed the balance of forces and gave rise to new and unexpected situations. The attempt to cope with these new situations by such techniques as direct financial incentives, joint consultation and new forms of paternalism was an attempt to escape from the real problems.

Both writers and men of action, such as generals and industrial managers, have examined past leaders on their own performance and drawn up lists of qualities which leaders should possess. Tead, for instance, in *The Art of Leadership* included physical and nervous energy, a sense of purpose and direction, enthusiasm, friendliness, integrity, technical mastery, intelligence, teaching skill, and faith. Barnard, in *The Functions of an Executive* listed physique, skill, technology, perception, knowledge, memory, imagination, and, additionally, individual superiority in determination, endurance and courage. It seems, however, that no two writers would give the same list and compilations of this nature serve no useful purpose. They merely state the obvious and, collectively, cover every human strength and virtue that has

[31] W. B. D. Brown: 'Leadership in Industry', in *Question*, Vol. I, No. 2 (Winter, 1948).

[32] In its publication *The Incidence of Neurosis amongst Factory Workers.*

ever been observed. Perhaps it is more profitable to discuss *leaders* rather than the abstract qualities of leadership. Lord Montgomery has stated in simple terms his conception of the leader: "... one who can be looked up to, whose personal judgment is trusted, who can inspire and warm the hearts of those he leads, gaining their trust and confidence, and explaining what is needed in language which can be understood".[33] Dr. Copeman in his study of British leaders[34] believed that many of the factors to which rise to leadership may be attributed have a medical or psychological slant, and include good health and 'boundless energy'. Very little seems to be known, however, of the causes of energy or what drives a man towards a more balanced and stable character whilst others "lapse into pettiness or nervous indecision".

Industrial leadership has often been contrasted with military leadership, but all leadership, as Field-Marshal Slim pointed out in his Elbourne Memorial Lecture,[35] is essentially the same, being a combination of *persuasion*, *compulsion* and *example*: all three elements are essential, and as Lord Slim says, "even in an army more is done by persuasion, encouragement and confidence than by shouting orders". But the leader must hold in reserve a determination "not to shirk the inevitable and mutual unpleasantness (or worse) of compulsion". Example means saying 'Come on', not 'Go on'. Lord Slim emphasizes the personal touch in leadership. In operation orders issued in his name Lord Slim always wrote one paragraph, usually the shortest, himself—the *intention paragraph*—a lesson which many industrial managers can take to heart. Subordinates must be quite clear as to what policy, plans and intentions are. Further, "the commander must be known throughout his command," not a vague figure, remote and inaccessible. "The head of any organisation, commander-in-chief, chairman, managing director, should be able to walk unannounced into any camp, bivouac, workshop or office under his command, and be at once recognised, and in this respect it is more important to be recognised than to be popular".

33 Field-Marshal The Viscount Lord Montgomery: *The Path to Leadership* (1961), pp. 9–10. For an example of the leader in action see Sir John Hunt: *The Ascent of Everest*, a book containing many lessons for management.

34 G. B. Copeman: *Leaders of British Industry* (1955), p. 152.

35 'Leadership', reproduced in *The Manager* (Jan. 1962).

A recent review of the research on leadership[36] to date discusses six 'principles' which will serve as a framework for practising managers:

(i) *Effective leadership contributes to the achievement of group goals.* Leadership means directing groups towards goals, and group goals are not necessarily the goals of the individuals who make up the groups but are the *raison d'être* of the groups—production, service, innovation, and so on. The leader must also try to control interactions within the group so that its cohesiveness and morale are enhanced.

(ii) *Effective leadership is a function of the characteristics of the leader, the group, the situation, and the inter-relations among these factors.* It is worth noticing here that a review of over one hundred studies dealing with the qualities or traits of the leaders revealed that only 5 per cent of the qualities listed by the different writers showed up in four or more of the studies.

(iii) *A leader's effectiveness depends on how well he and his organisation define his role and how completely they accept it.* This principle indicates three "environmental requirements" for effective leadership: (*a*) a proper organisational set-up; (*b*) careful definition of the leader's place within the organisation; (*c*) acceptance of this position by both the leader and those above him and below him.

(iv) *To be effective a leader must be able to analyse his group and determine what courses of action will best help to achieve the groups goals, and promote its morale*, i.e. the leader must understand both the work of his group and the group itself, and must know how these will be affected by his actions.

(v) *For the leader to be successful, it is important that his followers perceive him as effectively responding to the group needs.* No leader can be successful without the willing support of his followers.

(vi) *Finally, the leader's effectiveness must be judged in terms of the group's survival and its progress towards its goals.* This is clearly the most logical criterion of success.

In the next decade Britain will need leadership on every level,

[36] R. G. Wall and H. Hawkins: 'Requisites of Effective Leadership', *Personnel* (May–June 1962).

but especially in industry, where there must be a simultaneous attack on three fronts: long-term planning; the early recognition of potential leaders; and the bringing of management and labour to "a mutual recognition that they are not opponents, but allies fighting on the same side and, broadly speaking, for the same objectives" (Lord Slim).

A word may be said finally on *discipline*. All management discipline must begin with the self-discipline of the manager: the discipline which he then imposes on those under his leadership will then be more easily acceptable. The theory of 'prize and penalty' is regarded by some as old-fashioned, yet any system which offers no prize for outstanding performance or penalty for incompetence must finally disintegrate. Obviously there are some prizes and penalties which are insusceptible of monetary evaluation, but prizes and penalties have to exist.

Along with self-discipline go moral courage and acceptance of the view that, however much the manager delegates, he cannot divest himself of his own final authority and concomitant responsibility. One may indeed, distinguish between 'titular' leaders, who find it only too easy to delegate their own authority, and real leaders who also find it easy to delegate but realise that there is an ultimate residuum of authority and responsibility which cannot be delegated.

§ 14. Conclusion. Planning and Control—the Basis of All Effective Management

Planning is the intelligent anticipation of how an objective can be reached; controlling is the provision of a combination of measurement and discipline to ensure that the plan is put into effect and the objective achieved. A plan is a statement of the resources required—men, money and materials—and the requisite action to achieve a given end.

A statement of Lord Kelvin has often been repeated: "If you can measure what you are speaking about and express it in numbers, you know something about it; if you cannot express it in numbers, your knowledge is of a meagre and unsatisfactory kind". That is the scientist speaking: transferred to the industrial context, it implies that plans must be made as precisely *quantitative* as possible. Such quantitative planning is of use in even the simplest operations: a good example is the 'Planning and Instruction Sheets' for the Midland Bank Sports Day.[37]

Planning and control are the basis of all effective management and they must be based upon hard facts and figures as distinct from soft guesses. In this respect operational research will become of increasing importance in management, since it applies well-established logical principles to an existing body of data, in order to provide quantitative answers to meaningful questions. O.R. can tackle numerous problems, of which the following are important from the point of view of planning and control.

(i) How much of the product it will be necessary to make in order to keep pace with probable demand?
(ii) How many men will be required on what machines?
(iii) How much inward and outward stock will be required to ensure the smoothest flow under varying conditions?
(iv) Which of several competitive new machines will it be most profitable (*not* cheapest) to buy?
(v) What will be the most economical 'mix' of various raw materials to satisfy varying demands for a changing market?

Controls must be so established that they conform to the organisation structure. If the organisation structure is not clear, it will be impossible to say who is responsible, when deviations occur, for bringing them back to the planned norms. Control data should be simple and intelligible to the layman, and not couched in specialist jargon. The golden rule is to bear in mind the needs of the user, *e.g.* should a works manager in a branch receive all the information which goes to his subordinates as well as that which is relevant to his own purposes?

ADDITIONAL READING ASSIGNMENTS

1. Peter Drucker: *The Practice of Management*, chapt. 28, 'Making Decisions'.
2. W. H. Newman and C. E. Sumner: *The Process of Management*, Part III, 'Planning: Elements of Decision-Making'.
3. H. Kootz and C. O'Donnell: *The Principles of Management*, 23, 'The Process of Decision-Making'.
4. G. C. Copeman: *The Laws of Business Management*, 7, 'The Law of Business Strategy'.

37 See R. S. Edwards and H. Townsend: *Studies in Business Organisation: A Supplement to 'Business Enterprise'*, Appendix to Chapter 1, pp. 17–24.

5. M. H. Jones: *Executive Decision-Making.*
6. J. D. Williams: *The Compleat Strategyst.*
7. C. I. Barnard: *The Functions of an Executive*, chapts. 15 and 16.
8. H. A. Simon: *Administrative Behaviour*, Second edition, pp. 45–109.
9. A. J. Merrett and G. Bannock: *Business Economics and Statistics*, Introduction, 1 and 3.
10. G. L. S. Shackle: *Uncertainty in Economics.*
11. F. H. Knight: *Risk, Uncertainty and Profit*, chapt. 7.
12. H. W. Wage: *Manufacturing Engineering* (McGraw Hill 1963), chapt. 1, 'The Role of the Production Planner in Industry'; 6, 'Developing the Plan', and 12, 'Production Control'.
13. E. F. L. Brech: *Principles and Practice of Management*, Part IV, chapt. II.
14. *Management Succession* (Acton Society Trust).
15. M. P. Follett: *Freedom and Control*, chapt. VI.
16. H. B. Maynard: *Production Handbook*, Section 2, 'Production Planning and Control'.
17. T. G. Rose: *Higher Business Control*, Seventh Edition (1963).
18. *Better Factories* (Inst. of Directors Publication).
19. G. B. Copeman: *Leaders of British Industry.*
20. F. H. Albers: *Organised Executive Action*, Part Five, 'Leadership and Motivation'.
21. Sir John Hunt: *The Ascent of Everest.*

TOPICS FOR ESSAYS/DISCUSSIONS

1. "Decision-making is the central job of managers". "Planning and control are the basis of all effective management". Discuss these two statements taken together.
2. Examine Drucker's distinction between 'tactical' and 'strategic' decisions and discuss his statement that the latter are the "specifically managerial decisions".
3. "Alternative solutions are in effect our only tool to mobilise and train the imagination. They are the heart of what is meant by the 'scientific method'." Expand and explain.
4. What is the significance of the distinction between *risk* and *uncertainty*?
5. Write short notes on (*a*) Product Policy; (*b*) Purchasing Policy; and (*c*) Personnel Policy.
6. Write a short essay on "The Planning of Management Succession".
7. "Departures from an expressed profitability stem from a variety of causes". Discuss the main causal factors of variations which may supervene to upset a profit plan.

8. What are the essential steps in any control process?
9. Write a short essay on *one* of the following subjects: (*a*) Production Planning and Control; (*b*) Quality Control; (*c*) Environmental Control.
10. Is the 'power of leadership' different from the 'ability to manage'?
11. It has been said that higher productivity goes with democratic leadership, though in the short run autocratic management may achieve better results. What are your views?
12. Comment on Drucker's five processes of decision-making.

CHAPTER TEN

ORGANISATION STRUCTURE

§ 1. What is Organisation?

To organise means literally 'to furnish with organs' or 'make organic' (*Concise Oxford Dictionary*). The dictionary definition should be borne in mind, since to talk of organisation as the *framework* of management[1] tends to lead to the notion of organisation as something relatively rigid, as the bony framework of an organism. If we wish to have an analogy, it would be better to conceive of organisation as the anatomy and physiology of an enterprise—bones, muscles, arteries and specialised organs. It is worthwhile recalling here that the famous economist, Alfred Marshall, warned against talking about the economic *machine*: economic institutions behave more like organisms than mechanisms, and analogies should, therefore, be biological. Organisation must refer to the 'complete body' with all its correlated functions.

Organisation is synonymous with *associated effort*, and its first principle is co-ordination.[2] Organisation may be simply defined as "the form of every human association for the attainment of a common purpose".[3] The purpose of organisation is to create a network of positions and responsibilities through and by means of which an enterprise can carry out its tasks. The *policy* of an enterprise must first be clearly stated; activities must then be identified and *grouped* in a manner calculated to achieve the policy most effectively. This means that the duties, authority and responsibility of both groups and individuals must be carefully defined, and executive and procedural patterns most apposite to a given enterprise must be established.

There can be no such thing as the perfect organisation, self-running and self-regulating, with exactly the right number of sub-divisions and the right relationship of the latter to one another. It is possible for an executive to become a perfectionist as regards

[1] E. F. L. Brech: *Organisation: The Framework of Management.*

[2] James D. Mooney: *The Principles of Organisation*, Rev. Ed. (1947), p. 1.

[3] *ibid.* p. 3.

organisation and to begin to regard organisation charts, procedure manuals and internal operating rules as ends in themselves. Such a person will fail to realise that an over-emphasis on formality will destroy subordinates' initiative and power of independent thought, and will fail to appreciate the power of the *informal* organisation which inevitably develops among people who work together.[4]

The organisational structure of any enterprise must be kept constantly under review, if ossification and hardening of the arteries is to be prevented. During the period of early growth, when needs and opportunities are more easily appreciated, changes can be frequently and speedily made; with an increase in age, size and complexity, however, bureaucratic problems begin to appear.

§ 2. Authority and Responsibility

A useful definition of *authority* is "the power to make decisions which guide the actions of another".[5] An immediate distinction suggests itself—authority to deal with *objects* and authority to direct the *actions* of other *persons*. In the first case the authority is clear-cut, but authority over people can only be effective when they accept it. Many instructions are obeyed as a matter of course, or because a subordinate has certain direct satisfactions from his job, or simply because a given task gives him an opportunity for sociability. Yet it would be foolish to rely upon custom and direct satisfactions to ensure acceptance of authority and firms may have to resort to the use of power, the development of influence or reliance on personal leadership.

Authority must not be confused with *power*, which is the product of a personality (or personalities) in a given situation. "Authority can be delegated. Power cannot. It either exists or it does not. One may invest a person with authority, and with responsibility, but one can no more invest him with power than one can provide him with will, imagination or understanding".[6]

One should also distinguish between *authority of position*, which indicates the control over others which an individual may yield as a result of his position in an organisation (*e.g.* line

[4] See M. E. Dimock: *Administrative Vitality. The Conflict with Bureaucracy*, London (1960).

[5] H. Simon: *Administrative Behaviour*, p. 125.

[6] See F. Hooper: *Management Survey*, pp. 81–2.

managers); and *authority of the situation* which derives not from delegation but the individual's ability, through his knowledge and ideas, to induce others to accept his plan of action in a given situation. This is illustrated when an individual is informally accorded an authoritative position by reason of his experience, superior knowledge, or resourcefulness, or character.

Responsibility and authority are the basic concepts of all collective action, and both words are used in several different senses, but the most useful senses from the point of view of the executive are:[7]

Authority: the right or power to delegate responsibility* (the difference between 'right' and 'power' is the difference between *de jure* and *de facto* authority).

Responsibility: an accepted obligation to execute a certain task or incur a penalty.

Authority in a company emanates from the shareholders (who themselves derive it from the constitution and legal system) to the board of directors, whence it is passed down to designated persons who issue orders and instructions to subordinates.

§ 3. 'Kinds' of Authority

Authority may be viewed under three different headings:

FORMAL: authority conferred by law or delegated within an organisation;

FUNCTIONAL: based upon specialised knowledge or expertise;

PERSONAL: accorded because of seniority, popularity or leadership qualities.

As already stated, authority must finally rest upon the acceptance of orders and instructions by the person who receives them. Barnard[8] has indicated four conditions which must obtain before a person can and will accept a communication as authoritative:

(i) he must be able to *understand* the communication;

* Though the phrase 'delegate responsibility' is commonly used, strictly speaking one does not delegate responsibility but a *job* or *task*, holding the subordinate accountable for its performance.

[7] T. R. E. Johnstone: 'Responsibility and Authority', *The Manager* (June 1963).

[8] C. I. Barnard: *The Functions of the Executive*, Harvard University Press (1938).

(ii) he must believe that it is *not incompatible* with his own *personal* interest;
(iii) he must believe that it is *not inconsistent* with the *purpose* of the organisation;
(iv) he is *mentally and physically capable* of *complying* with it.

§ 4. Commanding or 'Inspiring'

One of the major elements identified by Henri Fayol was *commanding*, getting the workers to do the tasks assigned to them under the organisation. In modern times it seems that the word *inspire* is better than *command*, in spite of its rather sanctimonious associations, since the modern worker is no longer amenable to what might appear to be arbitrary orders. It is essential that those who share in the productive task believe it to be morally right: they must not only share the task, they must also share its satisfactions or its disappointments. Management fails if it merely secures passive obedience or unquestioning loyalty.

The disadvantages of issuing *arbitrary* commands are:[9]

(i) *possible contributions* from those directed are lost;
(ii) such directions are apt to cause *friction* between workers and foremen;
(iii) if a worker is asked to do something in a way which he thinks is not the best way, he will often lose all interest in the result (never interfere with a worker's *pride* in his work);
(iv) an arbitrary command decreases the *sense of responsibility*, thus lowering the chance of business success.

§ 5. Behaviour Patterns

If authority be viewed as the power to make decisions which guide the actions of another, then it is essentially a *relationship* between a superior and a 'subordinate'. Decisions are framed by the superior and transmitted to the 'subordinate' in the expectation that the latter will accept them. This relationship therefore involves a kind of behaviour on the part of both superior and subordinate, and only when such behaviour occurs can an

[9] See Mary Parker Follett: 'The Giving of Orders', reprinted in *Freedom and Co-ordination. Lectures in Business Organisation*, London (1949), Lecture II.

authority relationship be said to occur. Yet, as Simon points out,[10] two persons may stand in a relationship of authority at one moment and not at the next. Even if the 'superior-subordinate' relationship is recognised, it does not follow that all the communications of the superior are 'commands'. Simon distinguishes between *influence* and *authority*, and points out that *persuasion*, *suggestion* and *command* can be present in a single situation. If there is disagreement between two persons and it cannot be resolved by discussion, persuasion or other means of conviction, then it has to be decided by the authority of one or other of the participants. This "right to have the last word" is the usual meaning of *lines of authority* in an administrative organisation.

§ 6. The Structure of Organisation

As an enterprise grows the organisation structure must simultaneously expand both laterally and vertically. At any given level the expansion of the volume of work requires an increase in personnel to carry out the work; there is also vertical 'downward' growth as subordinates are acquired at managerial and supervisory levels and routine tasks delegated to them. It is important so to plan growth that both horizontal and vertical expansion take place hand-in-hand. There will usually be a third development—that of specialisation, or the grouping of tasks in certain fields of activity.

The 'vertical' growth of an enterprise gives rise to *levels of authority*, and the so-called *executive pyramid*. Growth means proliferation of both levels and positions, which have then to be cemented by delegation, *i.e.* entrusting part of management, supervision or operations to others. The practice of delegation creates a *chain of command* ('scalar' principle) and has a long history as an organisational device. In general, the number of levels of authority should be kept to a minimum, but this is a question that can be discussed only in relation to the 'span of control'.[11] If the span of control is narrow, the resulting organisation structure will be 'tall', with many levels; if the span is wide, the organisation structure will be 'flat', with few levels. Large organisations such as the Army require twelve or thirteen levels.

The essential problem of organisation structure is the *definition*

10 Simon: *Administrative Behaviour*, Chapter VII.

11 See Chapter Twelve of the present book on 'Delegation and Span of Control'.

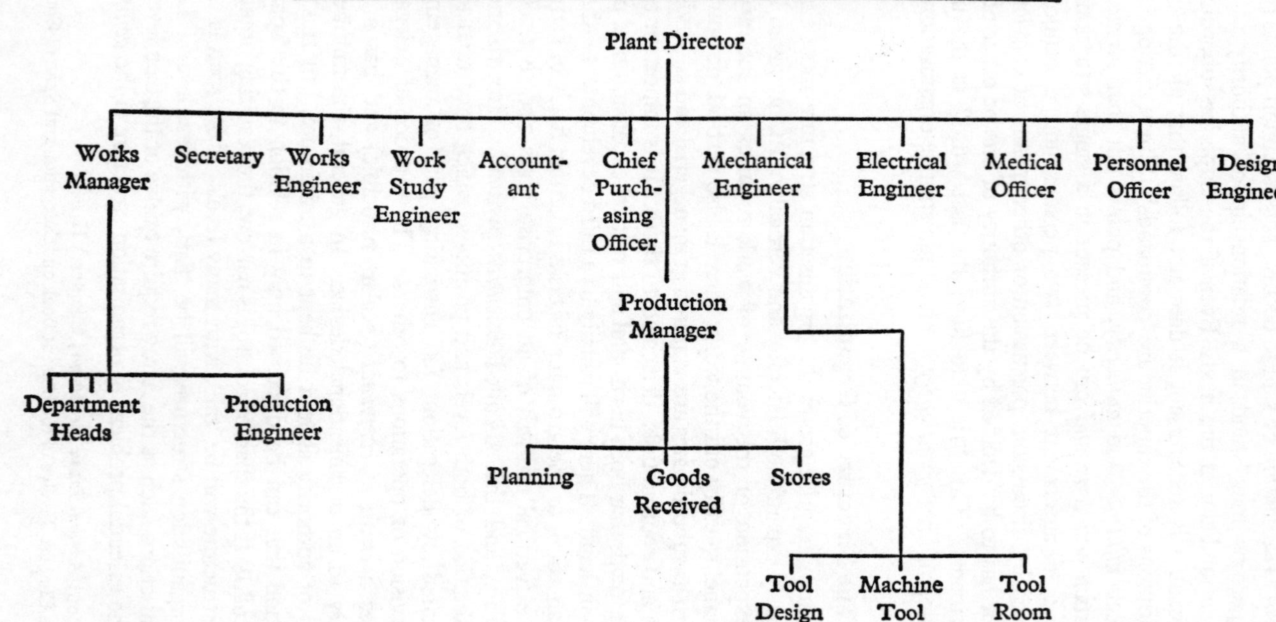
ORGANISATION CHART OF A LARGE ENGINEERING WORKS
Plant Director
Works Manager
Secretary
Works Engineer
Work Study Engineer
Account-ant
Chief Purch-asing Officer
Mechanical Engineer
Electrical Engineer
Medical Officer
Personnel Officer
Design Engineer
Production Manager
Department Heads
Production Engineer
Planning
Goods Received
Stores
Tool Design
Machine Tool Mandrel
Tool Room

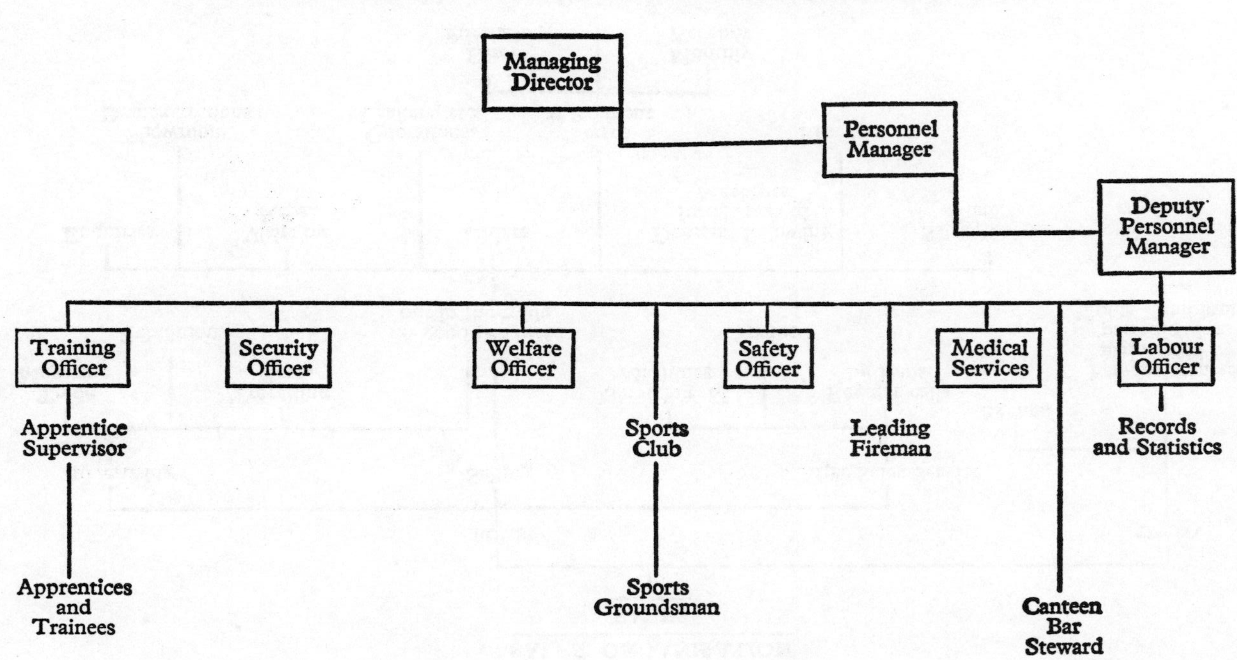
PERSONNEL ORGANISATION OF AN ENGINEERING FIRM
Managing Director
Personnel Manager
Deputy Personnel Manager
Training Officer
Security Officer
Welfare Officer
Safety Officer
Medical Services
Labour Officer
Apprentice Supervisor
Sports Club
Leading Fireman
Records and Statistics
Apprentices and Trainees
Sports Groundsman
Canteen Bar Steward

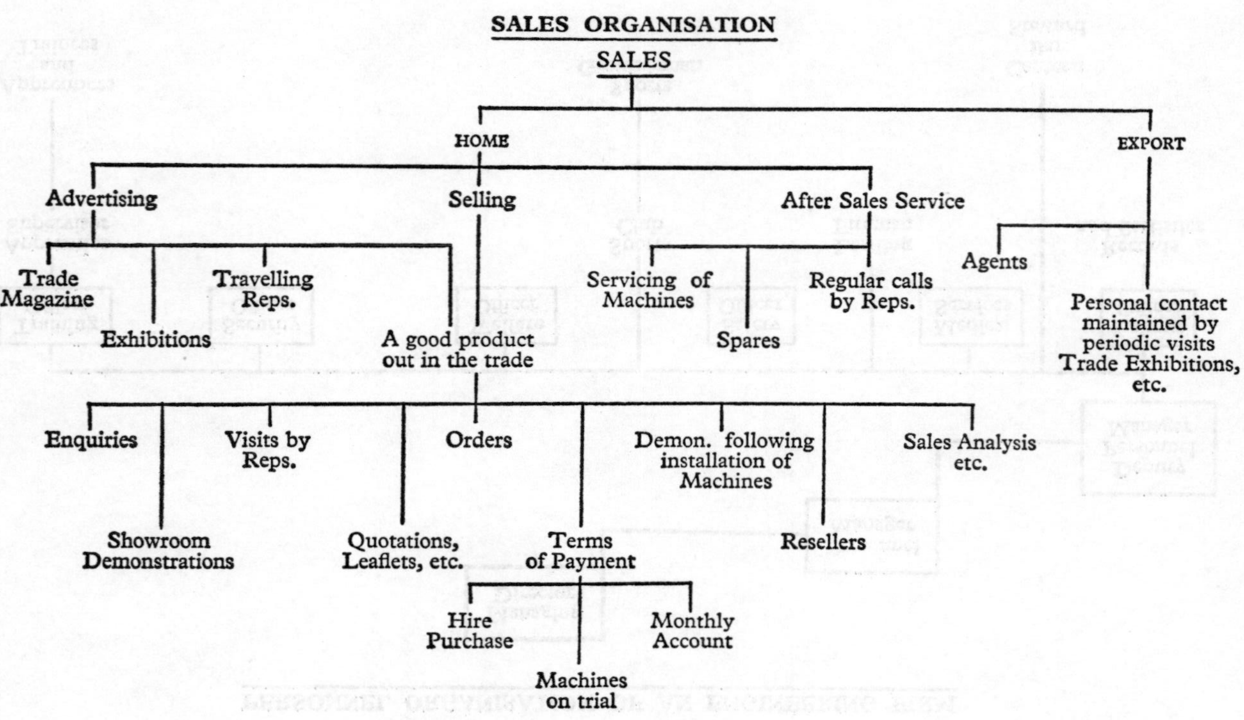
SALES ORGANISATION
SALES
HOME
EXPORT
Advertising
Selling
After Sales Service
Agents
Personal contact maintained by periodic visits Trade Exhibitions, etc.
Trade Magazine
Exhibitions
Travelling Reps.
A good product out in the trade
Servicing of Machines
Spares
Regular calls by Reps.
Enquiries
Visits by Reps.
Orders
Demon. following installation of Machines
Sales Analysis etc.
Showroom Demonstrations
Quotations, Leaflets, etc.
Terms of Payment
Resellers
Hire Purchase
Monthly Account
Machines on trial

DESIGN OFFICE ORGANISATION

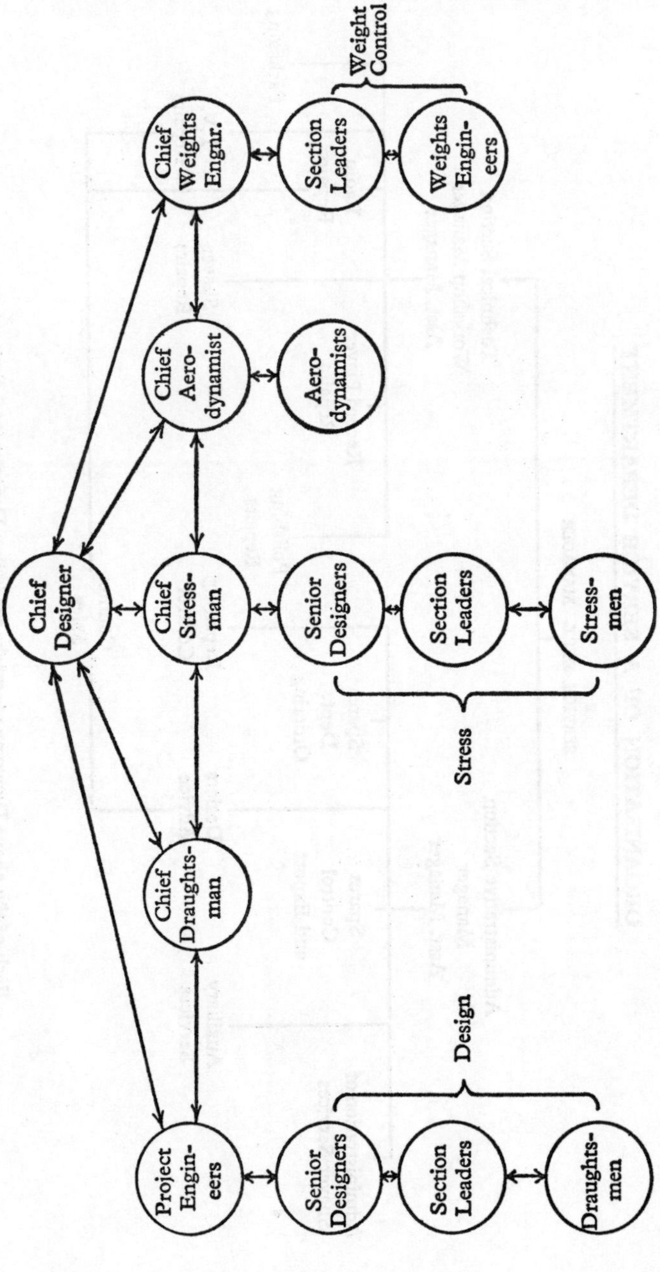

ORGANISATION OF A SERVICE DEPARTMENT

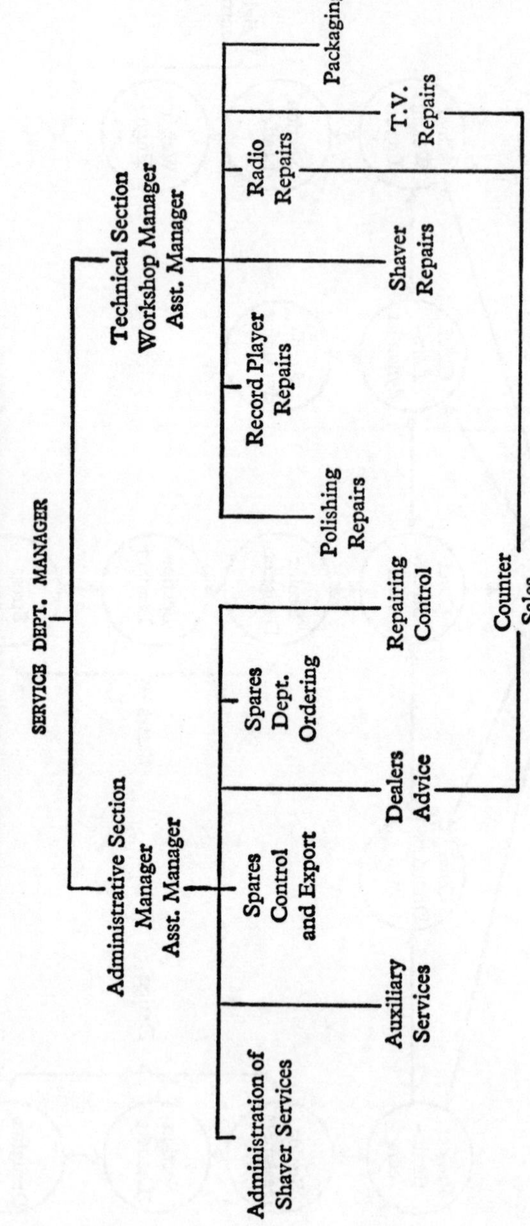

Each of the above Departments works through a Departmental Supervisor

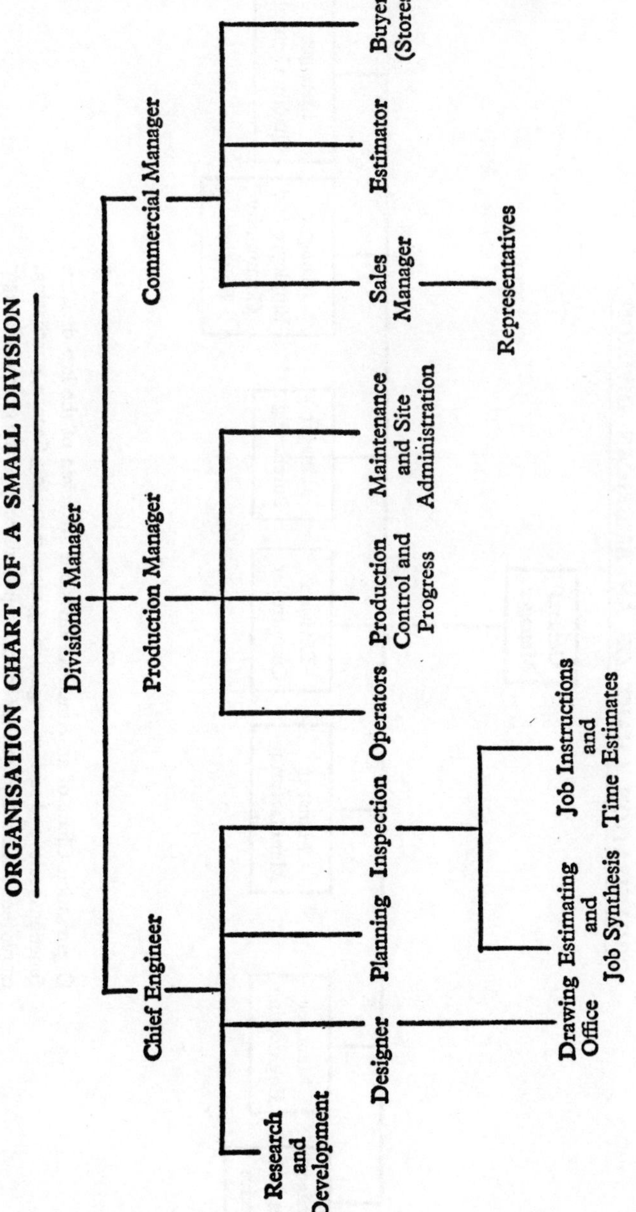

ORGANISATION CHART OF A SMALL DIVISION

ORGANISATION CHART OF AN AMERICAN DIVISION

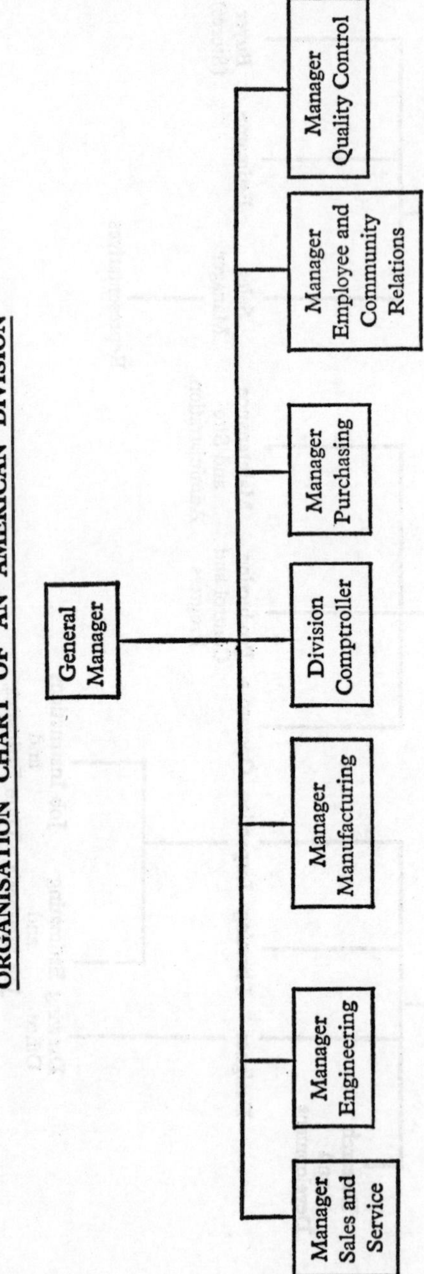

Organisation Chart of an American division: all seven of the key division functions; sales and service, engineering, manufacturing, finance, purchasing, employee relations and quality control report directly to the general manager of the division.

NATIONALISED INDUSTRY: ORGANISATION CHART OF AN AREA BOARD (GAS)

(Industrial Division)

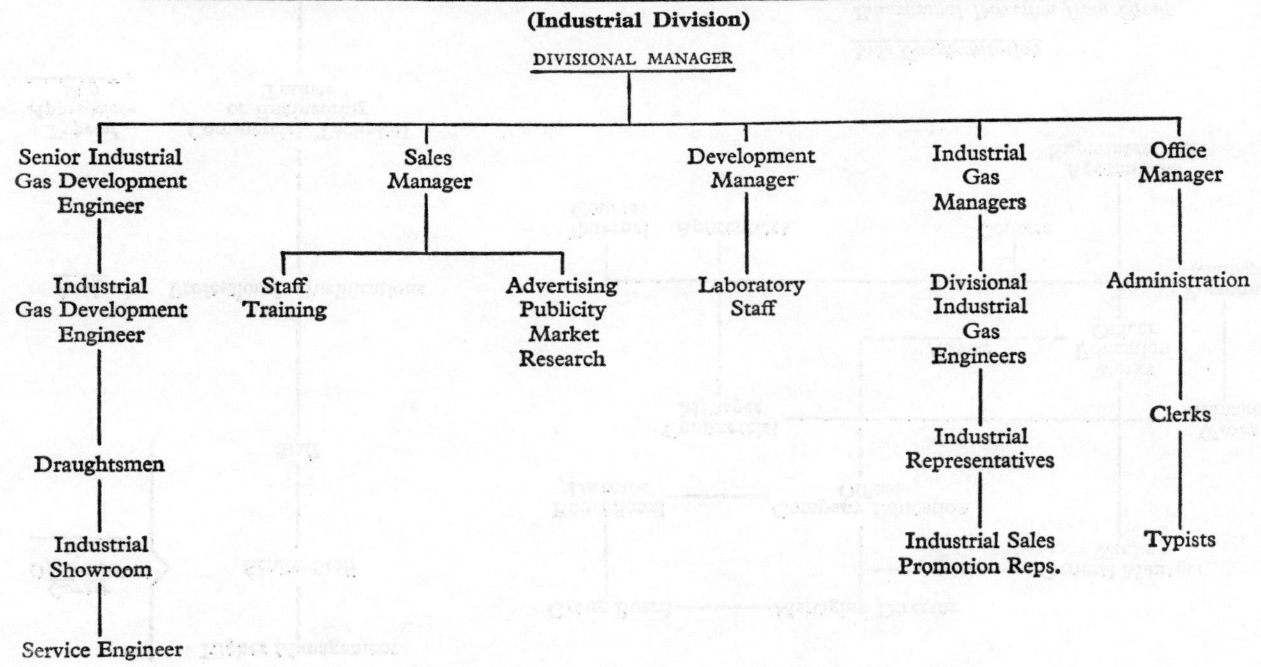

A GROUP EDUCATIONAL ORGANISATION

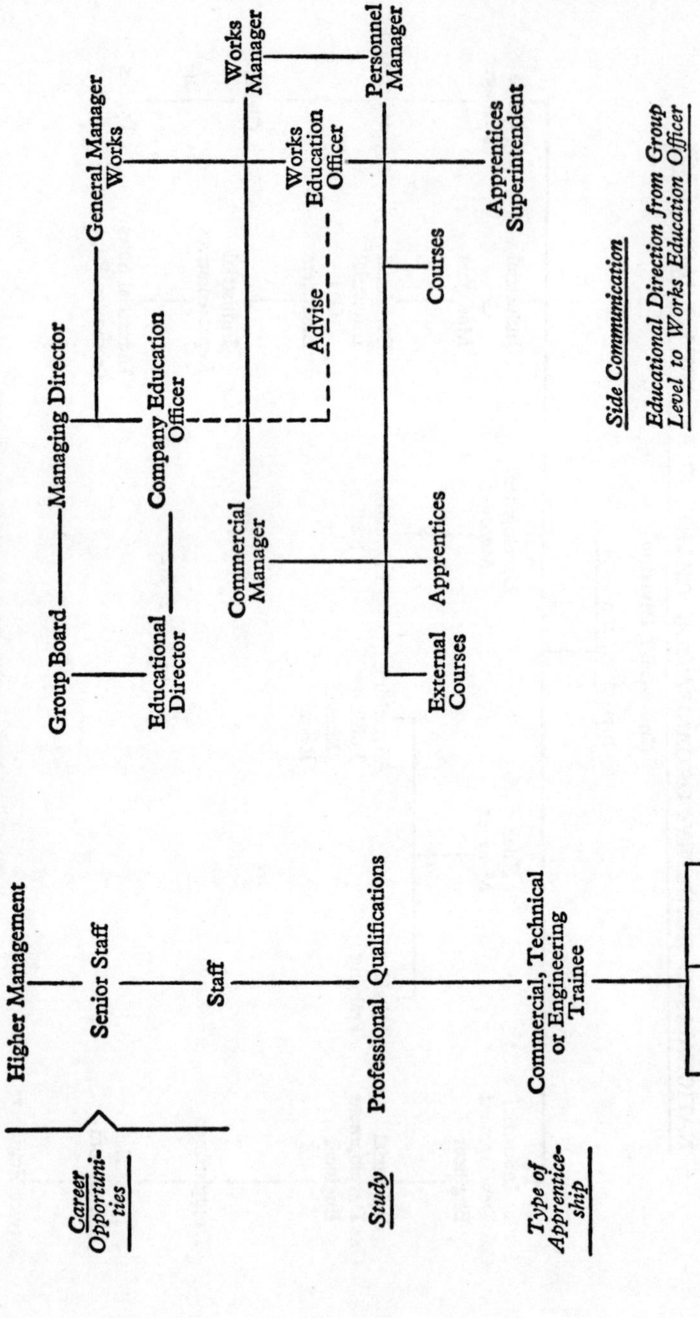

of responsibilities,[12] *i.e.* the determination of the content of given managerial positions and the formal relationships determined by their content. Such definition of responsibilities is the action required to realise the principle of delegation; the main difficulty is that of "so determining the over-all pattern of responsibilities that clearly-identifiable parts can be laid-out to promote sub-division of management action, yet at the same time preserving the unity of the whole management process properly integrated" (Brech).[13]

§ 7. The Management Team

The term 'top management' is generally taken to include the Board and its Members and a small number of the most senior appointments at the head of the major divisions of operation and service specialisation. It is to some extent an unsuitable term, since it is "less one of management in any day-to-day meaning than one of policy, direction and over-all control".[14]

The Board of Directors is a committee and the individual director as such has no functions, unless he is Managing Director. As the name implies, the function of the Directors is to direct the operations of an enterprise, determine its policy, lay down general guiding-lines for management, authorise unusual expenditure. Under the Companies Acts they also have certain legal obligations.[15] Individual directors may, however, have executive functions and be responsible for certain aspects of the work of the enterprise, *e.g.* sales policy, production policy. This does not alter the fact that the Board is collectively responsible for policy.

The Managing Director (Chief Executive). For a detailed discussion the student is referred to Brech's Schedule No. 21, which gives over thirty duties of the Managing Director.[16] His main

12 See Brech: *Organisation. The Framework of Management*, chapter IV, 'Can Responsibilities be Defined?'

13 For practical illustrations, see Brech, *op. cit.*, chapters VI and VII.

14 See Brech: *Organisation. The Framework of Management*, chapter VIII, 'The Responsibilities of Top Management'; also H. B. Maynard (Ed.): *Top Management Handbook*, esp. Parts VI and VII.

15 See A. Read: *The Company Director;* and F. H. Head: *Formation and Management of a Private Company*, chapter XII.

16 Brech: *op. cit.*, chapter VIII, pp. 240–42.

task is to carry into effect the Board's policy and ensuring that all members of the enterprise comply with it. When, however, the M.D. is a member of the Board, he shares their corporate responsibility for policy. If he is not a member, he will then be styled General Manager. The Chief Executive is the main co-ordinator, the main originator of reports and agenda for management meetings, and of broad operating instructions.

The Senior Managers (Senior Executives). Among these are usually included the works manager, the personnel manager, the sales manager, the purchasing officer, the chief accountant, the chief inspector, and other departmental heads who 'execute' the company's policy, translating it into more detailed lines of action. Frequent meetings with the M.D. are necessary so that the latter can co-ordinate their work and that they themselves can see where consultation with their fellow senior colleagues is necessary.[17] These senior executives constitute what is usually known as the 'management team' though, strictly speaking, the team includes personnel at a lower level. It is important to try to create a balanced team, avoiding excessive strength in one position and weakness in another. As Hooper emphasised[18] it is impossible to dispense with top management because of the frequent need for "an instant and flexible response to situations, alterations to plans, etc.".

The functional work required for the successful accomplishment of any task can, in a typical manufacturing enterprise, be divided into seven major "activity areas".[19]

1. RESEARCH AND DEVELOPMENT: designing the product
2. PRODUCTION: making the product
3. MARKETING: selling the product
4. FINANCE AND CONTROL: handling financial matters and controlling costs and profitability

[17] See particularly Schedule 30, 'The Works Manager', in Brech, *op. cit.*, pp. 213–15.

[18] Hooper: *Management Survey*, p. 70.

[19] For a full discussion see Maynard (Ed.): *Top Management Handbook*, pp. 14–22; and Part VI, 'Activity Area Management'.

5. PERSONNEL: providing labour and creating a favourable internal atmosphere

6. EXTERNAL RELATIONS: creating a favourable external atmosphere

7. SECRETARIAL AND LEGAL: seeing that there is compliance with the law

The Secretary. Under the *Companies Act* 1948 the Secretaryship of a company is a statutory function. The Secretary must convene the board and record its decisions. He must arrange the annual meeting and ensure that reports and accounts are properly presented and publicised. He is also responsible for the statutory registers of shareholders, and must keep them up to date. He has to supervise the transfer and transmission of shares, the issue of share certificates and the payment of dividends. In addition to these statutory and official duties, he will generally be the main medium of communication between the boardroom and the world outside. Since he has to keep the minutes, he will attend all board meetings whether as a member or not. It is his task to interpret the board's decisions and transmit them to the relevant executives and, if necessary, to public authorities.

Middle Management. This is a rather vague term, its interpretation varying from firm to firm. Included under this heading may be the assistants of the senior executives who take over full responsibility in the absence of the latter, and the most important 'sub-executives', *e.g.* deputy sales manager, assistant chief engineer, superintendent inspector.

Supervisors. This is again a term with a broad meaning, including anyone who literally 'keeps an eye on' (supervises) the work of others, with vague lines of demarcation at both the upper and lower level. In the past supervisors were often chosen because of their technical or operating skill, or their forbidding presence. It has been realised in recent times that they should be chosen mainly for their ability, actual or potential, as *leaders*. In recent years supervisors and foremen have rightly become concerned about their status and responsibility in relation both to their superiors and the shop-floor. Foremen attending courses believe, for example, that whatever the advantages of having a centralised employment policy, it weakens their authority *vis-à-vis* new employees. Again, the withholding of the power to suspend or discharge a man is viewed as a further weakening of their authority. The questions foremen ask show that they are concerned with their relationships with men both inside and outside the factory.[20] In general, they believe that they should be promoted outside their own shop, since a new foreman in his *own* shop tends to extremes of behaviour: he is either too strict or too lenient, both attitudes reflecting their uncertainty. Foremen used to give undue prominence to the technical abilities and know-how of a foreman, but a recent study by the Institute of Industrial Supervisors showed the following priorities in terms of total working time devoted to different aspects of the foreman's job:

RESULTS OBTAINED FROM QUESTIONNAIRE SUBMITTED TO 109 SUPERVISORS

	Percentage
1. PLANNING TASKS (allocating duties, arranging work ahead) . . .	40
2. TECHNICAL TASKS (advising on methods) .	21
3. PRODUCTION TASKS (actual work of the section)	18
4. INSPECTION TASKS (checking that the work has been properly done) . . .	11
5. PERSONNEL TASKS (discipline, 'awkward' people, etc.)	5
6. COMMUNICATION UPWARDS . . .	5

As regards the tasks which gave *most trouble*, the order was as follows:

Personnel:	in 27 per cent of cases
Planning:	„ 24 „ „ „ „
Production:	„ 19 „ „ „ „

Recently J. M. Fraser[21] has suggested that the task of the supervisor differs fundamentally from that of management. The supervisor is "the man between management, with its plans and eco-

[20] See M. S. Cousins: 'Questions Foremen Ask', *The Manager* (December 1956).

[21] J. M. Fraser: 'The Supervisor is Part of Management (or is he?)', *The Supervisor* (Aug. 1963).

nomic objectives on the one hand and the factory floor with its concern with the immediate job and wages on the other. The supervisor has the responsibility for putting management's plans into effective action. His task is to turn management objectives into individual tasks; to ensure that operators understand these tasks and see the point of them; to see that they apply their efforts effectively in achieving them". His function, therefore, it is asserted, is entirely different from making the plans and setting the objectives, though not less important. One of the conclusions reached from questions put to supervisors (though the writer recognised the limitations of such surveys) is that nearly nine out of ten agree that the supervisor is suspended between two conflicting points of view, although a similar proportion of the persons questioned believed that it was possible to achieve day-to-day working compromises between these two points of view. The present author has also frequently asked foremen and supervisors how they view their status, and several have recently replied that, in the last two or three years, they have begun to feel that they are "on the side of management", if only from the point of view that their seniors now "come down" to them and take pains to "put them in the picture".

§ 8. Methods of Internal Organisation

These vary a great deal from firm to firm, but a useful classification is into three 'types' or systems:

1. *Line* system (all-round men at top)
2. *Functional* or *Staff system*
3. *Line-and-Staff* (or 'Line and Functional')

Neither the line nor the functional type exists separately in its pure form in the typical modern firm, and all organisation must be of the third type, *i.e.* the main operational activities of the enterprise are as far as possible on the 'line' pattern, but there must also be room for specialised activities of a non-operational nature, for each of which a senior executive must be responsible. These senior executives will have subordinate personnel of their own, with whom their relationships will be of the line type.

The efficiency of such a *mixed* form of organisation depends upon adequate departmentalisation or division of the undertaking into departments, and upon the personality of the heads of these departments.

Line organisation was formerly termed also military organisation, though the latter is today very different from what it was in former times. The simple form of line organisation is found today only in small companies. The advantages of this form are its simplicity, stability, inherent possibility of quick action, the clearly-defined levels of authority, and the ease with which discipline can be maintained. Its disadvantages probably outweigh its advantages: they include inflexibility, inadequate division of labour, overloading of key-positions, dependence on 'key-men', conservatism.

'Line' refers to the '*line of authority*', *i.e.* there is a vertical gradation of authority, a series of superior-subordinate relationships, a single chain of direct command. Mooney's metaphor[22] is useful here: "Any duty in organisation that cannot be identified as an actual link in the scalar* process is an auxiliary function, adhering to the line like sidings along the main track. This means that every staff function must adhere to the line in some dependent relation, and could not otherwise exist". Earlier Mooney had remarked[23] " . . . the line represents the authority of *man*; the staff, the authority of *ideas*, and the use of the terms *line* and *staff* in conjunction "is intended to distinguish between the right of command and the function of counsel".

§ 8. Military Staff

The existence of a staff organisation is attested in ancient armies (Egypt, Rome) but the modern development was due initially to the Swede Gustavus Adolphus (1594–1632) and perfected by the Prussians from General Scharnhorst onwards. In modern armies there are three kinds of staff: the *general* staff, concerned with planning and co-ordination; the *special* staff, consisting of technical experts and administrators; and *personal* staff—aides, drivers, runners, etc.

The general staff includes all those activities (personnel, intelligence, operations and training, logistics) necessary to command a military unit; they are functions analogous to the 'organic' functions of industry, such as production, sales, finance. An industrial staff organisation concerned with these functions could

* The metaphor is mixed: *scalar* comes from Latin *scala*, a ladder, and 'link' should therefore be 'rung', but this terminology seems to have become accepted.

22 J. D. Mooney: *The Principles of Organisation*, p. 34.

23 *ibid.*, p. 34.

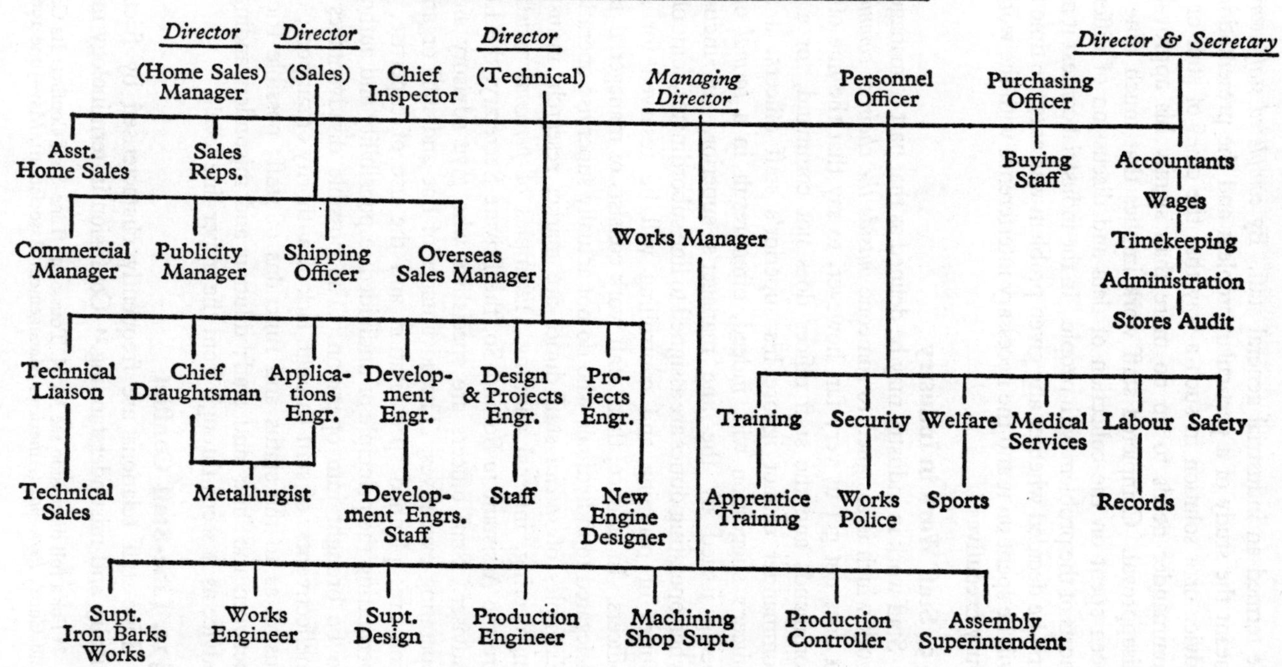
EXAMPLE: LINE-AND-STAFF ORGANISATION
Director
(Home Sales)
Manager
Director
(Sales)
Chief
Inspector
Director
(Technical)
Managing
Director
Personnel
Officer
Purchasing
Officer
Director & Secretary
Asst.
Home Sales
Sales
Reps.
Buying
Staff
Accountants
Wages
Timekeeping
Administration
Stores Audit
Commercial
Manager
Publicity
Manager
Shipping
Officer
Overseas
Sales Manager
Works Manager
Technical
Liaison
Chief
Draughtsman
Applica-
tions
Engr.
Develop-
ment
Engr.
Design
& Projects
Engr.
Pro-
jects
Engr.
Training
Security
Welfare
Medical
Services
Labour
Safety
Technical
Sales
Metallurgist
Develop-
ment Engrs.
Staff
Staff
New
Engine
Designer
Apprentice
Training
Works
Police
Sports
Records
Supt.
Iron Barks
Works
Works
Engineer
Supt.
Design
Production
Engineer
Machining
Shop Supt.
Production
Controller
Assembly
Superintendent
(plus Foremen and Charge-hands)

be termed an industrial general staff. By *completed staff work* is meant the study of a particular problem and the presentation of advice or a solution in such a way that the chief of staff or the commander needs to do no more than signify his approval or disapproval. Completed staff work implies that much time has been spent on the collection of data and discussion of different facets of the problem with people. In the industrial context it must first be decided whether any given problem warrants the time that will be spent on it and the necessary interference with the work of busy executives.

§ 9. Staff Work in Industry

Staff work in industry may be defined as that part of managerial work which is assigned to someone *outside the chain of command.* It does not get us very far, however, to say that the line officer commands and the staff officer does not command, for a line commander cannot ignore his superior's staff officers: a staff officer's suggestion will, indeed, often result in a *formal* order being issued by the line manager's superior. In industry, when operating duties are assigned to line subordinates, some of the duties of planning and controlling will be reserved for staff officers. In essence, then, staff work consists of managerial tasks delegated to individuals who do not actually supervise operations. Examples of *special* staff duties are market research, industrial engineering, internal auditing. Examples of *personal* assistants are the Assistant *to* So-and-So, the Private Secretary, the Legal Adviser. Staff officers are specialists who give advisory aid to operating executives. The advantages of line-and-staff organisation are: planned specialisation and the use of expertise, and permitting the principle of undivided responsibility and authority to be brought into operation. The possible disadvantages are ineffectiveness of staff through lack of authority or support; confusion as to the status and functions of staff; possible friction between the 'line' and staff; dilution and misunderstanding of advice as it seeps through from the upper line levels.

§ 10. Line-Staff Conflict

Line-staff relations are frequently characterised by friction, rivalry and misunderstanding.[24] Confusion in terminology might

[24] For a full discussion see M. N. Toussaint: 'Line-Staff Conflict: Its Causes and Cure', *Personnel* (American Management Association), May–June 1962.

be partly responsible for this, *e.g.* the personnel function has often been regarded by theorists as 'staff' whereas in actual practice industrial relations departments have often taken over, either deliberately or by default, responsibility for decision-making in such 'line' activities as hiring, firing, promotions, the negotiation of union contracts and the settling of grievances. Reasons for conflict may be: the apparently different responsibilities and goals (operating results—as against specialised function); background differences (the 'line man' may not have had much formal education); loyalties and identification may also be different ('line men' more concerned with their immediate working-group, staff men loyal to their professional colleagues and the company as a whole). How can these conflicts be resolved? The effort must come mainly from staff men who should endeavour to see problems in the line context; the advice given by staff men must not be armchair advice but must have been carefully considered and tested before it is given to the 'line'. Finally, staff men should avoid invoking their expertness on all occasions and flaunting it in the face of line managers; on the contrary, they should pay particular attention to the abilities and interests of their line colleagues and avoid outspoken criticisms.

§ 11. Functional Authority and Responsibility

The original use of the term *functional* in the 'low-level' industrial context is attributed to F. W. Taylor whose work has already been discussed in the chapter on Scientific Management. The meaning given to this term by the Institute of Industrial Administration[25] was "a specialised responsibility originating in expert knowledge": "the specialist official or executive is always consulted before decision is taken—but his actions must be directed through the executives and for supervision in the 'lines' of the organisation". As Brech stresses,[26] "the difficulties in the the working of functional responsibilities is widely recognised, but they spring from human deficiency, not from anything inherent in the notion itself".

The granting of formal authority is the most extreme technique for extending the influence of staff: either the superior executive

[25] Quoted by Brech: *Organisation, The Framework of Management*, see chapter III, 'Functional Responsibilities and Relationship—The Role of the Specialists'.

[26] *ibid.*, p. 32.

merely gives a formal stamp of approval to staff decisions and arrangements, or the staff man is even allowed to make recommendations in his own name to subordinate line executives. Confusion has arisen in some organisations because certain officers regarded as 'staff' (*e.g.* personal manager, purchasing officer) are in fact line executives. Functional executives may indeed, be line, staff or a combination of the two, *i.e.* they serve in a staff capacity to other departments but have line authority with reference to their own departments; they may also have certain functional decision-making prerogatives that cut across departmental boundaries.

§ 12. The Load on Top Management and the Use of 'Staff Generalists'

As Urwick has stressed, the main difference between business management and political government is that in the former "the issues of primary importance are executive whereas in the latter the question of administrative effectiveness in carrying out political decisions is secondary". In business, on the other hand, "the issue of executive effectiveness is paramount".[27] The failure to distinguish between policy-making and execution has sometime led in Britain to "awkward compromises by which no one individual is clearly indicated as responsible for the executive work of an undertaking and assigned commensurate authority". As a result, the burden of the individuals responsible for the executive work of an enterprise is greatly increased, and they have to spend too much time in co-ordination and, when they differ sharply, integration has often to be postponed until a management committee or board can be assembled. The weaknesses of *executive committees* are compromise, domination by a strong personality, lack of personal leadership over the non-participants, the tendency to avoid issues, and the element of instability.[28]

[27] L. Urwick: *The Load on Top Management*, p. 18 (an expansion of Urwick's views presented at the Torquay Conference, 1954) Urwick states that in a democracy the main question is, "are the purposes and policies of government acceptable to the majority of citizens". No exception can be taken to this statement, but one should also consider the statement of a civil servant that the essential character of government and of public administration, is the process of maintaining the unity of a political group (C. J. Sisson: *The Spirit of British Administration*, chapter 1).

[28] See Brech (Ed.): *Principles and Practices of Management*, Part V, chapt. 6, 'Committees in Management', by Brech.

In any medium or large enterprise, "co-ordination cannot be left to itself": Urwick argued that if functional specialisation runs right up to the top level of the organisation chart *below* the chief executive, then the latter will have no-one to whom he can delegate the constant burden of co-ordination. The alternative to committees, which are "an expensive palliative, not a cure",[29] is to place more emphasis on *unitary* forms of organisation, *i.e.* decentralisation on the basis of products or areas into what are virtually separate undertakings.

Urwick recommends also the appointment of *general* staff officers.[30] Whereas specialist staff officers in the army are usually concerned only with a particular function (medical, legal, engineering, etc.) and present to the commander their specialist points of view, general staff officers help the commander in carrying out *his* functions; their business is not to emphasise particular points of view but rather to help the commander to *reconcile* them. The experiments in business organisations along these lines have usually been in the form of 'Assistants to' . . . top management members, but a G.S.O. is not a personal assistant; he is an integral part of the system of control. The complexity and exacting nature of modern management at top level is such that general staff assistance is increasingly necessary in substantial businesses.

The task of 'staff generalists',[31] to use the American term, is not that of representing top officers in operating duties and daily tasks but of effecting improvements in "organisation, administration and managers", especially from the point of view of long-term improvements. "Not being involved in the day-to-day operations, he can spend the necessary time for his snail's pace approach, thus enabling him to think in larger terms and for more long-term results than executives." The approach of the staff generalist is that of *planned opportunism*—planned because it is positive and purposeful, and opportunism because the end is indeterminate and careful attention is given to timing. If a staff generalist has a problem which is too specialised for him to handle alone, he can invoke the aid of a specialist to work with him on a staff team basis.

29 Urwick, *op. cit.*, p. 30.

30 Urwick, *op. cit.*, pp. 40–45.

31 See R. C. Sampson: *The Staff Role in Management, Its Creative Uses*, chapt. VIII, 'The Staff Generalist'.

He must know enough about analytical tools[32] to be able to adapt them to a particular situation, but requires 'special personal tools': listening, observing, questioning, informing, encouraging and integrating.[33]

ADDITIONAL READING ASSIGNMENTS

1. T. H. Burnham and D. H. Bramley: *Engineering Economics*, Book II, Factory Organisation and Management, chapt. 1.
2. G. B. Carson (Ed.): *Production Handbook*, Second Edition, Section 1, 'Plant Organisation'.
3. E. F. L. Brech: *Organisation: The Framework of Management*, chapters VI, VII and VIII.
4. Wilfred Brown: *Exploration in Management*, chapters X–XV.
5. E. H. Anderson: 'The Functional Concept in Management', *Advanced Management* (Oct. 1960).
6. J. K. Louden: 'Line and Staff—Their Roles in the Organisation Structure', *Advanced Management* (June 1949).
7. R. C. Davis: 'What the Staff Function actually is', *Advanced Management* (May 1954).
8. R. C. Sampson: *The Staff Role in Management, its Creative Uses*, chapter VIII.
9. R. C. Dunnuck and R. J. House: 'Improving the Management Staff Function', *Personnel* (Nov.–Dec. 1962).
10. James D. Mooney: *The Principles of Organisation.*
11. M. N. Toussaint: 'Line-Staff Conflict: Its Causes and Cure', *Personnel* (May–June 1962).
12. L. Urwick: *The Load on Top Management.*
13. E. Dale: *Planning and Developing the Company Organisation Structure* (American Management Association), Part II, chapt. IX, 'The Organisation Chart'
14. M. E. Dimock: *Administrative Vitality*, Part I, 'Growth', Part II, 'Bureaucracy'.
15. H. Koontz and C. O'Donnell: *Principles of Management*, chapters 8 and 9.

TOPICS FOR DISCUSSION/ESSAYS

1. The meaning of 'Authority' and 'Responsibility'.
2. What 'kinds' of Authority are there?
3. Can responsibilities be defined?

[32] *ibid.*, p. 105, gives a list of 'analytical tools'.
[33] *ibid.*, p. 112.

4. Does the task of the supervisor differ fundamentally from that of management?
5. Staff work in Industry.
6. Line-Staff Conflict—Causes and Cure.
7. Organisation Charts and Manuals.
8. Give a management chart of *either* a works with which you are familiar, *or* a works, the nature of which you should specify, with about 1,000 employees. Define the work of *two* executives in the organisation: (*a*) a line manager; (*b*) a specialist. Do this by preparing complete entries for the firm's Organisation Manual.
9. The following is a quotation from a book on industrial sociology: "Organisation is like an organism: to develop it must become more and more differentiated; and this requires a central nervous system of increasing sensitivity and complexity to co-ordinate and control the specialised parts". Analyse this statement in relation to the growth of a modern factory.
10. Design an organisation chart for a company producing a range of hardware and small electrical products, 30 per cent of which are exported. Assume that the total number of employees is 1,500.

CHAPTER ELEVEN

COMMUNICATION

§ 1. Introduction

In the last decade communication became a fashionable word in industrial training circles and conferences. During this period many firms have spent much time and money in an effort to improve their internal communications, and in many cases have been disappointed at the results. One reason for this comparative failure has been a tendency to over-simplify the problem itself, due to viewing communication as a matter of information or persuasion. Both of these ingredients are necessary, but another essential ingredient is *participation*—the necessity of creating a permissive atmosphere in which everyone can make the maximum contribution from his experience and intelligence at *his level* to existing work and changes. As Michael Evans has said, there are still too many "peripheral gimmicks".[1]

As Barnard stressed, communication must occupy a central place in any exhaustive theory of organisation "because the structure, extensiveness and scope of organisation are almost entirely determined by communication techniques". It is wrong to regard communication merely as a 'tool of management': it is the foundation on which organisation and administration must be built.

Bell[2] has distinguished between *self-sustaining* communication and *operational* communication. The former is concerned with the individuals in the enterprise and should cover such matters as: the *aims* of the enterprise; the *policy; progress* (*i.e.* information about the operative side of the business); *external events* (anything affecting the social and economic context in which the business operates); *finance*; and *personal matters* (rates of pay, security of employment, pension and retirement benefit, etc.). Operational communication is concerned with *documents*, *meetings* and *external*

[1] M. Evans: 'Communications—after Ten Years', *Works Management* (April 1963).

[2] R. W. Bell: *Be Sure You Agree*, London (1960), chapt. VI, 'Communication in Business'.

communications. Bell has also stressed the importance of communication by *conduct*: methods of communication will fail to have the desired effect unless an individual's behaviour is consistent with his words.

The ability to communicate effectively must stand very high in any list of managerial qualities; it is also very important to know *when* and *how* to communicate, and *to whom*. 'Trouble spots' in industry are frequently the consequence of some failure in communication, either organisational or personal.

§ 2. Interpretation of Language

An attempt was made to establish what three different groups of people accepted as the meaning of several words in common use.[3] The three groups were samples of industrial psychologists, personnel administrators and manufacturing and inspection foremen. The results of the analysis and codification showed that no single word produced a definition on which there was universal agreement (the codification was based upon thought-content, not the actual words used); even within each group there was no word defined in a single or uniform way. This study showed that individuals attach a wide diversity of meanings to words, and specialised interpretations or word meanings vary very widely, even among groups with similar activities and work activities.

If there is no agreement upon the meanings of words, it is not surprising that communication is often ineffective. In some situations, admittedly, the vagueness of words can be an advantage to the user, but in others a positive handicap. Some of the causes of this are inherent in the very nature of language, whilst others operate only in special circumstances.[4] One of the principal causes of vagueness is the *generic* character of our words; again, words are never completely *homogeneous*, but may have several facets depending upon the context and situation in which they are used; a third cause of vagueness is lack of familiarity with the

[3] R. Bloom: *A Study of Communications: Based upon Group Differences in Language Abstraction.* Wayne State University (Detroit 1954). The words selected were: ATTITUDE, COMMUNICATION, EFFICIENCY, EMOTION, EMPLOYEE RELATIONS, FEELINGS, FOREMAN, INCENTIVE, JOB, MANAGEMENT, MORALE, MOTIVATION, OPINION, PERSONNEL, POLICY, PRACTICE, PRODUCTIVITY, PROFIT, QUALITY, RESEARCH, SCRAP, SECURITY, STANDARD, SUPERVISION, TRAINING, TURNOVER.

[4] See Stephen Ullmann: *Semantics: An Introduction to the Science of Meaning*, Oxford, Blackwell (1962), chapter 5.

things they stand for—a highly variable factor which depends on the general knowledge and special interests of each individual. It is also important to bear in mind the *emotive overtones* of language.

Every managerial or supervisory job is bound up with the establishment of relationships and the standard of spoken or written English can be judged only by the extent to which it creates the fullest understanding between individuals. Sir Ernest Gowers performed a salutary service when he wrote his book[5] "to help officials in their use of written English as a tool of their trade"; the golden rule, he said, concerned less the *arrangement* of words than the choice of them. The fundamental precepts given by Gowers are: BE SIMPLE, BE SHORT, BE HUMAN, BE CORRECT. As regards the *choice* of words he recommends that one should avoid the superfluous word (verbosity, padding), choose the *familiar* word and the *precise* word. "Language", said Ben Jonson, "most shows a man: speak, that I may see thee"; and Shakespeare wrote:

> "Mend your speech a little,
> Lest you mar your fortunes".

Compare the following two passages:

> "I returned, and saw under the sun, that the race is not to the swift, nor the battle to the strong, neither yet bread to the wise, nor yet riches to men of understanding, nor yet favour to men of skill; but time and chance happeneth to them all".
>
> (*Book of Ecclesiastes*).

> "Objective consideration of contemporary phenomena compels the conclusion that success or failure in competitive activities exhibits no tendency to be commensurate with innate capacity, but that a considerable element of the unpredictable must inevitably be taken into account."

Modern English, as George Orwell was at pains to point out,[6] is "full of bad habits which spread by imitation, and which can be avoided if one is willing to take the necessary trouble". Orwell gave *six rules* to follow if one is in doubt about the effect of a word or a phrase:

[5] Sir Ernest Gowers: *The Complete Plain Words* (H.M.S.O.), 'Prologue', pp. 1–7.

[6] G. Orwell: 'Politics and the English Language', in *Selected Essays* (Penguin Books, 1957).

(i) Never use a metaphor, simile or other figure of speech which you are used to seeing in print (because it will be hackneyed).
(ii) Never use a long word where a short one will do.
(iii) If it is possible to cut out a word, always cut it out.
(iv) Never use the passive where you can use the active.
(v) Never use a foreign phrase, a scientific word or a jargon word if you can think of an everyday English word.
(vi) Break any of these rules rather than say anything outright barbarous.

§ 3. Management's Responsibility for Communication

Chester Barnard said that "the *first* executive function is to develop and maintain a system of communication". Elton Mayo wrote[7] that communication problem "is beyond all reasonable doubt the outstanding defect facing civilisation today". Obviously, without communication a manager cannot fulfil his aim, which is to get things done through other people. Communication is, therefore, a basic skill which must be exercised daily through the medium of the spoken and written word in order to obtain understanding and action. Unfortunately, it is the most neglected skill and the growth in the size of firms tends to increase its complexity. Further, in industries which are technologically advanced and increasingly employ narrow specialists, there is need for a "common language" in order to co-ordinate ideas.

Communication is the art of transferring ideas, information, instructions and feelings from one person to another. In large industrial organisations anyone in a position of responsibility from the most junior position upwards must be skilful in communication if he is to do his job properly, since successful management depends upon *co-operation* and *team-work*. The basic elements of good communication are *clear thinking*, *clear speaking* and *clear writing*, but, in deciding upon the form and content of a given communication it is important first to decide what is the exact *purpose* of the communication, and make an appreciation of the knowledge, understanding interests and attitudes of the

[7] Elton Mayo: *The Problems of an Industrial Civilisation. Cf.* Lord Robbins (*An Essay on the Nature and Significance of Economic Science*, p. 34): "It is not an exaggeration to say that, at the present day, one of the main dangers to civilisation arises from the inability of minds trained in the natural sciences to perceive the difference between the economic and the technical".

recipients of the communication. Communication must be viewed from the aspect of *human* relations: it is easier to "communicate" with a person with whom one feels at ease and human relations will be improved when people understand the reasons for the orders and instructions which are passed to them.

It is not possible to deal with clarity of thought, speech and writing, but there are several brief, helpful books which the manager can consult. Anyone concerned with technology should read Kapp's book[8]: Kapp is concerned with 'functional English'—the writer of which spares his readers unnecessary effort; "he selects every item and places every sentence and word so that it will meet the function assigned to it, just as a designer of a girder selects and places every strut and tie-bar. Functional English presents facts and ideas simply and logically". A writer must keep his *reader* constantly in mind for the material used, its arrangement and lay-out, presentation and style will vary with the reader.[9]

The *logical approach* to problems can be developed by using the following five-stage method:

(i) Determine the objective;
(ii) Assemble the *facts*;
(iii) Weigh and analyse the facts leading to *decision*;
(iv) Take *action* on the decision;
(v) Check results.

It is obvious that the thinking process is not conducted in such rigid stages, but the above framework is useful until an orderly habit is required. Above all, beware of *excessive generalisation*, *begging the question* (assuming what you want to prove), *false analogy*, *prejudice* and *ambiguity*. Interesting examples of these will be found in the books listed below.[10]

§ 4. Sins of Communication

What J. W. Humble[11] has called the 'common deadly sins' of communication are:

[8] R. O. Kapp: *The Presentation of Technical Information.*

[9] Useful books are R. W. Bell: *Write what you Mean* (London, 1954); Sir E. Gowers: *The Complete Plain Words* (H.M.S.O.).

[10] Interesting introductions for the manager are R. H. Thouless: *Straight and Crooked Thinking*; Susan Stebbing: *Thinking to Some Purpose*, both obtainable as 'paperbacks'. On a more difficult level E. M. Emmet: *The Use of Reason* (1960) is recommended.

[11] In a talk given to the I.P.M. Course on Staff Management and Training, Harrogate, 1961 (see article in *Personnel Management*, 1961).

(i) *The tendency to confuse techniques and objectives.* Such methods as magazines, posters, committees, will prove sterile unless the *intention is clear* and there is a *receptive atmosphere.*

(ii) *Too much talking and insufficient listening.* Some managers view communications only as giving orders or influencing their subordinates.

(iii) *Faulty organisation*, such as lack of definition of responsibilities, too long chains of command, too wide a span of control.

(iv) *Mistaken view of human behaviour*—overstressing the logical nature and independence of men and insufficiently appreciating human behaviour in emotional, social and group terms.

(v) *Insincerity*—accepting a fashionable gimmick without really believing in it.

§ 5. How can a Manager Improve his Communication Skills?

Some guiding principles are:

(i) *Do your best to make your communications as clear as possible.* Decide what is the real objective of your communication and then how it can be most effectively expressed. Use language and style most in accord with the background of your reader or listener.

(ii) *Choose the most appropriate media of communication.* The 'grapevine' is a most unreliable medium and the use of it reflects managerial inefficiency. The choice of media must be governed by consideration of cost and desired effect. Media may be categorised as follows:

FACE-TO-FACE: conferences; interviews; conversations; meetings.

WRITTEN: individual letters or memos; employee pamphlets and publications; handbooks; manuals; general circulars; notice board bulletins; newsletters; suggestion schemes; press releases; advertisements.

VISUAL: posters; photographs; diagrams; films and film strips; charts; cartoons; television.

AUDIAL: telephone; 'Tannoy'; inter-communication system; radio.

(iii) *Aim at consistency.* Messages should be consistent with one another for the communication process is continuous, and one communication helps to condition those which follow it.

(iv) *Be selective in content.* If a communication is overloaded with detail its objective may not be clear.

(v) *Plan the timing.* Except in emergencies a communication should follow normal organisational lines: persons of similar status should receive communications as nearly as possible at the same time.

§ 6. Communication—Upward, Downward, Horizontal

It is often said that a serious flaw in management is the tendency to devote far more attention to the problems of communicating downwards than upwards. Yet, without effective upward communication it is not possible to assess the results of downward communication. Upward communication must not be a fortuitous matter, but should receive positive encouragement from top management. The *barriers* to *upward* communication are differences in type of work at different levels, differences in organisational and social status, education and language; the organisational structure may itself produce barriers, especially if the channels of communication are too long or ill-defined. There are fewer facilities for upward communication than for downward: subordinates may have few opportunities of consulting with their superiors or may be afraid of worrying them. The superior's power of reward or punishment is another factor which may inhibit subordinates. The question of loyalty to one's colleagues may also be a cause of reticence.

As Branton[12] points out, military authorities have devoted considerable attention to the techniques of issuing orders, but the problem has received little attention in management literature. *Oral* orders are to be preferred when a decision must be translated into action and, because of the face-to-face relationship, the superior can satisfy himself that the order has been understood. *Written* orders are better when complex details are involved. Sometimes written orders are regarded as more authoritative.

Horizontal communications are those between people in different departments at roughly the same level. To use the 'line' is both

[12] For a full, lucid discussion see Noel Branton: *Introduction to the Theory and Practice of Management*, London (1960), chapter vii.

cumbersome and time-consuming. Methods for such lateral communications include the circulation of documents and the use of the committee or conference. *Crosswise* communications are those between the subordinates of a given superior and the personnel in other departments who may occupy positions of equal, lower or superior status. The safeguards[13] to such communications are: an understanding between superiors that these relationships will be encouraged; that subordinates will not make commitments in excess of their authority, and that they will keep their superiors informed of their inter-departmental relationships. The barriers to crosswise relationships arise out of lack of knowledge about the organisation, lack of attention to human relationships (clashes of personality) and the fact that essential functions may not be in close proximity, so that activities have to be regrouped.

It must be stressed that 'the usual channels' do provide for an easy flow of lateral communication; a clear definition of functional responsibility is helpful to a person searching for a source of information.

§ 7. The Company Handbook

All new employees should be provided with information about the company to enable them to settle down more quickly, but such a publication should not be regarded as a substitute for a friendly, personal approach. Before deciding on the contents of a handbook, it must be asked for whom it is intended. If there are many different kinds of employees, jobs and educational levels it is doubtful if one handbook only will suffice. If a particular class of employee is in mind when the handbook is being prepared, it is possible to choose contents that are relevant, and to be more selective in the approach. A handbook should be neither a recruitment publication nor a book of rules; it should be a 'welcome' booklet, and not a legal document, its object being to explain, not to admonish nor exhort. It therefore seems better to explain regulations and conditions in simple, friendly words—to provide an interpretation of the rules rather than a literal transcription.

In general, the contents should fall into two broad categories:

13 Koontz and O'Donnell: *Principles of Management*, pp. 421–2.

P

(i) information about the company and group companies to which it belongs: history, organisational structure, products;

(ii) information about employee's relations with the company:

(*a*) regulations and conditions of service;

(*b*) benefits, services, facilities and opportunities the company has to offer.[14]

§ 8. Public Relations

Good public relations can help a firm to prosper, whilst the public's disapproval or lack of co-operation can harm it. "Public relations is the deliberate, planned and sustained effort to establish and maintain mutual understanding between an organisation and its public."[15] What is 'the public'? It includes shareholders, potential shareholders, City editors, financial writers, stockbrokers, employees and potential employees, their families, certain trade unions, employment officers, appointment boards, teachers, suppliers and potential suppliers of raw materials, trade associations, sub-contractors, wholesale and retail trade customers, potential customers, trade associations, consumer customers, actual and potential, other companies in the same industry, communities in which the companies operate, towns, M.P.s, editors.[16]

There is a threefold job in P.R.:

(i) keeping management informed of *public opinion*;

(ii) advising management on policies and action it should adopt in order to gain and keep *goodwill*;

(iii) applying P.R. methods to solve company problems in which its *reputation* is at stake.

The virtue of having a full-time P.R.O. is that the latter can advise, co-ordinate and execute in accordance with a clear, *long-term* plan. P.R. must always work simultaneously at two levels—"the adroit seizing of opportunities as they occur, within the framework of a continuing programme. . . . It is its long-term nature, together with a feeling that its results are intangible and hard to assess, which makes some companies reluctant to undertake any organised public relations."

[14] See B. Smith: 'Handbook for New Employees', *Personnel Management* (June 1962) for a more detailed statement.

[15] Definition authorised by the Institute of Public Relations.

[16] James Derrinan: 'The Two Levels of P.R.', *The Manager* (April 1963).

§ 9. Financial Information

Some firms (Rowntree, Shell, Renold Chains*) have made a practice for many years of putting their employees in the financial picture, but the presentation of financial information is still something of a novelty. The aim of giving this information is to foster among employees an understanding and appreciation of the company's affairs which might help them to identify their personal interests, to some extent, with those of the company, and thus stimulate them to give of their best. Financial information may also help to stop rumours and remove misconceptions.[17]

Undoubtedly it is no easy task to make financial analysis interesting to the non-specialist: this applies equally to the information produced by accountants for top management.[18] In general, it can be said that *actual figures* will not be remembered unless they receive unusual publicity; *too much* information should not be given at the same time; an effort should be made to relate figures to the employees' personal interests. The main source of financial information about a firm is the *Annual Report and Accounts*, and the Chairman's speech. Someone will have to translate these into language and pictures suitable for popular consumption, either in special reports, articles in the works magazine, or special meetings. 'Supplementary statements'—charts, graphs, visual aids and reports—may be incorporated in the Directors' Report, in order to make the information more palatable and digestible to the layman than the accompanying statutory accounts. Such supplementary statements also help to strengthen the bond between the boardroom and shareholders or debenture-holders, and lead to increased goodwill.

Philip Dyer gave the following example as being quite beyond the capacities of 'Mary Jones', who left school at 14, and offered a 'translation' which she might conceivably read *and* understand:

* See Sir Charles Renold: *Thirty Years of Joint Consultation*; for the history of the firm, B. H. Tripp: *'Renold Chains', A History of the Company and the Rise of the Precision-Chain Industry, 1879–1955*.

[17] Philip F. Dyer: 'Presenting Financial Information to Employees', *The Manager* (February 1957); see also *Presenting Financial Information to Employees* (B.I.M., 1957); F. H. Jones: 'Statements supplementary to the Annual Accounts of Companies', *The Accountants Journal* (June 1960).

[18] See *The Presentation of Information to Management* (Institute of Cost and Works Accountants Publication).

Part of Original Report

The importance of rapid turnover from raw materials to finished goods cannot be over-emphasized since bottle-necks and mounting stock cause additional money to be tied up which may even cause borrowing with the consequent payment of interest or slow payment of accounts, thus losing discount. At an extreme point shortage of money and high stock may cause cessation of production until the position is rectified.

"Translation"

We have to turn the cloth we buy into shirts and pyjamas, and sell these, just as quickly as we can. If we don't, we shall have to buy more cloth to make more shirts and pyjamas before we have got the money from selling the first batch. That means taking cash from the kitty. If the kitty isn't big enough, we might have to borrow money and pay interest on it. Or we might have to put off paying our bills for a bit, and so lose the discount that we get for prompt payment. Either way we should be out of pocket. And if the worst came to the worst, we might find ourselves with so much cloth and unsold shirts and pyjamas in the factory, and so little money in the kitty, that we should have to shut down the factory for a time until things righted themselves.

Confucius said that one picture was worth a thousand words, but diagrams have to be used with caution, and accompanied by a brief, simple explanation. All available means of communication must be used, and used *regularly*—not just once a year. In preference to mass meetings of all employees, greater progress might be made with smaller meetings of departmental heads, supervisors, joint consultative committees and shop-stewards; the process then merges imperceptibly into an educational programme, and can be integrated with executive and supervisory training.

Suggestion Schemes are one useful basis for practical co-operation between management and workers, since they restore to the worker some measure of initiative and make him feel that he can take part in the enhancement of efficiency and the general well-being of the firm.[19]

The essential objects of a suggestion scheme are:

[19] See *Suggestion Schemes*, published by Industrial Welfare Society, London (3rd ed., 1950).

(i) To arouse *interest* on the part of employees in the firm and its products, and to secure their *full co-operation* in the enterprise;

(ii) to obtain ideas valuable in the *actual conduct* of the business;

(iii) to train employees to think along *constructive lines* in order to make them more proficient at their work.

It is doubtful whether any suggestion scheme will be successful unless it has the support of management at all levels, especially that of supervisors and foremen. Apart from the financial gains which may accrue to a firm from suggestions, or the technical improvements which may be effected, there is the possibility that morale and industrial relations may be improved by a successfully working suggestion scheme.

HOW 89 FIRMS KEPT EMPLOYEES IN THE PICTURE

WHY FIRMS GAVE INFORMATION

	Number	*Percentage*
(1) Identification of interest with employer	51	57
(2) To stop rumours	27	30
(3) Helps understanding of company and economic affairs	27	30
(4) Improves workmanship	10	11
(5) Moral obligation	9	10
(6) Profit-sharing is received with more enthusiasm	3	3
(7) Good public relations	2	2
(8) Helps cut costs	1	1
(9) No answer given	23	26
	89	100

HOW FIRMS GAVE INFORMATION

	Number	*Percentage*
(1) Company magazine	50	56
(2) Annual report as issued to shareholders	49	55
(3) Committee meetings	49	55
(4) Publications specially designed for employees	25	28
(5) Annual report with illustrations and diagrams	24	27
(6) Personal contact with employees through supervisors	23	26
(7) Wall charts	10	11
(8) Works handbooks	8	9
(9) Films and film-strips	3	3
(10) Pay envelope inserts	3	3
	89	100

WHAT INFORMATION FIRMS GAVE

	Number	Percentage
(1) Forecast of future trading position	62	70
(2) Profit and loss account	57	64
(3) Balance sheet	46	52
(4) Sales £1 analysis	46	52
(5) Reserves	44	49
(6) Economic information about the industry in general	44	49
(7) New assets	40	45
(8) Sales turnover	38	43
(9) Return on capital employed	32	36
(10) Cost of employee services	34	36
(11) New machinery costs	32	36
(12) Labour costs	30	33
(13) Depreciation	27	30
(14) Product costs	25	28
(15) Analysis of unit selling price	18	20
(16) Added value	13	15
	89	100

(*The Manager*, Feb. 1957).

THE INFORMATION WORKERS WANT (Survey of seven firms)

Company	*Number interviewed*	*Interested in all items of information* %	*Interested in profits* %	*Interested in costs* %	*Interested in new developments and trade prospects* %	*Interested only in information affecting me personally* %
1.	161	26	3	(not asked)	53	15
2.	78	43	9	12	32	4
3.	89	33	15	4	47	(not asked)
4.	40	25	—	10	37	5
5.	165	39	4	7	42	7
6.	104	54	18	11	50	2
7.	194	40	20	6	27	7

(*The Manager*, Feb. 1957).

ESTABLISHING A COMMUNICATION PROGRAMME

EXAMINE the existing communication structure—both its weakness and its strength in the different departments of the company. This will enable you to establish priorities for the programme.

OBTAIN top management support for the programme. Ensure that communication is regarded as an important function of management. If top management is insincere in its intentions towards good human relations and communication no programme will be wholly successful.

MAKE full use of training facilities. Include communication skills as a subject in training courses. This can make a valuable contribution to the efficiency of a manager or supervisor. It can also assist the young scientist and the salesman in selling his product.

PLACE all company policies, services, benefits and conditions of employment on paper either in the form of a manual or a handbook. A published statement implies honesty and good faith on the part of the company. This can improve working confidence and eliminate confusion in the minds of all staff.

MAKE full use of existing media. It may be easier to put new life into joint consultation rather than to devise a new communication technique.

From The Manager, Feb. 1959.

§ 10. Conclusion: the Communication Process

A Manager

TRANSMITS (says, issues, writes)

MESSAGES (orders, ideas, encouragement) to

PEOPLE (individuals, groups, the public) in order to evoke

ACTION (understanding, reply, behaviour)

"In fact, a manager is at the centre of a complex communications system. He receives a flow of orders and instructions from his general manager which require personal action and, suitably amended and focused, are passed on to his subordinates. Suggestions, ideas, grievances, reports and control data return to him and there is, after editing, some feedback of vital matters to the general managers" (J. W. Humble).

Fayol's 'Ladder' or 'Bridge'. In order effectively to carry out duties assigned to each line there must be contact, communication and relationship between individuals at *each level* of authority in the two converging lines:

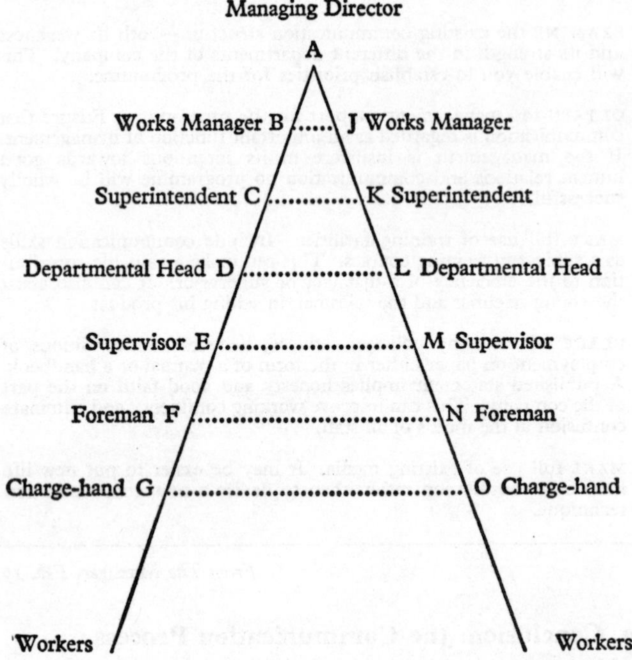

Fayol's 'Ladder' or 'Bridge'

These cross-relations may be concerned with *jurisdiction* (determining which line is to do certain work); co-ordination of policies and operation methods; *review and criticism* of work; *division* of overlapping authorities. Fayol said that executives at any level of authority may contact one another, reach decisions and initiate action, provided that contact is initiated only with the consent of the *immediate line superiors*, and the latter approve of any proposed action *before* it is taken.

ADDITIONAL READING ASSIGNMENTS

1. *Communications and Management* (H.M.S.O. 1963).
2. B.I.M.: *Communication: A Study of Employee Information in Twelve Companies*. Information Summary No. 73, London (1958).

3. *Suggestion Schemes* (Industrial Welfare Society, 1950).
4. C. E. Redfield: *Communication in Management*, University of Chicago Press (London, C.U.P., 1959, revised ed.).
5. C. Chisholm (Ed.): *Communication in Industry*, London (1955).
6. James Brown: *Cases in Business Communication*, Belmont, California (1962).
7. R. W. Bell: *Be Sure You Agree*, London (1960), chapt. VI.
8. R. W. Bell: *Write What You Mean*, London (1954).
9. Sir Ernest Gowers: *The Complete Plain Words* (H.M.S.O.).
10. J. D. Edwards: *Managers: Making or Marring Them*, London (1957), chapter VIII.
11. F. C. Dyer: *Executive's Guide to Effective Speaking and Writing*, London, Prentice-Hall (1962).
12. F. Anstey: *Committees: how they work and how to work them*, London (1962).
13. George Copeman: *The Role of the Managing Director*, London (1959), chapter 15.
14. M. Ivens: *The Practice of Industrial Communication*, London (1963).
15. Eric Moonman: 'The Manager and the Organisation', London (1961), Part One, *The Manager*.
16. Wilfred Brown: *Exploration in Management*, London (1960), Part Three, 'Communication'.

PUBLIC RELATIONS

Institute of Public Relations: *A Guide to the Practice of Public Relations*, London (1958).

David Finn: *Public Relations and Management*, New York and London (1960).

N. Ellis and P. Bowman: *The Handbook of Public Relations*, London (1963).

S. Black: *Practical Public Relations*, London (1962).

QUESTIONS FOR ESSAYS/DISCUSSIONS

1. "The more levels between top management and the work force, the greater the difficulties of communication" (Brown).
2. "Within most large organisations the chief problem is over-communication—the tendency for documents to multiply to excess and for too much to be spent on meetings" (Bell).
3. "The manager does not handle people; he motivates, guides, organises people to do their own work. His tool, his only tool, to do all this is the spoken or written word or the language of numbers" (Drucker).
4. "It is better to tell too much than not enough" (Falk).

5. "The object of public relations is co-operation, based on goodwill, and in this it differs from propaganda, a purely one-sided operation" (J. Derriman).
6. "The higher you rise in management the more time you spend in communication. Your success becomes ever more dependent upon the ability to communicate."
7. "Communication is successful when it is understood in the fullest sense, that is both in verbal meaning and intention. A manager cannot become good at it by learning a number of gadgets or techniques" (R. Stewart).
8. Discuss the value of (*a*) Suggestion Schemes; (*b*) Company Handbooks; (*c*) House Journals.
9. Discuss the human problems of shift operation. (See for example, P. C. Reid's article in *The Manager* (April 1961).

SIX MAJOR REQUIREMENTS OF EFFECTIVE DELEGATION

Check items that are deficient in your office	A Check List on the Fundamentals of Management That Create a Climate for Effective Delegation
	1. Overall Company Objectives and Policies
....	Is there a written statement of the company's objectives?
....	Are the company's general policies formulated?
	Is there a common understanding of the criteria used
....	by the Board for appraising overall performance?
	Are there well-defined controls (ratios and standards)
	established for appraising the accomplishments of the
....	organization and each major department?
	2. A Sound Organization Structure
	Is the company's organization chart well-designed and
....	interpreted uniformly by all members of management?
	Are departmental charts interpreted to the respective
....	members of each department and kept current?
	Is there a common understanding of lines of command
....	and channels of communication?
....	Are line and staff relationships adequately understood?
	3. Clear-Cut Position Descriptions
	Are accurate, brief, and complete position descriptions
....	maintained with respect to all key positions?
....	Are the objectives of each position clearly stated?
	Do the position descriptions indicate clearly to whom
	the incumbents report to, and who they are responsible
....	for?
....	Are position descriptions currently kept up-to-date?
	4. Standards of Performance
	Are standards of performance developed for each
....	position?
	Are criteria developed which facilitate self-appraisal
....	of the incumbent of each position?
	5. Periodic Appraisals of Performance
	Is there a systematic program of performance appraisals
	carried out by the manager or supervisor of every
	organizational unit, with respect to all employees who
....	report to him?
	Is there an adequate overall review of departmental
....	appraisals for conformity with established standards?
	6. Delegation
	Is maximum use made of delegation of responsibilities
....	for the purpose of:
	Relieving the "boss" to perform his most important
....	work of managing?
	Developing personnel through the assignment of
....	increased responsibility?
....	Are the techniques of effective delegation observed?

SIX MAJOR REQUIREMENTS OF EFFECTIVE DELEGATION

A Check List of the Fundamentals of Management that Create a Climate for Effective Delegation	*Check items that need improvement in your office*
1. Over-all Company Objectives and Policies	
Is there a written statement of the company's objectives?	....
Are the company's general policies in writing?	....
Is there a common understanding of the criteria used by the Board for appraising over-all performance?	....
Are there well-defined controls (ratios and standards) established for governing the administration of the organization? and each major department?	....
2. A Sound Organization Structure	
Is the company's organization chart well-designed and interpreted uniformally by all members of management?	....
Are departmental charts interpreted to the respective members of each department, and kept current?	....
Is there a common understanding of 'lines of command' and 'channels of communication'?	....
Are line and staff relationships adequately understood?	....
3. Clear-Cut Position Descriptions	
Are accurate, brief, and complete position descriptions maintained with respect to all key positions?	....
Are the objectives of each position clearly stated?	....
Do the position descriptions indicate clearly to whom the encumbents report to, and who they are responsible for?	....
Are position descriptions current—kept up-to-date?	....
4. Standards of Performance	
Are standards of performance developed for each position?	....
Are criteria developed which facilitate self-appraisal by the encumbent of each position?	....
5. Periodic Appraisals of Performance	
Is there a systematic program of performance appraisals carried out by the manager or supervisor of every organization unit, with respect to all employees who report to him?	....
Is there an adequate over-all review of departmental appraisals for conformity with established controls?	....
6. Delegation	
Is optimum use made of delegation of responsibilities for the purpose of:	
Releasing the 'boss' to perform his most important work of managing?	....
Developing personnel through the assignment of increased responsibility?	....
Are the techniques of effective delegation observed?	....

CHAPTER TWELVE

DELEGATION AND THE SPAN OF CONTROL

§ 1. The Specification of Responsibilities

Any sound organisation structure must rest on a clear definition of responsibilities at different levels; there must be effective delegation, horizontal and vertical co-ordination and the integration of functional groups, so that the lines of responsibility or command are not impaired. The limits of responsibility may be fixed in relation to *subjects*—the *functional* method; or in relation to *processes* and *types of equipment*—the serial method; or in relation to *persons, numbers, areas, e.g.* a foreman may be in charge of one of several teams, or vehicles, or a particular portion of the shop floor—the unitary method.

The definition of responsibilities and the relationships that follow form the organisation structure. Defining responsibilities is a necessary prelude to the process of delegation.[1] Work must be divided up, an integrated pattern of managerial and supervisory positions must be designed, and suitable individuals appointed to fill these positions.[2] In the case of a new firm such *organisation planning* is possible from the start; in the case of an established firm it is desirable to review the organisation structure from time to time, and to place positions before personalities. Obviously, basic positions or activities cannot be determined before objectives have been set, and initially there will not be more than two or three—production, sales and, perhaps, finance.

§ 2. The Process of Delegation

Delegation is the process whereby an individual or group transfers to some other individual or group the duty of carrying out some particular *action* and, at the same time, taking some particular decision.

1 For a good discussion, especially with regard to the problem of 'personalities' and 'status' see Brech: *Organisation*: *The Framework of Management*, chapter IV, 'Can Responsibilities be Defined?'.

2 See E. Dale: *Planning and Developing the Organisation Structure*, 'Determining the Objectives and Dividing the Work Accordingly', pp. 28–49.

Delegation means the entrusting of some part or aspect of the work of management or operations to subordinates.

Delegation must not be confused with the *surrender of responsibility*: no manager, by delegating, divests himself of *ultimate* responsibility. It is more correct to say that *tasks* or *jobs* are delegated, and the superior holds the subordinate *accountable* to him. The subordinate is responsible for *doing* the job, but the superior is responsible for *seeing* that the job *is* done.

The superior must be sure that his subordinate has sufficient *authority* to carry out the task that has been delegated to him.[3] Authority is a word used in several different senses: *legal* authority, *technical* authority, *ultimate* authority, *operational* authority.[4] The delegation of authority means simply granting someone the *permission* to do something; the delegation of operational authority should never be made, however, without the superior's indicating *how* the authority is to be used, *i.e.* delegation of authority is intimately related to *duties* and *obligations*.

The process of delegation can be viewed from three aspects:

(i) A manager *assigns duties* to his immediate subordinates.

(ii) He grants *authority* to make commitments, use the firm's resources and take any action which he thinks necessary adequately to carry out his duties.

(iii) He creates an *obligation* on the part of each subordinate for the *satisfactory performance* of the task (accountability). "In theory at least", says Newman, "the three aspects of delegation are inseparable, and a change in one normally implies a corresponding adjustment in the other two."

§ 3. The Limits of Authority

The limits of authority must be defined; every delegation has either expressed or implied *limitations*. A common restriction is that any action taken must accord with the policies, procedures and programmes of the Company, but specific limitations may also be imposed.[5] A distinction must also be made between

[3] Yet, if a superior asks certain subordinates to be accountable to him for certain tasks, he must necessarily also be giving them the authority to do what he is asking—see Brech: *Organisation*: *The Framework of Management*, pp. 54–8.

[4] *ibid.*, pp. 159–63.

[5] For examples, see Newman, *Administrative Action*, p. 168.

authority and *influence*.[6] In any given situation there may be simultaneously elements of *suggestion*, *persuasion* and *command*, and a superior may choose suggestion or persuasion rather than a direct order. The main characteristic of a 'subordinate' position is that it establishes an 'area of acceptance'—the subordinate is willing to accept the decisions made for him by his superior. Self-restraint of the superior may often be as important in maintaining the relationship as the subordinate's acceptance. The use of authority may lead to mere acquiescence on the subordinate's part, and other means of influence, leading to conviction, are often to be preferred.

Every superior must be clear about the limits of his own authority, and should deliberately avoid weakening his authority by exercising it where it may be *challenged* or *ignored*.

§ 4. Unity of Command

An old adage is that 'no man can serve two masters', and it has often been regarded as an organisational principle that *dual subordination* must be avoided—no individual must have more than one line supervisor. Yet, so long as orders are non-conflicting there is no reason why a subordinate should not receive two sets of orders, *e.g.* the authority of a line superior may determine the programme, that of the accountant determine what financial records shall be kept. How can conflicts in authority be prevented or resolved? A subordinate may receive orders from several superiors but recognise only one whom, in the case of a conflict, he is expected to obey. There may also be *division* of authority—each unit in the organisation may be assigned some specific area over which it has authority. Finally, there may be a system of *rank*—subordinates are subject to the authority of all other individuals of a certain rank. As Simon pointed out, these procedures are not mutually exclusive, and may even be used in combinations in a single organisation.

§ 5. An Old Device

The organisational device of delegation is very old; perhaps the first mention of it is in *Exodus* xviii. 25, 26:

> "And Moses chose able men out of all Israel, and made them heads over the people, rulers of thousands, rulers of hundreds, rulers of

[6] Simon, *Administrative Behaviour*, chapter VII, 'The Role of Authority'.

fifties and rulers of tens. And they judged the people at all seasons: the hard causes they brought unto Moses, but every small matter they judged themselves."

The advice which Moses received from his father-in-law is one of the most practical passages in the Bible, for Moses was trying in his own person to judge and govern all the people. Jethro said: "Thou wilt surely wear away, both thou and this people that is with thee; for this thing is too heavy for thee; and thou art not able to perform it thyself alone". He then suggested the delegation of duties, and Moses acted as above. Delegation is also seen in Caesar's army, the Roman Catholic Church, medieval monarchies and the fleet of Columbus.

As a business grows its various phases which formed an essential unity assume separate form; the problems of the running of the plant, finance, stock and purchasing, accounting and personnel become separate problems, and the delegation of functions is necessary, whilst supreme authority and responsibility remain at the top. Although there are various devices for co-ordinating action, the process of delegation provides the skeleton of the formal organisation structure.

§ 6. Delegation and the Reduction of the Work-Load

Delegation becomes necessary when the burden of a managerial position exceeds the *physical and psychological capacities* of the manager. Delegation is a necessary consequence of authority or leadership and is inherent in the very nature of the superior-subordinate relationship. As soon as any objective requires the organised effort of more than one person, there is always leadership and delegation of duties. Delegation reduces the managerial work-load, but may also add to it if by increasing the number of subordinates and hence the 'span of management'. If an individual's span is exceeded an additional *level* of management may have to be created.

The question of span of management or control is discussed in some detail later in this chapter.

§ 7. The Psychology of Delegation

Probably the most important test of true leadership is the way it delegates its authority, and three different types or attitudes may be distinguished:[7]

[7] Mooney & Reiley: *Onward Industry!* pp. 38–9.

(i) Persons who find it easy to delegate their *authority* and would also like to delegate their *responsibility*. Such persons find their responsibility and obligations distasteful, and are poor leaders.

(ii) The real leaders find it easy to delegate authority, but remain conscious of the fact that they cannot delegate their ultimate authority and responsibility. It is this consciousness of *ultimate* responsibility which makes them ready to delegate specific tasks as soon as the total task becomes too onerous.

The above two 'types' represent extremes, but there is a third type which may present a formidable obstacle to organised growth.

(iii) Persons who fail as organisers because they are unable to utilise the capacities of others. Whilst they are often compelled to delegate portions of the total task, they will try to withhold, as long as possible, the authority which must go with the delegation of duties. "One of the tragedies of business experience is the frequency with which men, always efficient in anything they can *personally* do, will finally be crushed and fail under the weight of *accumulated* duties that they do not know and cannot learn how to delegate."[8]

§ 8. The Risks of Delegation

As already stated, the superior does not divest himself of ultimate responsibility by the act of delegation. The superior often has to take a *calculated risk* on the abilities of his subordinates, which means that he must, to some extent, supervise their activities, at least until such time as he knows his subordinates. Supervision does not, however, mean breathing down their necks. In a highly centralised organisation, a superior may be able to absorb some of his subordinates' mistakes, and thereby reduce their impact, but one of the main arguments for decentralisation is the need to develop self-reliance and initiative among subordinates by creating 'long' spans of management and making greater delegation inevitable. It is the fear of possible results through delegating to imcompetent subordinates that explains many managers' reluctance to delegate. One can justifiably complain about one's subordinates in the short run, but not in the long run,

[8] *ibid.* (my italics).

since an essential aspect of the art of delegation is that of training one's subordinates.

§ 9. Reasons for Delegation

The law-making body of Britain is Parliament but, owing to its increase in business in the twentieth century, the practice of delegated legislation has grown up, *i.e.* passing down the authority for making rules and regulations to Ministers or Government Departments. The Select Committee[9] which was set up to investigate the practice of delegated legislation gave three reasons why it is necessary: because of (i) pressure on Parliament's time; (ii) the complexity and technicalities of legislation, and (iii) emergency situations (*e.g.* 1914, 1931, 1939).

The same arguments apply to delegation in industry: it is necessary because of lack of time and energy; to deal with the crises (especially the minor ones) that constantly recur; a further reason is that in many cases, especially in technologically complex industries, the rate of advance of knowledge and techniques is such that, under the strain of *general* management, many managers quickly become out-of-date, and have to rely upon younger specialists. To these three reasons given in the Report another must be added: delegation for *education* and *training*. A progressive firm will constantly have in mind the question of management succession at all levels.[10] This is doubly important: a firm must progressively train its personnel to assume greater responsibility and decision-making; by doing so it tends to boost the morale of its younger personnel, who feel that they are being watched and 'groomed'.

What has been said above applies particularly to plants with a complex technology. Miss Woodward has suggested[11] that the ability to delegate increases with the complexity of the technology, for two reasons:

(i) In a highly technical environment (*e.g.* an oil refinery) many of the factors influencing managerial decisions are within control (because technical) and decision-making is thus a more rational process.

[9] *Report of the Select Committee on Delegated Legislation*, H.C. 310–1 (1952).
[10] On this question see *Management Succession* (Acton Society Trust).
[11] J. Woodward: *Management and Technology* (H.M.S.O. 1958).

(ii) In such industries a high proportion of the managers at all levels are scientific specialists, and possess a high degree of confidence in one another's competence. Hence, a senior manager can feel that in a given set of circumstances his subordinates would make decisions substantially the same as he himself would make. Both the above factors facilitate delegation.

§ 10. How and When Should a Manager delegate?

There are four simple steps which are helpful in the practice of delegation:

(i) *Makes sure that the subordinates accept and understand.* Having delegated a job or given an instruction, the superior should have the subordinate 'play it back' and show that he accepts the accountability for the results expected.

(ii) *It is useful to state the end-result first.* If the superior states the end-results *first*, *i.e.* before going into details of the assignment, delegation will be much more effective. Details and instructions may become so involved that the end-results are never clarified or understood by the subordinate.

(iii) *Leave the subordinate to get on with the job,* having first discussed the *time-limits* for the job, any 'check points' for progress reports, the standards of performance expected, and where the subordinate may turn for help.

(iv) '*Follow Through*'. This is necessary for ensuring that progress is in accordance with the time schedule and standards previously agreed upon, and for the purpose of deciding whether it is necessary to make any changes in the original assignments.

In practice delegation is often unsatisfactory: it may be only *partial* delegation (inconsistent with the result expected; it may be *pseudo*-delegation, which only *appears* to delegate authority). Superiors may 'hover' over their subordinates and refuse to let them use their authority. These weaknesses become more serious when the subordinates themselves are weak or untrained. An American has drawn up an amusing list of 'business-birds' to parody these weaknesses. Thus, the 'white-shirted hoverer' is a bird who gives a subordinate a job to do and then perches on his shoulder; the 'duck-billed double-talker' is a bird who never really makes clear what he wishes to delegate; the 'black-and-white organisation creeper' delegates authority and then creeps round to lower-level subordinates and thereby nullifies the delegation; the 'red-headed fire-fighter' thinks he is delegating authority when he makes his subordinates check with him before making even the most innocuous decisions.

It is helpful to have some method of deciding *where* and *when* the need for delegating arises, before failure to delegate causes a crisis. The following guide[12] will be helpful: each of the eighteen personal symptoms is usually due to, or will lead to, under-delegating.

DO YOU NEED TO DELEGATE MORE ?

1. Do you have to take work home almost every night? . YES NO
   Why?........................ Outline actions you can take to cut this down.
2. Do you work longer hours than those you supervise, or is usual for hourly-paid workers in the business? . YES NO
   Steps you could take to change this to a 'No' answer
   ....
3. Do you have little time for appointments, recreation, study, civic work, etc.? . . . . . . YES NO
   Time could be obtained by..................................
4. Do you need two or more telephones to keep up with the job? . . . . YES NO
   How did this happen to come about?......................
   Plans for doing something about it.........................
5. Are you frequently interrupted because others come to you with questions or for advice or decisions? . . YES NO
   Why? ....
   Strategies for cutting down these interruptions...........
6. Do your employees feel that they should not make work decisions themselves, but should bring all their problems to you . . . . YES NO
   Examples ....
   Actions you might take to avoid this.......................
7. Do you spend some of your working time doing things for others which they could do for themselves? . YES NO

12 See Laird and Laird: *The Techniques of Delegating* (1957), chapter 3.

Such as ....
Actions you might take to avoid this.......................

8. Do you have unfinished jobs accumulating, or difficulty meeting deadlines? . . . . YES NO
Examples ....
The jobs could be finished in time by.....................

9. Do you spend more of your time working on details than on planning and supervising? . . . . . YES NO
Why? ....
For a better balance, you could...............................

10. Do you feel you must keep close tabs on the details if someone is to do a job right? . . . . . . YES NO
Examples ....
Different plans for control of results would be..............

11. Do you work at details because you enjoy them although someone else could do them well enough? . . . YES NO
Such as ....
What to do about this...

12. Are you inclined to keep a finger in everything that is going on? . . . . YES NO
Examples..
Procedures to try instead......................................

14. Are you too conscientious (a perfectionist) with details that are not important for the main objective of your position? . . . . YES NO
Examples..
New plans to try for this.......................................

15. Do you keep job details secret from workers, so that one of them will not be able to displace you? . . . YES NO
Examples..
New plans for action...

16. Do you believe that an executive should be rushed in order to justify his salary? . . . . . . YES NO
Why? ....
An executive's principal job is?...............................

17. Do you hesitate to admit that you need help to keep on top of your job? . . . . YES NO
Examples of help you could use..............................
List of subordinates who could be trained to give this help
....

18. Do you neglect to ask workers for their ideas about problems that arise in their work? . . . . YES NO
Examples..
To change this you could.......................................

It is a salutary exercise for anyone in a managerial position to carry out the above self-analysis. Wherever possible details must be delegated, and delegation must be pushed as far down the line as possible. In order to simplify a managerial position the following questions should be asked:

Simplifying a Managerial Position:

(i) What *details* are constantly recurring in my job?

(ii) What *minor* decisions do I make most frequently?

(iii) What job *details* take up the biggest proportion of my time?

These first three questions are inter-locked and relate to the *easing of the pressure* on the manager. The next questions relate to re-designing one's position to bring it more in accord with one's talents, energies and capabilities.

(iv) What parts of my job am I *least qualified* to handle?

(v) What job *details* do I dislike the most?

(vi) What job *details* make me *underspecialised*?

(vii) What elements in my position make me *overspecialised*?

A useful way of breaking down one's position to find the details that should be delegated is the following: take a piece of paper and divide it into four columns. The first column is headed *What I do*, giving details of duties and responsibilities.

When you are satisfied that it is a complete list[13] re-write it, placing the most important details—which, in ordinary circumstances, you would never delegate—at the top, in order of priority. The next column, which will require some honesty and soul-searching, is headed *Why do I do it*? In some cases you will discover no convincing reason; you might have to say, if you are honest, "Because I like doing it"; or you may simply have 'inherited' the detail when you took over the job—it is a 'sacred cow'. The third column is headed *Who could do it for me now*?, and the fourth, *Who could do it for me after training*?

Self-Analysis

THE ART OF DELEGATION

It is suggested that if your answer to three or more of the following

[13] The student should look at one or two detailed examples of descriptions of management positions ('illustrative schedules') in Brech: *Organisation*: *The Framework of Management*, pp. 144–215, e.g. Schedule No. 7: 'The Factory Manager' (pp. 170–173) which lists no less than 44 responsibilities; Schedule No. 11, 'The Superintendent', (pp. 184–186), 40 responsibilities, Schedule No. 15, 'The Chief Inspector' (pp. 194–5), 19 responsibilities.

questions is YES, you should begin to re-appraise your supervisory methods.

	YES	NO
1. Are *unexpected* emergencies *constantly* arising in the operation you supervise?		
2. Do you find that your daily job consumes so much of your time that you have no time to *plan*? . .		
3. Do you tend always to be bogged down in *detail*? .		
4. Is there much *friction* or *dissatisfaction* among the members of your work-group? . . .		
5. Do *simple* jobs take a long time to get done? . .		
6. Do you *complain* or *criticise others* when the work of your group does not go as you planned? . .		

	YES	NO
7. Do subordinates or employees *always wait* for you to *give the sign* before they *begin* a job? . . .		
8. Have workers *stopped* coming to you to get *your reaction* to their ideas?		
9. Do your employees display *little or no enthusiasm* or *spontaneity* in their work?		

(See 'The Noble Art of Delegation', *Foreman,* No. 10 (1962).

§ 11. The Art of Delegation

This art rests upon certain basic attitudes on the part of the superior:[14]

(i) *Personal receptiveness*: willingness to give a hearing to subordinates and discuss their ideas with them;

(ii) *Willingness to release decision-making to subordinates*: it has often been observed that when a person moves up the

[14] See Koontz and O'Donnell: *Principles of Management*, pp. 91–3, for a fuller statement.

managerial ladder he wishes to continue to make the decisions appropriate to the position from which he has moved—the superintendent wishes to continue acting as foreman. A reason for this may be that he is familiar with the job, and possibly thinks he can do it better than anyone else. But an individual will contribute most to a firm if he concentrates on those tasks which are of most importance from the firm's point of view, and delegates to subordinates the less important tasks, even if he can carry them out more efficiently than his subordinates. Progress 'up the ladder' should lead to a wider, more general vision, and a progressive shedding of detail.

(iii) *Willingness to let subordinates make mistakes*, so long as the mistakes do not imperil the company or the subordinate's position in it. True delegation is impossible if the superior is constantly checking the subordinate.

(iv) *Willingness to trust subordinates*. This is allied with the previous attitude: there cannot be effective delegation unless there is an atmosphere of mutual trust and confidence.

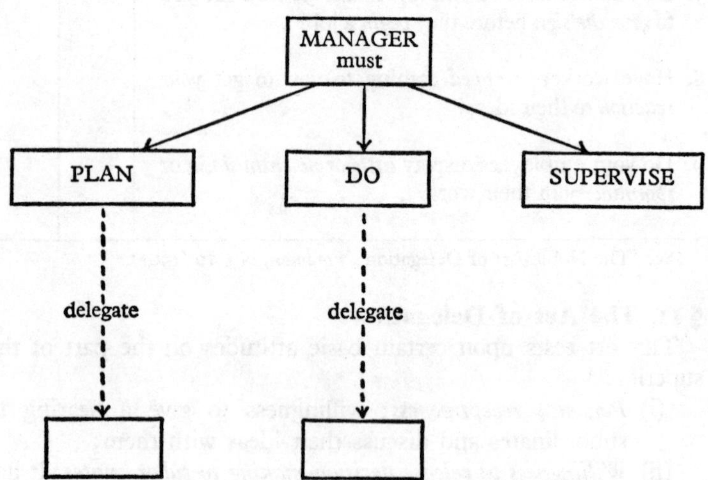

THE SPAN OF MANAGEMENT

(or Span of Control)

§ 12. The 'Span Principle'

The 'span of management' (or 'span of control') is a principle which has long been accepted as a practical concept in military organisation. General Sir Ian Hamilton stated: "The average human brain finds its effective scope in handling three to six other brains", and Sir William Robertson in his memorandum of 1915 wrote: "The number of general officers commanding with which the Chief of the Imperial General Staff should deal should not exceed the number which experience shows to be possible—about half-a-dozen".[15] It should be stressed, however, that the data at present available on the span of management should warn against any dogmatic conclusion as to numbers. There can be no general rule for determining the 'right span' (*i.e.* positive, numerical definition) for any particular situation, though it is probably true to say that spans should be smaller at higher managerial levels than at supervisory levels. (It should be stressed that the phrase does not refer to subordinate *operating* personnel, but only to executive or supervisory subordinates over whom a given individual has authority: the phrase 'span of (management) responsibility' might, as Brech suggested, be preferable.)[16]

Any 'principles' of management are valid only as guides to effective practice: they must embody commonsense and gain acceptance through the support given them by practising managers in the light of their individual experience. As regard the 'span of control' Urwick wrote: "All my own practical experience in industry confirms its validity. Time after time I have seen greater effectiveness and smoother human relations result from a determined effort to apply this principle and reduce the excessive number of subordinates whom some executive imagined he was controlling. Vanity, personal ambition, inability to delegate, mistrust of people—all the human failings with which we have to try to deal."

15 Quoted by L. C. Urwick: *Problems of Growth in Industrial Undertakings*, B.I.M. (1960), p. 7.

16 Brech: *Organisation: The Framework of Management*, p. 77.

§ 13. Real Significance of the Principle

The importance of the principle lies in its recognition of the fact that there is, generally speaking, a limit to the number of subordinates whom a manager can *effectively* control, but the exact number is indeterminate in any given circumstances and will vary with such factors as:

(i) the ability and training of the subordinates;
(ii) the clarity of policies and plans;
(iii) the degree of delegation exercised;
(iv) the degree to which objective standards or 'yardsticks' are used;
(v) the effectiveness of communications.

The arguments in favour of the principle do, in fact, seem to be nothing more than commonsense, but there is also a 'contradictory proverb of administration' which can be supported by arguments of equal plausibility.[17]

Administrative efficiency is enhanced by keeping at a minimum the number of organisational levels through which a matter must pass before it is acted upon. Simon regards this as "one of the fundamental criteria that guide administrative analysts in simplifying procedures", but points out that in many situations it leads to results that are "in direct contradiction to the requirements of the principle of span of control, the principle of unity of command and the principle of specialisation". The dilemma thus arises that in a large organisation, a restricted span of control will produce excessive red tape, since matters will have to be carried "upward through several *levels* of officials for decision and then downward again in the form of orders and instructions".

§ 14. The Theory of Graicunas

A Rumanian consultant, Graicunas, made an interesting analysis of basic relationships in the span of management in his paper first published in the *Bulletin of the International Management Institute* (Geneva, 1933). He analysed the problem of *superior-subordinate* relationships and couched his theory in mathematical terms to show the astronomical proliferation of relationships as the number of subordinates increases.

17 Herbert A. Simon: *Administrative Behaviour*, p. 26; see the two examples he gives on pp. 26–8.

He began his argument by showing that there are three types of superior-subordinate relationships:

(i) *Direct Relationships*—between a superior and his immediate individual subordinates, *e.g.* if A has three subordinates, X, Y, Z, there are three direct single relationships.

(ii) *Direct Group Relationships*—between a superior and every possible combination of subordinates, *e.g.* X with Y, X with Z, Y with X, Z with X, X with Y and Z (with three subordinates there are nine possible group relationships—what are the other four?).

The X with Y relationship differs from the Y with X relationship because in one case a problem is addressed primarily to X and in the other case to Y.

(iii) *Cross Relationships* exist when the subordinates of a common superior consult together, *e.g.* X to Y, X to Z (with three subordinates there are six possible group relationships). Graicunas couched this reasoning in mathematical form. The maximum number of all possible relationships is given by the formula:

$$n\,(2^n/2 + n - 1)$$

where n is the number of subordinates.

The following table gives some examples of the application of the formula. It is, of course, only an amusing illustration of a tendency pushed to its maximum extent, but it serves to illustrate the complex social situation which can arise if a manager has more than a few subordinates.

TOTAL RELATIONS WITH INCREASING NUMBER OF SUBORDINATES

Number of subordinates	*Total number of relationships*
1	1
2	6
3	18
4	44
5	100
6	222
12	24,708!
18	2,359,602!
24	201,327,144!

It is not so much the actual number of relationships which is important as the *frequency* of their occurrence and the extent of the demand they make on the manager's time; if the latter is excessive, co-ordination will be neglected. The table gives, however, the *maximum possible* number of relationships and it is extremely unlikely that the maximum number will, in fact, develop.

The theory shows:

(i) The problem facing a superior *vis-à-vis* his subordinates is both an *individual* and a *social* problem—social, because the manager has also to deal with *groups*.

(ii) Hence, the behaviour of subordinates must be studied in terms of *social interaction* and *group sentiments*: if there is a hostile clique or friction between individuals teamwork will suffer.

(iii) If a superior pays constant attention to the *training* of subordinates there should be *fewer* relationships requiring his attention, since a well-trained subordinate will require both fewer contacts with his superior and with other subordinates with whom he is in proximity. Training minimises the need for direction and control.

(iv) In general an executive should choose a lower rather than a higher number of subordinates, otherwise he will lack the time to fulfil all his duties—answering queries, assigning jobs, co-ordinating the work of his department, intervening in altercations. If the span is too wide leadership may become ineffective or wholly fail.

(v) There is no particular magic in the figure of 5 or 6 which is often quoted; every manager must consider the problem in relation to his own particular organisation, and he should concern himself only with subordinates who are reporting *directly* to him.

(vi) In order to decide on the 'best' span, a superior must take many factors into consideration, including the *competence* of his subordinates, the degree of *de-centralisation*, and the extent to which tasks are *repetitive* or *varied*.

§ 15. The Executive and Queues

Queueing theory is concerned, among other things, with the psychological factors which tend to increase disorder, exacerbate the queue effects.[18] The manager should frequently consider whether or not he is becoming a 'bottleneck', causing long waits to persons who wish to see him and thus holding up production or other operations. People may have to wait too long for managerial decisions; the executive himself, through having too many problems on his mind, will be subjected to increased 'load stress', with the result that wrong decisions, which later have to be rectified, are made. Again, if there is a queue, he may make decisions too speedily, without proper consideration of the factors involved. It is particularly when the work-load begins to exceed his physical and psychological capacity that the manager must delegate decision-making as much as possible, reserving only crucial decisions for himself.

On any given problem a manager may allow his subordinates to participate to varying degrees.[19] At the bottom there is no participation. The first level of participation is when the manager makes a decision and merely tells the subordinate to *implement* it. A higher level is when he says to his subordinate that he is *about* to make a decision but first asks the subordinate *what his reaction is*. At a still higher level, the manager may actually ask his subordinate for *advice*. Still higher is an invitation for the subordinate to *share* in making a decision. Highest of all (full delegation) is when the manager tells the subordinate to make the decision and says that whatever the decision may be, he, the superior, will support it.

TOPICS FOR ESSAYS/DISCUSSIONS

1. Outline the theory of Graicunas and discuss its significance.
2. "The leader . . . is the one who can organise the experience of the group and get the full power of the group. The leader makes the team. . . . Men with this ability create a group power rather than express a personal power." (Mary Parker Follett).
3. "The span of control, we are told, cannot exceed six or eight subordinates. The span of managerial responsibility, however, is determined by the extent to which assistance and teaching are needed. It can only be set by a study of the concrete situation.

[18] See Kenneth J. Shone: 'The Queueing Theory—5: 'The Executive and Queues', *Time and Motion Study* (April 1961); see also W. Brown: *Exploration in Management*, pp. 30–31.

[19] See H. B. Maynard (Ed.): *Top Management Handbook*, McGraw-Hill, New York (1960), chapter 4, 'The Art of Managing'.

Unlike the span of control, the span of managerial responsibility broadens as we move upwards in the organisation. . . . The span of managerial responsibility is, therefore, wider than the span of control, and where good practice would counsel against stretching the span of control, a manager should always have responsibility for a few more men than he can really take care of. Otherwise the temptation is to supervise them, that is, to take over their jobs or, at least, to breathe down their necks . . ." (Peter Drucker). Discuss this distinction between 'span of control' and 'span of responsibility'.

The following diagram is an example of the 'inverse span of control'. The Managing Director has eight subordinates, and his subordinate D has only two sub-managers reporting to him. Is this generally satisfactory?

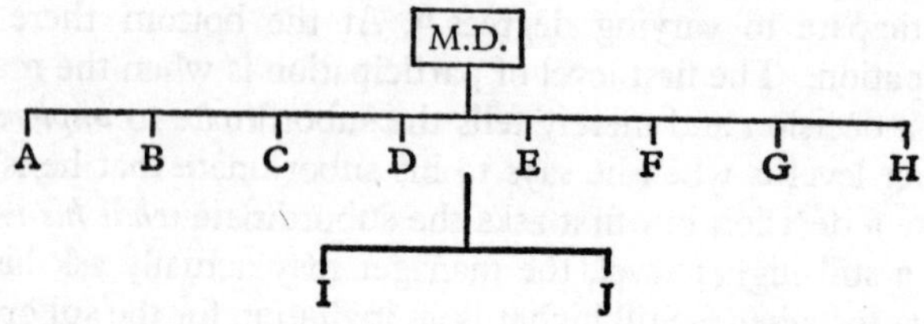

APPENDIX TO CHAPTER TWELVE

'PRESCRIBED' AND 'DISCRETIONARY' WORK-CONTENT

Dr. Elliott Jaques has asked the question: can 'principle' replace the law of the jungle as a guide to wage agreements? What he has termed the *time-span* of *discretion* provides the basis both for an equitable and acceptable pattern of differentials and for a national wage policy.[20]

[20] See E. Jaques: *The Measurement of Responsibility* (1956), and *Equitable Payment* (1961); also articles 'The Impact of the Production Engineer upon the Structure of Work and Payment in Industry' (paper presented to the Institution of Production Engineers, 18th October 1956, and reproduced in *Production Engineering*; 'An Objective Approach to Pay Differentials', *The Manager* (January 1961); 'Objective Measures for Pay Differentials', *Harvard Business Review*, January, February 1962); and Wilfred Brown: 'What is Work?', *Harvard Business Review* (September–October 1962).

Available jobs and the payment attaching to those jobs may be modified by the introduction of changes in production engineering. Jaques suggests that the basic feature of production engineering work is to modify what is *discretionary* in an operation, so that the operation becomes increasingly *prescribed*. The design of tooling and of standardised forms introduces limitations on discretion. Thus, *drill-jigs* eliminate the discretionary component involved in marking off for drilling; *standardised fixtures* eliminate the need for repeated design of tools or parts having similar basic components; *automatic feeds and stops* eliminate the need for judgment as to the speed and extent of a given operation. This process of 'prescribing discretion' has culminated in *automatic machine tools* in which most, if not all, of the operating discretion has been built in. On the other hand, a new type of discretion is emerging—that of the increasing complexity of judgment required in setting and machine-minding. Hence there is an interplay of judgment on discretion and of the prescribed or non-discretionary or prescribed elements of production work.

A new method for assessing the *level of work* or *responsibility* in jobs, by careful assessment of the prescribed and discretionary components, has been worked out by Jaques at the Glacier Metal Company. An important result is that 'responsibility' or 'level' can be measured by the so-called 'time-span of discretion', which is defined as "the maximum period of time during which any employee is authorised and expected to exercise *discretion* in his work without that discretion being *subject to review* by his superior".

The *prescribed content* of a job consists of those elements of the work about which the worker is left no *authorised choice*. The *discretionary content* consists of all those elements in which the choice is *left to the judgment of the operator*. Responsibility in industry, says Jaques, seems to attach to the discretionary content of work, not to the prescribed content: "we feel weight of responsibility in terms of the discretion or judgment that we are called upon to use", and the actual measure of responsibility can be obtained in terms of the maximum period during which a person is relied upon to use his own judgment. The period can be assessed by discovering the mechanisms which a superior uses to review the quality of discretion or judgment which a subordinate uses. A superior can use either the method of *direct review* by himself or someone acting on his behalf; or *indirect review* through the medium of reports.

The *time-span of discretion*, then, is the *longest* period that can pass before a superior makes an effective check on a man's work. It seems that Jaques has discovered social norms of what constitutes *fair payment* for different levels of work, so that jobs and salaries can be automatically linked. Once a man's career is under way it is possible to make approximate predictions of the different levels of work he will be capable of doing at different points in the future. The advantages are that superiors and subordinates have now realistic terms in which to talk about salaries, and that the range of personal judgment is narrowed down. The time span, however, is not the only factor determining level of work: some jobs require more education, greater speed of thinking or greater powers of concentration, but the scheme of Jaques allows for these requirements.

If Jaques' conclusions are accepted a new type of wage policy may emerge—a policy of fixing salary and wage brackets in connection with *level* of work alone. The scale of differential payment will then be fixed nationally on the principle of a genuine 'rate for the job'. The conclusions also seem to bear important implications with regard to the problem of *delegation*: a superior who has a clear idea of the level of responsibility of his subordinates and their time-span of discretion will be able to delegate with an easier mind, and will be able to conserve his own energies by knowing that, in all normal circumstances, no interference or 'review' is needed within a given period. Subordinates, in turn, knowing that they are receiving a differential for their capacities of judgment, will be readier to accept delegated assignments of increasing difficulty and importance.

Some Measured Ranges of Time-Span Discretion for Various Jobs[21]

1. Low-level manual and clerical jobs: half a day to a full day.
2. So-called skilled craft jobs (e.g. machine-tool fitting work): one week to a few months.
3. Foreman positions: six months to a year, depending on the responsi-

[21] Elliott Jaques: 'Objective Measures for Pay Differentials', *Harvard Business Review* (January–February 1962), p. 134.

bilities connected with work throughput, forward orders and forward planning for work input.

4. Research technologist jobs: weeks, months or years, depending on the maximum length of the project assigned to the worker.
5. Sales management: months to years, depending on the time required to cover territories, to open markets, to introduce new products, and so on.
6. Top management (i.e. managing director roles): several to many years.

"Generally speaking, the higher the position is in an executive system, the longer is its time span because of the increased connection with longer term planning". Jaques points out, however, that the above time-spans "do not mean that there is no managerial intrusion at all during the periods covered". The time span of discretion can be measured at *any position at all* in the hierarchy. Further, since the measure refers only to the time dimension of work, and not to job content, it can be used for direct comparison of work levels between any jobs, whatever the industry or content of the work.

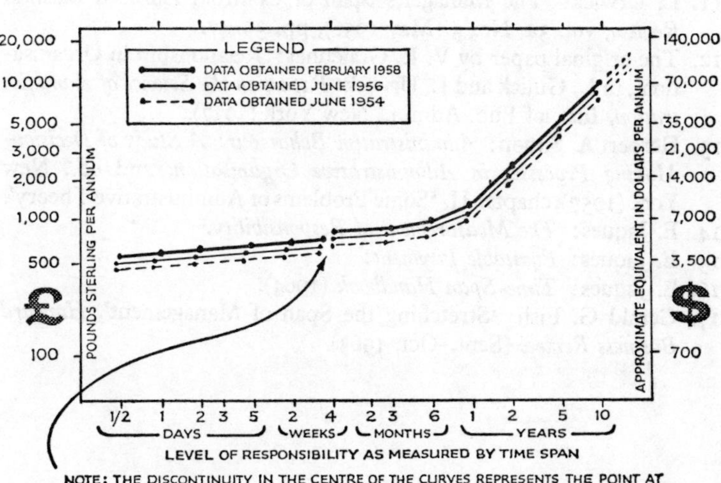

NOTE: THE DISCONTINUITY IN THE CENTRE OF THE CURVES REPRESENTS THE POINT AT WHICH PEOPLE STOP THINKING IN TERMS OF OVERTIME, AND THEREFORE EXPECT HIGHER BASIC PAY.

ADDITIONAL READING ASSIGNMENTS

1. D. A. and E. C. Laird: *The Techniques of Delegation* (1957).
2. J. M. Black: *Developing Competent Subordinates*, American Management Association (London, Bailey Bros. and Swinfen; 1961).
3. W. H. Newman: *Administrative Action*, London (1958), chapter 10, 'The Process of Delegation'.
4. E. F. L. Brech: *Organisation: The Framework of Management*, chapters IV, VII, IX.
5. H. A. Simon: *Administrative Behaviour*, chapter VII, 'The Role of Authority'.
6. E. Dale: *Planning and Developing the Company Organisation Structure*, American Management Association, New York (1950), especially Part One.
7. Koontz and C. O'Donnell: *The Principles of Management.*
8. L. Urwick: *Problems of Growth in Industrial Undertakings;* (Brit. Inst. of Management, 1960), Introduction to Paper, pp. 5–8.
9. E. F. L. Brech: *Organisation: The Framework of Management*, chapter V, 'The Principles of Organisation'.
10. H. Koontz and C. O'Donnell: *Principles of Management: An Analysis of Management Functions* (McGraw-Hill Book Co., New York, 1959), chapter V, 'Span of Management'.
11. L. Urwick: 'The Manager's Span of Control', *Harvard Business Review*, vol. 34, No. 3 (May 1956), pp. 39–47.
12. The original paper by V. L. Graicunas: 'Relationship in Organisation', in L. Gulick and L. Urwick: *Papers on the Science of Administration*, Inst. of Pub. Admin., New York (1937).
13. Herbert A. Simon: *Administrative Behaviour: A Study of Decision-Making Processes in Administrative Organisation*, 2nd ed., New York (1957), chapter II, 'Some Problems of Administrative Theory'.
14. E. Jaques: *The Measurement of Responsibility.*
15. E. Jaques: *Equitable Payment:*
16. E. Jaques: *Time-Span Handbook* (1964).
17. Gerald G. Fish: 'Stretching the Span of Management', *Harvard Business Review* (Sept.–Oct. 1963).

TEN TESTS OF MANAGEMENT CO-ORDINATION

Co-ordination is a must for management if an organisation is to have close harmony among its executives, supervisors, and employees. Only by consulting each other and by democratic participation of appropriate management groups can a smooth-working team be created.

How satisfactorily, in your opinion, does Management maintain adequate co-ordination of over-all activities in our organisation?

Place a check mark in those spaces which indicate your true appraisal of our present attainment in each of the areas listed below.

OUR PERFORMANCE

1. EXCELLENT
   No changes needed now
2. ADEQUATE
   Little improvement needed
3. FAIRLY SATISFACTORY
   Some improvement needed
4. WEAK
   Considerable improvement needed
5. LACKING
   Much improvement needed

	5	4	3	2	1
1. **Consultative Management.** Are the principles of consultative management and good human relations carried out effectively by all key executives?..................	...	...	...	...	...
2. **Viewpoints.** Is there adequate co-ordination of management viewpoints regarding: objectives, policies, plans, programs, and schedules; does the Management Team "sing the same song; out of the same book; at the same time—in harmony?"..................	...	...	...	...	...
3. **Communications.** Are communications satisfactory; up and down and across all organisational levels?	...	...	...	...	...
4. **Flexibility.** Is the Management Team adequately equipped to adjust itself quickly to meet new conditions, trends, and/or management problems?..................	...	...	...	...	...
5. **Interpretation.** Does Management assist supervisors and employees to interpret how the impact of changes and new events affects them?..................	...	...	...	...	...
6. **Recognition.** Does Management appreciate fully the wide gap between telling employees what the aims and objectives of an organisation are, and giving them an opportunity to participate in creating objectives and standards?..................	...	...	...	...	...
7. **Self-discipline.** Are Top Management Controls so designed and co-ordinated that they enable subordinates to detect problems and to effect corrections before it becomes necessary for Management to take remedial action?..................	...	...	...	...	...
8. **Balance.** Do department heads maintain a wholesome balance between their respective specialisations and the organisation as a whole?..................	...	...	...	...	...
9. **Reports.** Is adequate co-ordination made of all Management reports which are prepared by various executives and supervisors?	...	...	...	...	...
10. **Operations.** Are all functional activities and interdepartmental operations co-ordinated most effectively by Top Management in order to achieve the best results for the organisation as a whole?..................	...	...	...	...	...

Date....................19........

CHAPTER THIRTEEN

CO-ORDINATION

§ 1. Definition

By *co-ordination* is meant the *synchronisation* of effort, and the *relating and integrating* of tasks to achieve *unity of effort*. A manager must group the activities for which he is responsible, assign some of them to subordinates (ensuring that they have the requisite authority) and provide for the co-ordination of their efforts. Co-ordination has been regarded as the 'first principle' of organisation, the very essence of the manager's job containing within itself all other principles, and "expressing all the aims and purposes of organisation, in so far as these purposes relate to its internal structure".[1]

Co-ordination is the process of timing activities and re-uniting sub-divided work, of combining activities in a consistent and harmonious action. Simple examples are a gang of men hauling a heavy object or moving an awkward piece of furniture; more complex examples are the integrated activity-patterns of a football team or a symphony orchestra. Co-ordination is seen at its most complex in the case of the human brain: the *cerebellum* is a 'great special exchange' which times and co-ordinates muscular movements through a comprehensive series of connexions with all other parts of the brain and of the body in general. In the absence of a co-ordinating or timing system the working of a machine would be haphazard, irregular and completely unreliable.[2] Co-ordination has its own principle and foundation in *authority*, the supreme co-ordinating power. Mooney and Reiley drew attention to what they called the 'psychic' (*i.e.* psychological) aspects of co-ordination:

(i) True co-ordination must be based upon a real *community* of interest in the attainment of the desired object.

(ii) Such a real community of interest can only come through a *real community of understanding*: both management and

[1] Mooney and Reiley: *Onward Industry!*, chapter 3.

[2] See Sir Adolphe Abrahams: *The Human Machine*, Penguin Books (1956), 'Co-ordination and Timing'.

workers must understand each other and understand what the *real purpose* is.

(iii) *Faithful co-operation and mutual participation*; by mutual participation is meant that everyone's right to participate should extend beyond his own job.

All individuals and groups in an enterprise are affected by co-ordination. The quality and effectiveness of co-ordination, however, depends upon the leadership, insight and awareness of top management. Top management must see the details as part of a *whole.*

Co-ordination is not the mere *sum* of *separate* plans; it implies the merging of details and the development of the whole (or combination of details) into a *common policy* or *plan.*

§ 2. Specialisation and Division of Responsibilities

As an enterprise grows and specialisation and division of responsibilities develop, there is a progressive need for co-ordination. In a small organisation where everybody knows everybody else, team-work and co-ordination are likely to develop 'naturally', but in a large organisation the complexity of the task is such that co-ordination will require the full attention of top management. For this reason product departmentation or territorial divisions will be sometimes imposed on a functional system in order to effect a better co-ordination of all activities relating to a particular product or a particular branch.

Unity of effort depends upon the relating and integrating of tasks, which implies that every individual knows the scope and significance of his particular job, as well as some appreciation of the tasks of his fellow-workers. Co-ordination is often poor because of *failure of communication.* It has often been said that co-ordination must be achieved 'horizontally' rather than 'vertically': the *conditions* for co-ordination may be created from above, but it is not possible to compel people to co-operate. Sources of conflict include the 'We–They' attitude, the creation of departmental interests and loyalties, and the limited vision of narrow specialists and the empire-builders who desire other people to co-operate with them but are not prepared to extend co-operation to others.[3]

[3] N. Branton: *Introduction to the Theory and Practice of Management*, pp. 15–16.

The aim of co-ordination is to bring about a smooth, harmonious flow of work, to eliminate frictions and delays. *Teamwork* is organised effort, and requires careful timing if the aim is high productivity. Co-ordination, then, includes all the steps taken by a manager to ensure that the working operations are correctly timed and are smoothly integrated. The manager has a continuous responsibility for seeing that the activities for which he is responsible are properly synchronised. It must not be thought that co-ordination can be effected once and for all, requiring no further attention. Every time a new situation arises a fresh effort of co-ordination is required, and others must be advised of any change which may affect co-ordination.

Simon distinguishes between *procedural* and *substantive* co-ordination.[4]

Procedural co-ordination: establishing lines of authority and outlining the *sphere of activity* of each member of an orgnisation.

Substantive co-ordination: specifying the content of the work of each member.

§ 3. Individual Jobs and the Goals of the Enterprise

It is obvious that the best co-ordination will take place when individuals are able to see how their jobs and aims harmonise with the dominant goals of the enterprise. This means that everyone must have knowledge and understanding of the major goals of the enterprise. If managers and their subordinates are not sure what the dominant goals are (*e.g.* profit, quality, innovations) then it is impossible to co-ordinate their activities, since each person will tend to be guided by his own conception of what is in the interest of the enterprise, or, if he has no such conception, will tend to work for self-aggrandisement and the furtherance of his own ends. In order to mitigate the effects of such disintegrating influences, the dominant goal or goals of the enterprise must be clearly stated and interpreted to everyone concerned. There can be no effective unification unless there is frequent contact with one's subordinates, so that both major and minor matters can be discussed and natural collaboration can ensue. The importance of a clearly recognised *common objective* is seen in the case of

[4] H. A. Simon: *Administrative Behaviour*, p. 11.

General Motors or General Electric U.S.A., which are decentralised and split up into engineering, production and selling in product divisions. The management of each division can then co-ordinate these functions since the dominant goal of each unit is to be successful in its particular product line. It seems true, as Urwick[5] pointed out, that a 'functional perspective' is more disruptive of unity than a 'product perspective'. Moreover, product departmentation creates co-ordination centres at the *lower* levels of management.

§ 4. The Tasks of the General Manager or other 'Chief Executive'

One of the main tasks of the chief executive is to obviate or prevent the separatism which tends to arise in an organisation because of "the inclination of the specialist managers or officials to over-estimate their own particular activity, and to neglect their obligation to contribute co-operatively to the well-being of the organisation as a whole."[6] Brech gives two instructive examples: firstly, of a small firm employing 70 people in which the Managing Director serves in three capacities—those of General Manager, Sales Manager and Technical Director or Manager; secondly, of a larger firm employing 2,300 people in which the Managing Director effects co-ordination by means of:

(i) *Defining in writing* the responsibilities of both major and second-line executives.
(ii) Maintaining *daily contact* with each of the top-line executives.
(iii) Having a *fortnightly progress-meeting* with top executives (and second-line executives called in when necessary)—a meeting which follows a definite agenda and exists primarily for the purpose of co-ordination.
(iv) By using a *budgetary control scheme* for the control of all costs and expenditure by pre-determined standards.

§ 5. The Principles of Co-ordination

The most original and constructive thought to the 'principles' was given by Mary Parker Follett, who sifted principles from

[5] Urwick: *The Load on Top Management—Can it be Reduced*? London (1954).

[6] See E. F. L. Brech: 'The Unity of Management', pp. 851–856 of *Principles and Practice of Management*; see also George Copeman: *The Role of the Managing Director*, 'The Managing Director as Co-ordinator and Final Decision-Maker'.

techniques and clearly discussed what conditions were necessary for synchronised effort.[7]

The 'four fundamental principles of organisation' are:

(i) Co-ordination as the *reciprocal relating* of all the factors in a situation.

(ii) Co-ordination by *direct contact* of the responsible people concerned.

(iii) Co-ordination in the *early stages*.

(iv) Co-ordination as a *continuing process*.

Principle 1. Miss Follett said that this principle "shows us just what the process of co-ordination actually is, shows us the nature of unity." She gives the following example: "Take four heads of departments. You cannot envisage accurately what happens to them by thinking of A as adjusting himself to B and to C and to D. A adjusts himself to B and also to a B influenced by C and to a B influenced by D and to a B influenced by A himself—and so on." The goal of all attempts at co-ordination should be "this interpenetration of every part by every other part and again by every other part as it has been permeated by all"—a goal which is never reached. Not only do A, B, C and D adjust themselves to each other, but also "to every other factor in the situation." Miss Follett emphasised that this reciprocal relating, co-ordinating, unifying, does not require sacrifice on the part of the individual. The good of a department must not be subordinated to the good of the whole undertaking. A "departmental view is needed in the whole and must be *reconciled* with all the other points of view, but it must not be abandoned"—"I should say to the heads of departments that they should not *de*-departmentalise themselves but *inter*-departmentalise themselves. . . . Whether we are talking of the individual man or individual department, the word should never be *sacrifice*, it should always be *contribution*. We want ever possible contribution to the whole." (my italics).

Principle 2. If the process of co-ordination is one of 'interpenetration' it is impossible to impose it by an outside body—"no-one can issue a fiat by which I am adjusted, I can only help to adjust myself." The same applies to a group of executives: since the process here, too, is one of self-adjustment "it is essential that they should have the opportunity for *direct contact*".

Principle 3. Granted the importance of direct contact, it is essential that it should begin in the *earlist stages* of the process. If managers

[7] See Mary Parker Follett: *Freedom and Organisation*, chapters V and VI.

confront one another with 'finished policies' it will be difficult to come to any agreement and they will begin to 'play politics', "But if these heads meet *while they are forming their policies*, meet and discuss the questions involved, a successful co-relation is far more likely to be reached. Their thinking has not been crystallised. They can still modify one another. "You cannot . . . make policy forming and policy adjusting two separate processes. Policy adjusting cannot begin after the separate policies have been completed".

Principle 4. Co-ordination cannot be enforced, must be a self-activity and must begin in the early stages; it must also go on all the time: continuous machinery must be provided for co-ordination and people should not "try to write only when difficulties arise."

Miss Follett also discussed three factors which make for the greater unity of an enterprise:

(i) *The System of Cross-Functioning between Departments.* By cross-functioning is meant the inter-relation of departments, *i.e.* a 'horizontal' rather than a 'vertical' authority, 'conferences of parallel heads'. *Committees* are a form of cross-functioning. But whatever form of discussion or consultation is adopted there will always be antagonistic policies and methods, "each wanting right of way". Differences can be settled by *domination, compromise* or by *integration.* It is integration, the third way, which is important, and one must recognise this and not let one's thinking stay within the boundaries of two alternatives which are mutually exclusive. In other words, never let yourself be bullied by an either-or situation. Never think you must agree to this or that. Find a third way."[8]

(ii) *The Co-Relation of Executive and Expert* (specialist). The executive should give every possible value to the information of the expert, but the latter's opinion must not be allowed automatically to become a decision. The problem is "to find a way by which the specialist's kind of knowledge and the executive's kind of knowledge can be joined". This is not easy, and line managers and supervisors complain that although their authority is nominally maintained, in practice important decisions directly affecting this work are made for them by functional specialists, forcing

[8] Follett, lecture on 'Co-ordination'.

them to 'rubber-stamp decisions' which ought to be genuinely theirs. It has, indeed, been suggested[9] that any organisation depends on the type of technology and that while the line-and-staff organisation may be suitable for mass-production, it is perhaps less appropriate to process industry.

(iii) *Collective Responsibility*. Miss Follett pointed out that the functional form of organisation made joint responsibility imperative. She referred to the development of *group* responsibility which was helping to increase the sense of collective responsibility. An enterprise has a much greater chance of success if men or groups "think of themselves as not only responsible for their own work, but as sharing in a responsibility for the whole enterprise".

The importance of co-ordination is likely to increase rather than diminish. The pyramidal structure of management has become much wider and flatter, owing to the increase of departments and functions and a larger number of executives and staffmen justling one another on similar *levels* of responsibility. These specialists tend more and more to serve one another rather than a higher boss. George Copeman[10] gives the example of a Sales office: the customers' orders do not usually arrive directly in the hands of the top man, but to the Sales office, whence information about them or related to them is passed to many different departments. Thence there is a direct information channel, almost a line of command, *across* the firm, joining all those engaged in some aspect of serving the customers: there are numerous individuals working 'in parallel'.

§ 6. Co-ordination and Communication

The problems of co-ordination are essentially those of communication since, without efficient communication, no coordinated effort is possible. The defects of communication may be considered under the headings of time, space and the natural divisions of the enterprise.[11]

[9] Joan Woodward: *Management and Technology*, D.S.I.R. Problems of Progress in Industry.

[10] George Copeman: 'Some Future Trends in Management Practice', *Stock Exchange Gazette*, 18th January 1963.

[11] J. A. C. Brown: *The Social Psychology of Industry*, chapter IV.

(i) *Defective Communication due to the Time Factor* occurs mostly in establishments engaged on shift work. The main shift may consider itself to be the most important (the 'money maker') and regard other shifts as merely serving to keep down costs by the maximum utilisation of plant and machinery. There is little or no contact between the workers on the various shifts who may never meet except during the brief period of overlap. "Under these circumstances, a vicious circle of grievances may develop, and there may be deliberate attempts to shelve problems or even create them for the next shift to solve."[12]

(ii) *Defective Communication due to Spatial Segregation, i.e.* when the units of a company are geographically dispersed, or even widely separated over the same piece of ground. The danger here is that each unit or department regards itself as the most important. "In general, the greater the spatial separation of the units of an organisation, the greater the difficulty in co-ordinating work activity; spatial distance is likely to lead to social distance".

(iii) *Defective Communication due to Functionally Separate Units.* By functionally separate units is meant divisions and departments, line and staff organisation, or departments and sections at the same horizontal level. In general, co-ordination is easier when units are engaged upon similar work than when their work or functions are dissimilar. 'Horizontal' divergencies of interest may arise and there will be problems of trying to reconcile simultaneous attitudes of competition and co-operation.

It is important to stress that when a manager communicates information, instructions, interpretations or directives to a subordinate, he must be sure that the latter understands and accepts—"telling alone is not enough. It is necessary to make a periodic check of needs and current practices in communication, to fill in gaps and eliminate overlaps. Bad communications will have a direct effect upon the quality of co-ordination".

There is often failure to transmit information *upward*, because subordinates do not realise what information the superior needs for his decisions. This is a major communication problem: much

[12] See the interesting article by Peter C. Reid: 'The Human Problems of Shift Operation', *The Manager* (April 1961).

of the information relevant to high-level decisions originates at lower levels and may never reach the higher levels "unless the executive is extraordinarily alert".[13]

§ 5. Consultative Management

Consultative management is based upon the attitude that an individual manager cannot be an expert at everything, and that the experience and judgment of subordinates must be used whenever practicable. Chester Barnard wrote:[14] "The real executive sets up, fosters and maintains the system of co-operative effort, and then guides and stimulates and energizes the group in its effort to work together within that system. When the executive moves from managing persons, over to stimulating and energizing and guiding them, he will get larger results than when he seeks primarily to think up all the solutions himself. Consultative management furnishes the executive with devices which he needs for changing his emphasis from managing persons to maintaing a system of co-operative effort where *each person manages more and more of his own effort*." A simple administrative technique is always to ask for a subordinate's *own* ideas and recommendations before answering his question regarding an operating problem.

§ 6. Co-ordinating Committees and Conferences

Urwick believed that the use of the committee is over-rated, and that the necessary integration should be a natural consequence of the organisation. Obviously co-ordination will be impossible if the individuals concerned do not accept a *common objective*. If there are individuals who pursue private aims inconsistent with the performance of tasks assigned to others they may continue to act in this manner whilst sitting on a committee, although the existence of a committee may make it difficult for them to 'get away with it'. However, group discussion *does* enable individuals who have been entrusted with certain activities related to a common task to review their own activities in relation to those of others and to try to make necessary *adjustments*.

A distinction must be made between an ordinary staff meeting and a well-planned and conducted conference. A few simple

13 H. A. Simon: *Administrative Behaviour*, p. 163.

14 Quoted by D. Carlson: *Modern Management Principles and Practices*, p. 84.

techniques are required for the co-ordination of group participation:[15]

(i) The stage must be set and the purpose of the conference clearly stated by the leader, who must ensure that everyone understands the facts of the situation to be discussed.

(ii) The leader must motivate and guide the discussion so that the *group* identifies the main factors in the situation that are unsatisfactory or could be improved.

(iii) The group is then led to identify the cause(s) of the situation and to clarify the problem(s).

The remaining stages are a discussion of alternative solutions, the best solution, how the solution shall be put into effect, the appraisal (when will the results be reviewed) and the follow-up.

§ 7. Programmes as Instruments of Co-ordination

The administrative device of programmes may have either an economic or an organisational purpose (*e.g.* programmes in the world of entertainment or railway-timetables). The function of the programme as an instrument for the co-ordination of productive activities is most obvious at the level of the individual firm. "Inputs of materials and components as well as of labour have to be adjusted to the outputs eventually required; and the longer the interval between input and output and the greater the variety of materials and components incorporated in the finished product, the more difficult it is to place orders without a production programme. Such a programme, when drawn up, covers a fixed period of time, and shows the outputs of various commodities which it is planned to produce during that time. This allows all operations to be phased and co-ordinated in relation to the outputs to be produced. It also reveals any shortages in labour and materials that are likely to arise and any future bottlenecks in capacity. For this reason it provides a basis for the recruitment of labour, and for inventory control, ordering of materials and new investment in additional capacity."[16]

In addition to such a *production* programme a firm may also

[15] See D. Carlson: *Modern Management Principles and Practice*, Paris (1962), Session V, 'Co-ordination'.

[16] See A. K. Cairncross: *Factors in Economic Development*, chapter 19, for a full discussion.

have a *buying* programme, a *sales* programme and an *investment* programme, but there will be differences in time-span, *e.g.* the investment programme is likely to cover a longer period than its production programme.

Programmes serve five distinct functions:

(i) they register decisions;
(ii) they communicate decisions;
(iii) they clarify and force decisions;
(iv) they provide a measure of success of earlier decisions;
(v) they allow decisions to be delegated.

§ 8. Examples of Information required by General Management to Achieve Effective Co-ordination between Sales and Production

A useful report prepared by H. L. Bingham[17] gives different types of business and the sets of 'co-ordination information' characteristic of each type. Six types are given, but it is recognised that many firms do not fall neatly into these categories. The findings are summarised in the following Table:

[17] H. L. Bingham: 'The Information required by General Managements of Different Types of Company', *The Manager* (December 1956). (Preliminary Findings of an investigation conducted under the Auspices of the Joint Management Statistics Committee of the Association of Incorporated Statisticians and the B.I.M.)

I TYPE	*II* SUMMARY OF CHARACTERISTICS OF FIRM	*III* *Methods* OF CO-ORDINATING SALES AND PRODUCTION	*IV* EXAMPLES OF THE *information required* FOR CO-ORDINATION
A	*Long-term quantity producer:* the firm makes, and sells intensively, one or a few products of its own choice made in advance of orders for current sale (*e.g.*, mass-produced popular cars.)	Co-ordination built into *long- and short-term plans*; co-ordination of current activities achieved by ensuring that actual performance is in line with plans.	Plans are based on long- and short-term forecasts of *general economic trends*, of *demand*, of the *supply of physical and financial resources, etc.* For current co-ordination: information showing whether actual performance is in line with plans (*e.g.*, budgetary control information). Information is required on the *inflow and outflow of money*.
B	*Stock-level producer:* the firm sets out to make and maintain a comprehensive range of products for sale from stock, production in each line being planned on a *short-term basis* with a view to *maintaining predetermined levels of stocks* (*e.g.*, producers of a wide range of screws, nuts and bolts, *etc.*).	Conditions for co-ordination are set *in advance* by establishing maximum and minimum stock levels for each item, these levels being revised when necessary to take account of changes in demand. Current co-ordination is achieved by initiating production on a *short-term basis* in the light of *stock changes* within the *previously determined levels*.	For setting stock levels: information on *sales and stock turnover* by items, on the general demand for the company's products. For current co-ordination: information on *current sales, stock* and *production*. Information is required on the inflow and outflow of money.
C	*Wide-range manufacturer producing to customers' orders:* the firm offers, on a catalogue of equivalent basis, a wide range of products which are *produced to customers' orders* (*e.g.*, manufacturers of a wide range of electric switches).	Co-ordination is necessarily *short-term*; it depends on the firm's ability to obtain sufficient orders to fill its capacity, and to *integrate current inflow of new orders into existing commitments* in such a way that *quick deliveries* can be achieved, thus maintaining good customer relations, avoiding the danger that costs may rise should long deliveries have to be quoted, and also avoiding accumulations in work-in-progress.	Information both on *current rate* and on *long-term* trends of order inflow in relation to orders executed; on *major cost* items, and on *money inflow* and *outflow*.

I TYPE	*II* SUMMARY OF CHARACTERISTICS OF FIRM	*III* *Methods* OF CO-ORDINATING SALES AND PRODUCTION	*IV* EXAMPLES OF THE *information required* FOR CO-ORDINATION
D	*Manufacturer specializing in the production of large quantities of products to customers' orders and specifications:* (*e.g.*, manufacturers of industrial goods such as customer-designed packaging material).	Co-ordination is achieved by 1. Planning production for a *considerable time ahead* in the light of forecasts of customers' requirements and estimates of the rate of order inflow at different times. 2. Checking that actual order inflow is *as estimated* and if necessary directing the sales force to make special efforts to obtain orders for which capacity was originally earmarked.	1. Information on *customers' requirements* before firm orders have been obtained. 2. Estimates of the *rate of order inflow* at different times, and information on actual order inflow. 3. Detailed analysis of *available production capacity.* 4. Information on the *inflow and outflow of money.*
E	*Contract—manufacturer* (*capital goods*): contracts are in respect of capital goods of high unit value which take a form agreed between the customer and the manufacturer. Contracts usually take a considerable time to complete (*e.g.* manufacturers of large electrical generating plant).	Co-ordination is built into *long- and short-term production plans* covering all contracts in hand. These plans take account of the need to meet delivery dates quoted, and to use production resources economically; they will also indicate any spare capacity. Quotations for new contracts are made on the basis of an *assessment of the work-content and financial commitments* involved, so that contracts obtained can be *integrated* into *existing plans.* Current co-ordination is achieved by ensuring that actual performance and inflow and outflow of money are as planned.	For planning: detailed information on *contracts in hand, production capacity,* and on *work-content and financial commitments of possible new contracts.* For current co-ordination: information on actual as against planned production and deliveries, and on the inflow and outflow of money.
F	*General or jobbing manufacturer:* The firm offers a production service in a specific field, producing to customers' orders and specifications and accepting orders for small quantities regardless of whether such orders are large enough to make long production runs possible (*e.g.*, jobbing foundries, jobbing printers, general engineering shops).	Co-ordination is necessarily *short-term*; it depends on the firm's ability to obtain *sufficient orders to fill its capacity*, and to integrate current inflow of new orders into existing commitments in such a way that quick deliveries can be achieved, thus maintaining good customer relations, avoiding the danger that costs may rise should long deliveries have to be quoted, and also avoiding accumulations in work-in-progress.	Information both on *current rate* and on *long-term trends of order inflow* in relation to orders executed; on *major cost items*; and on *money inflow and outflow.*

T

§ 9. Co-ordination with the External World

So far discussion has centred on *internal* co-ordination, but the enterprise must also have co-ordination with the outside world. One can begin by viewing the enterprise as a little world of its own, then as part of the *wider industrial world*—associated industries, service organisations and functionally related markets. This is the first 'arc'. The second arc is the national economy, the third is the *geographical* world or physical setting for any enterprise; the fourth and outermost arc is the *world* of thought, ideas and resources.[18] Examples:

Co-ordination with the Industrial World: shipping co-ordinated with transport agencies; relations with banking and insurance firms; preparation of literature—catalogues, directories, statistical reports.

Co-ordination with the National Economy: here the co-ordinating mechanisms are institutional—finance, marketing and the price system.

Co-ordination with the Geographical World, i.e. with the local community and other geographical areas in which the enterprise is active, *e.g.* membership of local government, clubs.

Co-ordination with the World of Thought, Ideas and Resources: i.e. with the forces of science, technology. This is, perhaps, the most difficult aspect of co-ordination with the outside world. It is a matter of long-range planning for the individual enterprise to be brought into a working relationship with this 'distant' external world.

§ 10. Co-ordination and Government

The problem of co-ordination is a universal one; it exists in central and local government[19] no less than in industry. The Cabinet, for example, must have its devices for direction and co-

[18] Bethel, Atwater, Smith and Stackman: *Essentials of Industrial Management*, McGraw-Hill, New York (1959), chapter 19.

[19] Co-ordination in central government can be studied in Chester and Wilson (Eds.): *The Organisation of British Central Government 1914–1956*, and H. Morrison: *Government and Parliament*.

ordination and is aided by its own committees, the hierarchy officials beneath these and a permanent Secretariat. The Secretariat is also a 'junction' for Departments and the inter-Departmental bodies by which ministers are assisted. The Secretariat keeps in touch with the 'private offices' of ministers and heads of Departments, and keeps in touch with important inter-Departmental committees. Devices for introducing a 'level' between the Cabinet and Government Departments have been developed, *e.g. ad hoc* and standing committees of the Cabinet; the appointment of co-ordinating Ministers (*e.g.* Lord Privy Seal), the creation of co-ordinating Departments (*e.g.* Treasury, Ministry of Defence). At the level of local government which employs specialists co-ordination is also necessary and is brought about by the Town Clerk[20] whose job it is to see that the chief officers are not at cross purposes with one another, and that the different Departments do not duplicate one another's work. Even so, the Town Clerk's capacity as a co-ordinator is limited in its scope; the O and M Division of the Treasury recommended that the Town Clerk should have the power to interfere with the work of other Departments in order to bring about co-ordination of council activities.

ADDITIONAL READING ASSIGNMENTS

1. Mary Parker Follett: *Freedom and Co-ordination*, London (1949), V ('Co-ordination'), and VI.
2. N. K. Sethi: 'Mary Parker Follett: Pioneer in Management Theory', *Journal of the Academy of Management* Vol. 5, No. 3 (December 1962).
3. American Management Association: *Co-ordination between Engineering, Production and Sales*, New York (1950).
4. A. K. Cairncross: *Factors in Economic Development*, London (1962), Part IV, 19, 'Programmes as Instruments of Co-ordination'.
5. E. F. L. Brech: *Organisation the Framework of Management*, chapter X.
6. Robson: *Nationalised Industry and Public Ownership*, chapter 4, 'Organisation and Management'.
7. W. H. Newman: *Administrative Action*, chapter 10.
8. L. Urwick: The Load on Top Management—Can It be Reduced? London (1954).
9. G. Copeman: *The Role of the Managing Director.*

[20] See article by T. Headrick: 'The Town Clerk as Co-ordinator', *Public Administration*, Vol. XXXVI (Winter 1958).

TOPICS FOR ESSAYS/DISCUSSIONS

1. "Many analysts of managership separate co-ordination as an essential function of the manager. It seems more accurate, however, to regard it as the essence of managership . . ." (Koontz and O'Donnell).
2. "Every man's success in business depends largely, I believe, on whether he can learn something of this process (*i.e.* 'unifying'), which is one neither of subordination nor of domination, but of each man learning to fit his work into that of every other in a spirit of co-operation, in an understanding of the methods of co-operation." (Mary Parker Follett).
3. "The problem of co-ordination is largely one of communication, for without efficient communication no co-ordinated effort is possible." (J. A. C. Brown).
4. Discuss the organisation for co-ordination and delegation in a large industrial group (see, *e.g.* Appendix on the Royal Dutch/Shell Group, in Edwards and Townsend: *Business Enterprise*, pp. 342–53).
5. "Co-ordination is . . . dependent upon effective controls." (D. Carlson).
6. Discuss the value of the committee or conference as a co-ordinative instrument.
7. Discuss Simon's distinction between *procedural* co-ordination and *substantive* co-ordination. (See Simon: *Administrative Behaviour*).
8. "Co-ordination should be secured at the lowest possible level." Consider the following extract:

   ". . . policy is adjusted much more easily if it is adjusted in the actual process of formation. If each one of four separate countries considers a problem with international reactions from its own point of view, develops a national policy, begins to give it expression in administrative arrangements, fortifies it with ministerial decisions and Cabinet Authority, adjustment will prove almost impossible. Four rigid and developed policies will confront each other. . . . If a settlement is arrived at in these circumstances it will probably be after a contest in which the bargaining strength of the disputants has been measured, rather than the intrinsic merits of the case. But if the national points of view can be explained while they are still developing, if policies can be brought into contact while they are still plastic and still unformed, agreement will be easier and probably better."

   (A. Salter: *Allied Shipping Control*, p. 179).

CHAPTER FOURTEEN

PROBLEMS OF GROWTH AND SIZE

§ 1. Large and Small Firms

For most industries there is a size of plant which can be regarded as 'typical', *e.g.* plants in the iron and steel industry tend to be large; those in cotton-spinning 'medium', those in baking 'small'. There has, in recent times, been an increase in average size: thus in 1935 in Britain there were 64,649 establishments employing a total of 7,203,000 persons—average 111.4; in 1955 there were 56,313 establishments employing a total of 7,833,000 persons—average 140.1: an average increase of nearly 26 per cent.[1] Not only establishments but also *firms* have been increasing in size in the last twenty years. The Census of Production for 1949 showed that small establishments were no longer typical, but still existed. Of the total of 137,000 establishments of all sizes, 90 per cent employed fewer than 100 workers, and over 50 per cent has less than 11 workers. In spite of this, large-scale production predominates in Britain. Thus, some 2,300 establishments employing more than 500 employees are of such a size that they employed about 42 per cent of the total manufacturing labour force; of the latter, the 340 largest, with more than 2,000 employees, accounted for about 20 per cent of total employment in manufacture. The most important large-scale industries are vehicles, iron and steel, engineering and chemicals, coal, electricity and gas.

§ 2. Scale of Business

Peter Drucker[2] usefully distinguished *four stages of business size*:

(i) The *small* business, distinguished from the one-man business by requiring a level of management (*e.g.* superintendent, accountant) between the man at the top and

[1] McGivering, Matthews and Scott, *Management in Britain*, 'Size of Units', pp. 14–22. On questions of definition ('industry', 'firm') see A. Beacham and L. J. Williams: *Economics of Industrial Organisation.* Many firms started as family businesses—see Roger Falk: *The Business of Management*, Penguin Books (1961), chapter 7, 'Family Firms'.

[2] P. Drucker: *The Practice of Management*, London (1955), chapter 18.

the workers. The man at the top may, in addition to running the business, have a function such as sales manager.

(ii) The *fair-sized* business, probably the commonest type and one of the most difficult. It is distinguishable from the small business in that the man at the top is fully occupied in *general* management, and does not occupy an additional functional position. A fair-sized business requires a chief-executive team, and has to cope with the problem of the relationship of *functional managers* to top management. There is also the problem of organising *technical specialists*, and of settling their relationship to top and functional management.

(iii) The *large* business. When a firm reaches a certain size one or other of the *chief executive jobs* has to be organised on a *team-basis*: either the "top-action job" (as Drucker calls it) or the "setting overall objectives job" becomes too large for one man and has to be split. In such large businesses "the federal principle of management organisation is always the better one. This raises a problem of the relationship between top management and the autonomous managers of federal businesses".

(iv) The *very large* business. When a firm grows even larger both the 'top action job' and the 'setting overall objectives job' will have to be organised on a team basis, and each job will require the services of several people. Such a firm can again only be organised in a federal manner, and the organisation of the 'chief executive' and the relation of the latter to operating management tend to become the major problems.

Study the following Table:

GROWTH IN THE NUMBER OF LARGE COMPANIES IN BRITAIN

Analysed by total employment size, 1935 and 1958: private sector enterprises in manufacturing industry employing 5,000 or more persons:

Size of enterprise	Number of Enterprises		Employment (000)	
	1935	1958	1935	1958
50,000 and over . .	—	8	—	547
20,000–49,999 . .	9	24	273	750
10,000–19,999 . .	21	42	308	566
5,000– 9,999 . .	58	106	413	709
Total—5,000 and over	88	180	994	2,571

(Source: 'Size and Diversification of Industrial Enterprise', *Board of Trade Journal*, 8th March 1963.).

§ 3. The Economies of Scale[3]

Every textbook of economics contains a section on the economies to be enjoyed from large-scale production—both internal and external economies.

Internal economies can be grouped under the headings *technical*, *managerial*, *commercial*, *financial* and *risk-spreading*.

External economies include the economies of *concentration*, of *information* and of *disintegration*.

In spite of these advantages, however, numerous small firms exist because there is little scope for *capital-intensive techniques*; or because of the time required for considerable growth; or because there are always numerous individuals ready to start new businesses; there are also managerial, market and financial obstacles to growth.

A very broad generalisation is that large firms tend to be inefficient in administration, but efficient in the use of capital, whilst small firms tend to be efficient in administration and inefficient in the use of capital. In small firms top management is likely to tolerate circumstances which do little more than enable the directors, as working executives, to get a living wage out of the business. This is indicated by the *return on capital employed* which, in many

[3] For a full discussion see Cairncross: *Introduction to Economics*, chapter 8, 'Large Scale Production', or Benham: *Economics*, chapter 8.

small firms, may be only 5.7 per cent *before* the Inland Revenue intervenes. Another cause of inefficiency is the lack of management training and management knowledge among the executives of small firms. Many firms are begun by men with technical *know-how* and ability to make a special product, but they may survive and grow to a size at which *management skill* becomes necessary, but which they cannot afford, even if there were sufficient people of management calibre to meet the needs of 40,000 firms employing less than 100 persons. Not only is there frequently a lack of *costing*, but also of *management action to control costs*. "A great deal of detailed work is involved when management by *instinct and rule-of-thumb* is to be changed to management '*by exception*' from known standards. . . . A complete revolution in the methods of managing a business is involved, and it usually takes an outside person to initiate a spirit of change and progress and to reconcile conflicting interests within the management. In the worst cases it is not enough to make some cursory improvements; it is necessary to evaluate *proper standards* for the future health of the business."[4]

Hutchesen and Lee give an example of the wider effects of work study connected with increased output and turnover which become possible if increased productivity is matched by increased sales. The turnover of capital in the example given increased from $1\frac{1}{2}$ times to $2\frac{1}{4}$ times, and the return on capital increased from $7\frac{1}{2}$ to $31\frac{1}{2}$ per cent.

The main problem of small firms is that they cannot usually afford the management they need, and even the fair-sized may be too small to offer its managers sufficient inducement; further, it will not offer the challenge and scope which the large business can offer. In both small and fair-sized businesses there will tend to be a gap between the *demands* of management and the *competence* of management. The problems of such businesses may be so serious that there is "only one solution: expand the business by merger with another small or fair-sized company, or by the acquisition of another such company" (Drucker).

§ 4. Growth and Profitability

It is probably true that most firms wish to grow in terms of

[4] G. A. Hutchesen and O. R. J. Lee: 'Inefficiency in Small Firms', in *The Stock Exchange Gazette* (January 18th 1963). (My italics).

output and employment, and that the best measure of 'success' is the long-run growth of the firm—the *average percentage growth* from one year to the next.[5] As Barna has shown growth is correlated with profit: a high percentage rate of growth depends upon a high percentage rate of capital employed (rate of profit=total profits related to total capital employed). At the National Institute of Economic and Social Research a sample of 70 firms from two industries, electrical engineering and food manufacturing, was studied. The best measure of growth seems to be some measure of *assets*, both fixed and total assets (total assets=fixed assets+working capital *minus* current liabilities). The following results were obtained:

RELATIONSHIP OF GROWTH AND PROFIT

(averages over 9 or 10 years)

Growth Rate per cent per annum	*Number of Firms Profit ratio per cent per annum*					
	30 and over	*25–29*	*20–24*	*15–19*	*Under 15*	*Total*
20 and over .	4	1	2	2	—	9
16–19 . .	3	5	2	4	—	14
12–15 . .	1	4	4	4	1	14
8–11 . .	1	2	5	5	9	22
Under 11 .	—	1	3	1	10	15
Total .	9	13	16	16	20	74

Two conclusions were drawn from these figures:

(i) There seems to be a wide difference in both the rates of growth and of profit of individual firms over a period as long as 9 or 10 years, and it is the *character of management* which is likely to determine both the rate of growth and the profitability of a firm.

(ii) The difference between the two industries was not great. The relationship between growth rate and profit rate was

[5] T. Barna: 'What is a Successful Business?' *The Manager* (June 1960). (It should be realised, however, that there are cases where growth may be undesirable, e.g. over-diversification of product may lead to uneconomic batch sizes, and the increase in sales volume may impose unexpected costs of market development.)

the same in both industries, and there is a tendency for firms with a given rate of profit to grow at the same rate.

It does not necessarily follow that growth is *caused* by profits, but it is believed that both profits and high rates of growth can be explained by the *aims and attitudes of management*.[6]

Not all giant companies grow quickly, but large companies tend to expand more quickly than small: in the period 1948–53 the fast and slow growers among the giant companies were as follows:[7]

FAST AND SLOW GROWERS AMONG THE GIANT COMPANIES

1948–53

(Percentage change in net assets per annum)

Fast	*Rate*	*Slow*	*Rate*
1. Albright & Wilson (Chemicals)	29	Associated British Picture	—1
2. A. E. Reed (Paper)	26	Odeon Theatres	—1
3. Monsanto (Chemicals)	24	Kemsley Newspapers	0
4. De Havilland (Aircraft)	24	Charrington (Brewery)	0
5. Hawker Siddeley	24	Bovril (Food)	1
6. English Electric	24	M. Burton (Clothing)	1
7. Babcock & Wilson (Boilermakers)	24	Walker Cain (Brewery)	1
8. Rolls Royce	21	Barclay Perkins (Brewery)	1
9. British Oxygen	20	Bass Radcliff (Brewery)	1
10. Steel Co. of Wales	20	Debenhams (Stores)	2

Study the following Table which is an analysis of British firms according to the number of employees:

[6] On 'profitability' as a more correct criterion of management success than 'profit' in the ordinary accounting sense see Brech (ed.): *Principles and Practice of Management*, Part V, chapter VII, 'Criteria of Success'.

[7] A. S. J. Prais: 'The Financial Experience of Giant Companies', *Economic Journal* (June 1957).

No. of employees	*Establishments*		*Employees*	
	Number	*Per cent of total*	*Number (000s)*	*Per cent of total*
11–24	14,874	53	258	10
25–49	14,625		516	
50–99	11,520	20	810	10
100–249	8,759		1,351	
250–499	3,293	24	1,141	46
500–999	1,524		1,048	
1,000–1,999	742		1,021	
2,000–4,999	328	3	959	34
5,000 or more	74		631	
Total with 10 or more employees	55,739	100	7,735	100

(Source: *Ministry of Labour Gazette*, September 1959)

In the past industrial progress has depended upon the development of specialisation or *division of labour*, opportunities for further specialisation arising as a firm grows. If, however, customers require special attention and tailor-made products, division of labour is not possible to the same extent as in the case of a *standardised* product. Again, a limit may be set to specialisation by the *technical nature* of the industry. When a firm grows, the gains it can obtain are limited to those processes in which *sub-division* is possible as output increases. *The economies of size* (or economies of *scale*) are not, therefore, limited to division of labour. Several individual operations may be combined and this—the *integration* of processes—is the reversal of the division of labour. When processes are spread over several separate concerns and these firms are linked up ('vertical integration') economies can be obtained similar to those obtained from the integration of processes in a single industry.[8]

§ 5. Advantages and Disadvantages of Large Organisations

The best discussion of this is by Edwards and Townsend[9] of which the following is a summary:

[8] On the economy of large outputs see R. H. Edwards and J. Townsend: *Business Enterprise*, chapter VII.

[9] *ibid.*, chapter VIII, 'The Merits of Large Organisations'.

ADVANTAGES:

(i) *Managerial ability* can be used to the full.
(ii) Large firms have advantages in *staff recruitment.*
(iii) Large firms are better placed with regard to *securing finance.*
(iv) Large firms can spread their risks over several ventures and reduce their vulnerability to changing circumstances.
(v) Large firms can reduce the risks of *fluctuations in technical success*—"diversification may indeed be essential to survival".
(The above five are *cost-saving* in nature.)
(vi) "Size may carry with it power and the advantages that power brings", *e.g.* a hearing from *Government Departments,* power over *suppliers,* over *employees,* over *customers.*

DISADVANTAGES:

(i) With the growth in size, the problem of *co-ordination* becomes more difficult. "The men at the top have more things over which they may divide their attention. More managers have to be managed".
(ii) The problem of *morale* also becomes more difficult.[10]
(iii) *Inflexibility, red-tape* and '*empire-building*' (Parkinson's Law).

Growth is not always and unequivocally desirable, especially if it is based upon wide diversification of product, which will cause difficulties to arise both on the production and sales side. Nor must one forget the costs of growth: if a new product is launched (or a new department set up) the cost will be mainly if not wholly written off as a current cost of running the business when it is, in fact, a *cost of growth.*[11]

§ 6. The Problem of Size

Economists and others have discussed the relationship between the size of a firm and its economic efficiency. As a firm grows three phases of development may be distinguished:

[10] See Acton Society Trust pamphlets: *Size and Morale* (London, 1953); *Size and Morale II* (1957).

[11] George Copeman: *Laws of Business Management,* Appendix C, 'The Process of Capital Accumulation in Large Firms'.

*Phase 1: Increasing returns** due to greater specialisation of personnel and capital and more efficient utilisation of indivisible resources (i.e. those which cannot be sub-divided without complete or partial loss of efficiency).

Phase 2: Further growth may result in *constant returns** rather than *increasing returns, i.e.* a 10 per cent increase in size may bring about a 10 per cent increase in output.

Phase 3: Still further growth may cause *diminishing returns**. The usual argument has been that an increase in size beyond a certain point reduces managerial efficiency. More managers and supervisors are required; both vertical and horizontal relationships inevitably become more complex; the increasing number of *levels* of management causes difficulties and time-lags in communication; owing to the remoteness of top management from the seat of operating conditions, decisions often have to be made on the basis of second-hand information. Hence there is a decline in economic efficiency.

The *optimum size* of a firm is that at which *costs per unit are lowest*. It has been argued that the main factor limiting the size of firms is that of *management* or *entrepreneurship*. The manager or entrepreneur is a single unit; further, there is a limit to his skill and ability and, as increasing amounts of other factors are applied to the 'fixed factor' of managerial ability (co-ordination), a point must be reached when costs increase. Because of this it has been argued that a firm must reach an 'optimum' size because the factor of management is fixed.[12]

The notion that decreasing returns to scale is inevitable has, however, been to some extent disproved by the experience of numerous American industrial corporations. Large organisations have been sub-divided into autonomous operating units by *departmentation* according to *product* and *territory*, and large organisational changes have been made to cope with the greater

* The student will familiarise himself with the meaning of these terms during his economics studies.

12 See especially E. G. R. Robinson: *The Structure of Competitive Industry* (Cambridge Economic Handbooks). Robinson defined the 'optimum firm' as "the firm which in existing conditions of technique and organising ability has the lowest average cost of production per unit, when all those costs which must be covered in the long run are included."

problems of co-ordination, communication and control. Much of the responsibility for decision-making has been delegated to lower levels of the organisation.

The argument that co-ordination is a 'fixed' factor was based upon the commonsense deduction that single-minded direction is limited in its possible scope because of the limited abilities and capacities of any single human being. Yet a firm can alter its administrative structure so that non-routine management decisions requiring real judgment can be made by many *different* people without destroying the firm's essential unity. Operating control can be effected through accounting devices which, though highly centralised, take the place of co-ordination in an entirely different framework and permit the use of highly mechanised techniques.[13]

Divisionalisation or the sub-division of a company into a number of integral cells has sometimes been carried out as a deliberate, preconceived policy, but in other cases it is simply the logical consequence of the pressure of circumstances.

In the past a large company may have been run as a whole by a single manager of genius, but such a situation has probably become very rare. When the 'personal touch' has disappeared consideration should be given to divisionalisation, so that smaller units are created where the managers can exercise closer control. A possible indication that this point has been reached is when the accountant finds that top management can no longer find time to examine any but the broadest statistics of activity, with the result that inefficiencies are left unattended. From the accountant's point of view "the critical moment is reached when owing to the ramifications and size of the business the sources of profit and loss have become confused behind a welter of arbitrarily-spread expense."[14]

§ 7. Departmentation

This means the grouping of activities into convenient management units. The need to divide up work was recognised long ago by Aristotle (*Treatise on Politics*, Book 2, chapter II): "Where the

[13] E. T. Penrose: *The Theory of the Growth of the Firm*, Oxford (1959), pp. 18–19.

[14] A. H. Taylor: 'Management by Division', *The Accountant's Journal* (May 1960).

State is large, it is more in accordance with constitutional and democratic principles that the offices should be distributed among many persons. . . ." At each managerial level work must be subdivided, the units becoming progressively smaller until the operator is reached. The need to re-assign work arises constantly as a firm grows.

The most usual forms of departmentation are functional departmentation and the grouping by geographical divisions or areas, products, customers or functions:

(i) *Functional Departmentation* is based upon the primary functions of production, sales, finance, engineering and personnel, and departments covering the latter are responsible for a functionally defined objective. Some functions will be essential in some industries and companies, but not in others, *e.g.* research and advertising; in some companies the main departments will be of roughly equal importance, but in others the success of the company will depend greatly upon the efficiency of one department. The relative importance of a functional department will be shown by the level which its top executive occupies in the hierarchy. The following Table shows the main types of executives reporting directly to the President in a hundred large American companies:[15]

[15] Ernest Dale: *Planning and Developing the Company Organisation Structure*, Research Report No. 20 (American Management Association, 1950), p. 58 (partial table only with 15 other functions below advertising).

TYPES OF EXECUTIVES REPORTING TO THE PRESIDENT IN 100 LARGE COMPANIES

Function	*No. of companies*
Production, Operations, Manufacturing	94
Marketing, Sales	88
Industrial Relations, Personnel Administration	64
Legal Counsel, General Counsel	55
Controller, Comptroller	46
Treasurer	45
Finance	42
Purchasing	38
Research, Development, New Products	38
Plant Managers	37
Assistant to President	37
Engineering	37
Secretary	37
Public Relations	34
Executive Vice-President	29
Advertising	15

Size is an important consideration in determining the extent to which functional departmentation may take place, and some departments will not, therefore, be found in small organisations. The growth of a firm will, however, generally lead to a greater degree of functional specialisation, and the centralisation of a particular function, *e.g.* research and development, will give it a higher status.

It has been assumed throughout most of this century that functional organisation is preferable if it can be set up, since specialisation and efficiency have been regarded as synonymous, but modern developments, both at the higher and lower levels, have tended to modify this attitude. Thus, at the top level, there has been a growing emphasis on team-work, which is more difficult to arrange when workers are narrow specialists; at the lower level there is the tendency towards *job enlargement*, *i.e.* workers (either individually or as a team) completing a given job from beginning to end, and this means increasing the *variety* of work assigned to workers.

How should work be divided? There are two approaches: the '*top-down*', starting with the duties of top management and working downwards; or the '*bottom-up*', grouping work operations into individual jobs, combining workers engaged on similar jobs into sections, and combining sections into divisions. Both approaches have their advantages: the top-down approach necessitates a critical analysis of all operations, the bottom-down approach means that careful attention must be paid to workers. As regards the top executives, a useful method is to distinguish between sub-divisions which are centres of major operations, and those which are auxiliary services. There is a tendency for auxiliary divisions to grow unnecessarily large, but if services are clearly identified it is easier to justify their size and existence in terms of their usefulness to primary operations.

(ii) *Geographical divisions.* Manufacturers of bulky products divide their work on a territorial basis, each area or district being served by a separate plant. Chain-stores, banks, automobile assembly and oil-refining are further examples. The main reasons for territorial departmentation are to avoid *absenteeism* and to take advantage of the *economies of localised operation.*[16] *Absenteeism* in this context means the tendency of a firm's officials to ignore local factors in decision-making. Plants for manufacture and assembly may be so located as to reduce transport costs. Further, the district, area or branch can be used as a training-ground for managers. Sometimes false reasons are adduced for territorial departmentation, *e.g.* poor communication facilities (no longer valid), or the need for taking prompt action (but the distant officer can act just as promptly as the local one).

[16] See Koontz and O'Donnell: *Principles of Management*, pp. 106–11, for a full discussion.

The Sales Activity. The organisation of this activity on territorial bases may be for reasons of paying attention to local preferences of making economic gains, and for management training purposes.

The Finance Function. There are no good arguments for area departmentation of finance; on the other hand, great economies may accrue from the centralisation of finance activities.

(ii) *Departmentation by Product.* Product departmentation has proved successful in all functions except finance and industrial relations. Even small companies may find it advantageous to set separate production units for each product, but product divisions are typical of large corporations, *e.g.* General Electric, with departments for electric light bulbs, generators, household appliances, jets. Many enterprises which adopted this form of organisation were originally organised on a functional basis, but growth led to such inflexibility and complexity that product departmentation became necessary, permitting top management to delegate wide authority to a plant or division over manufacture, sales and service functions relating to a particular product. An automobile firm may divide its activities between private cars, commercial vehicles, tractors and spares. Such divisions as dyestuffs, plastics, man-made fibres, paints, insecticides and so on are typical of a large chemical firm. The main reasons for departmentation by product are: maximum use of personal skills and knowledge, the use of specialised capital goods; the grouping together of activities relating to a particular product may also facilitate co-ordination.

(iii) *Departmentation by Customer* as found, for example, in sales departments that have both large and small customers, or sales to both wholesalers and industrial buyers. It is a useful basis for grouping the sales activity of those who cater for customers with different needs. There are two possible disadvantages of customer departmentation: the difficulty of co-ordinating a department so organised with other departments organised differently; and the possibility of under-employment of plant and labour during slack times.

(iv) *Departmentation by Process or Equipment.* The main purpose of grouping activities round a process or type of equipment is to achieve economies. This is particularly true when a process is based upon heavy specialised equipment and it is not possible to make use of small units. Boot and shoe manufacture, for example, may be sub-divided into checking, closing, press cutting, lasting, finishing, glossing and cleaning.

§ 8. Centralisation and Decentralisation

These terms may be used with reference to the allocation of managerial work within a single company (firm) or within an entire organisation, such as a nationalised industry. *Decentralisation* within a company refers to the passing of managerial work downwards to the operating levels; *centralisation* is the retention of a large amount of the managerial work at the top management level.

Newman and Sumner[17] have given seven guides to the *degree of decentralisation* that is appropriate to a specific situation. The following factors should be carefully weighed in choosing the best place in the executive hierarchy for each category of decision-making:

(i) Who knows the facts on which the decision will be based, or who can assemble them most readily?

(ii) Who has the ability to make sound decisions?

(iii) Must speedy, on-the-spot decisions be made to meet local conditions?

(iv) Must the local activity be carefully co-ordinated with the other activities?

(v) How significant is the decision?

(vi) How busy are the executives to whom planning tasks might be assigned?

(vii) Will initiative and morale be significantly improved by decentralisation?

Often the factors pull in opposite directions—the need for speed may suggest greater centralisation, while the desire for co-ordination may dictate greater decentralisation.

[17] Newman and Sumner: *The Process of Management*, pp. 49–51; see also E. F. L. Brech: *Organisation: the Framework of Management*, chapt. IX, 'Centralisation v. Decentralisation'.

Profit Decentralisation means the sub-dividing of a company into product divisions or regional divisions, each of which is responsible for its *own* profit or loss, so that there are several 'little businesses' operating within the parent company. It is held that such decentralisation has a great advantage in its stimulating effect upon the morale of the key-men in the self-sufficient and semi-autonomous divisions. The 'little businesses' are of manageable proportions and communications are, therefore, facilitated. Co-ordination and control are also improved.

§ 9. The Nationalised Industries

The 'Fleck' and 'Herbert' Reports have been regarded as the classic exposition of the contrast between doctrines of centralisation and de-centralisation yet these Reports do not conflict all along the line. The Fleck Report did not suggest that *everything* should be centralised; indeed, it approved the basic structure of an organisation which delegated considerable powers and functions to its subordinate units, *e.g.* the basic project planning work was given to the 48 Area Headquarters which, the Fleck Report recommended, should be strengthened. The Herbert Committee, however, recognised that the central organisations had very important functions of direction and co-ordination.

A general guide as to what should be devolved to a lower level is to ask whether at that level there will be enough experienced and competent staff to carry the responsbility; this, in turn, will depend on whether there is *enough* work to devolve and whether it would come in a flow sufficiently regular to allow experience to be accumulated. But even if subordinate units in a large organisation are given very comprehensive formal powers, they may frequently have to consult specialists at headquarters if they lack experience.

The 'Fleck' Report on the Coal Industry. In 1946 the National Coal Board was functional, but after 1951 Board members without departmental duties and concerned mainly with *policy* were appointed. The Fleck Committee proposed that there should be a return to a functional Board; the proposal was accepted by the Minister. The Board is responsible for policy, and the day-to-day management of each department is in the hands of an Executive Head at Headquarters. There are five *levels* of management—

Headquarters, Divisions, Areas, Groups and Collieries—and the General Directive of July 1955 set out the responsibilities of each level of management. The task of the managers of the first three levels is "to control and co-ordinate the work of subordinate authorities" and to "help, guide, and stimulate them, and . . . hold them to account". At the first three levels there is a *functional* division into departments, and the responsibilities of each Head of Department at these levels are:

(i) To advise on the *framing of policy* in his field.

(ii) To set in motion the execution of policies in his field.

(iii) To *co-ordinate* the *specialist work* of his department, not only at his *own level*, but also at the *next level* of management below him.

(iv) To *advise*, *guide* and *stimulate* the department at his *own level* and at *all levels* of management below him.

(v) To keep himself *fully informed* about the work of his department, and to satisfy himself that the policy in his field is being carried out punctually and efficiently, both at his *own level* and at *all levels* of management below him.

The Board empowers all Departmental Heads at Headquarters to issue to functional Divisional Heads instructions as to how policies are to be implemented; the Divisional Heads have similar powers; Area Heads are empowered to issue instructions to Group Managers on established policy matters.

The General Directive emphasised the need for the Board to express its policies "fully, specifically and, where necessary, in detail. Each level of management must avoid interfering in the day-to-day work of the level of management below it, but should exercise control by means of modern management techniques. . . ."

The 'Herbert' Report and the Electricity Supply Industry. The Central Electricity Authority was formed in 1955, and became responsible for the general policy, supply of electricity and the generating stations and main transmission. Each of the 14 Area Boards was responsible for the distribution of electricity to its own customers. Generation and bulk transmission were divorced from distribution. The Herbert Committee believed that these functions should continue to be separated, but was not in favour of the mingling of supervisory and executive functions in the C.E.A. The Committee recommended that the Central Authority should retain its supervisory powers, but lose its responsibility for generation and transmission. It also recommended that a new statutory body, the Central Generation Board, should be set up, to take over from the C.E.A. the responsibility for generating electricity. More authority should be delegated by the Central Authority to its own Divisions and power-stations. Because of the national grid system it was essential to centralise the electricity supply industry. In 1958 a Central Electricity Generating Board was established, which took over the assets and responsibility for generation and bulk transmission.

It is recommended that the student should study one of these Reports which vividly illustrate the problems under discussion (*e.g.* Fleck Report, chapter 8).

§ 10. Conclusion

Before 1939 it was generally believed that every firm had an 'optimum' size, at which any further *economies of scale* were offset by the inability of management to *co-ordinate*. Now it appears that there is no evidence for *diseconomies* of size. Co-ordinative ability sets a limit only to the *rate* at which a firm can grow; size in itself, it appears, sets no problem that cannot be solved by decentralisation, though it may be desirable to hive off part of a rapidly-growing firm so that the part may itself expand as rapidly as possible. Many of the difficulties of growth are due to the difficulties of delegation. Both co-ordination and delegation are discussed in separate chapters of this book.

ADDITIONAL READING ASSIGNMENTS

Two short studies:

1. L. F. Urwick: *Problems of Growth in Industrial Undertakings*, and
2. Sir Charles Renold: *The Organisation Structure of Large Undertakings.*

   (Both are published by B.I.M.).
3. R. H. Edwards and J. Townsend: *Business Enterprise: Its Growth and Organisation* (London 1957), chapters VII and VIII.
4. Peter Drucker: *The Practice of Management*, chapter 18, 'The Small, Large and Growing Business', and chapter 19, 'The Small-Scale Business'.
5. R. B. Heflebower: 'Observations on De-centralisation in Large Enterprises'. *Journal of Industrial Economics* (November 1960).

6. I. McGivering, D. Matthews and W. H. Scott: *Management in Britain*, 'Size of Units', pp. 14–22.
7. Acton Society Trust pamphlets: *Size and Morale* (London 1953), and *Size and Morale II* (London 1957).
8. A. S. Mackintosh: *The Development of Firms*, Cambridge University Press (1963). A study of 36 Birmingham manufacturing firms; the author found that the commonest limiting factor to growth was *finance*.
9. G. E. Milward (Ed.): *Large Scale Organisation.*
10. R. Evely and I. D. M. Little: *Concentration in British Industry: an Empirical Study of the Structure of Industrial Production, 1935–51*, Cambridge University Press (1960). Shows that the major firms had grown primarily by *external* expansion.
11. National Coal Board: *Report of the Advisory Committee on Organisation* (1955) ('Fleck' Report).
12. C. A. Roberts: 'The National Coal Board and the Fleck Report', *Public Administration*, vol. xxxv, Spring 1957.
13. H.M.S.O. *Report of the Committee of Inquiry into the Electricity Supply Industry*, Cmd. 9672 (1956). ('Herbert' Report.)
14. R. J. S. Baker: *The Management of Capital Projects*, London (1962). (Choose *one* of the three industries for study.)
15. E. T. Penrose: *Theory of the Growth of the Firm*, Oxford (1960).
16. Roger Falk: *The Business of Management*, chapter 7, 'Family Firms'.
17. R. M. Lawless and P. R. Haas: 'How to Determine the Right-Size Plant', *Harvard Business Review* (May–June 1962).
18. E. F. L. Brech: *Organisation: the Framework of Management*, chapter IX, 'Centralisation v. Decentralisation'.
19. J. Kornas: *Over-Centralisation in Economic Administration*, Oxford (1959).

TOPICS FOR ESSAYS/DISCUSSIONS

1. Discuss the advantages and disadvantages of large-scale organisations.
2. What are the main forms of departmentation? Discuss any *one* in some detail.
3. "... the larger the organisation the greater the problem of maintaining the sense of belonging and participating in the fortunes and performance of the organisation." (Edwards and Townsend).
4. Discuss the following 'temptations of large scale': (*a*) The temptation to do one's 'best'; (*b*) the temptation to delegate too much; (*c*) the temptation to promote amalgamations; (*d*) the temptation

to build a one-man show; (*e*) the temptation to appoint yes-men (see Edwards and Townsend, pp. 197–9).

5. Outline the main arguments of *either* the 'Fleck' Report *or* the 'Herbert' Report.
6. What is meant by 'balanced organisational growth'? Do you agree that this phrase, "though unexceptional as a generalisation, means very little in specific cases"? (N. Branton).
7. "... the family firm today presents a unique set of management situations" (R. Falk). What are they?
8. "... all these pyramidal charts encourage in a way that will hardly be believed the development of water-tight compartments" (M. Guigoz: 'Organisation Charts and People', *Management International* 1961/I).
9. Is there anything of value in the concept of the "optimum" firm?

APPENDICES

APPENDIX I

THE MAIN SPHERES OR PHASES OF ACTION OF ENTREPRENEURIAL ACTIVITY

(A delimitation of the field of management)

1. The determination of the *business objective* of the enterprise and the *change* of those objectives as conditions require or make advantageous.
2. The *development and maintenance* of an enterprise including *efficient relationships* with subordinates and employees.
3. The securing of *adequate financial resources*, the *retention* of them, and the nurture of *good relations* with existing and potential investors.
4. The acquisition of *efficient technological equipment* and the *revision* of it as new machinery appears.
5. The development of a *market for products*, and *the division of new products* to meet or anticipate consumer demands; and
6. The maintenance of *good relations with public authorities*.

(Arthur C. Cole: 'An Approach to the Study of Entrepreneurship', reprinted in *Enterprise and Social Change*, ed. Lane and Riemersma, London, 1953.)

APPENDIX II

WHAT THE JOB OF MANAGEMENT REQUIRES OF EVERY EXECUTIVE

Place a check mark in those spaces which indicate a true appraisal of your present attainment in each of the areas listed below

MY PRESENT PERFORMANCE

1. EXCELLENT
Little improvement needed
2. GOOD
Some improvement needed
3. FAIRLY SATISFACTORY
More improvement needed
4. WEAK
Much improvement needed
5. UNSATISFACTORY
Major changes needed

	5	4	3	2	1
1. To what extent have your organization's over-all objectives and policies been prescribed in written statements?........	...	...	...	...	...
And how effectively have these statements been interpreted by you to your subordinates?	...	...	...	...	...
2. To what extent are definite criteria used by your organization for the measurement of the company's over-all results?........	...	...	...	...	...
And, are these criteria understood by you and adapted insofar as practicable to the measurement of your own activities?........	...	...	...	...	...
3. Do you have a written statement that clearly defines the end results for which you are responsible? and accountable?........	...	...	...	...	...
4. To what extent have you developed a written summary of the activities which are currently required of you in order to achieve the results for which you are accountable?........	...	...	...	...	...
Are they listed in sequence of importance?........	...	...	...	...	...
And grouped by related functions?........	...	...	...	...	...
5. To what extent are you thoroughly acquainted with the principles and techniques of sound organization and staffing?........	...	...	...	...	...
And, to what extent have these principles and techniques been applied to the organizational design?........	...	...	...	...	...
And the staffing of your present department?........	...	...	...	...	...
6. To what extent are you familiar with the principles and techniques of sound delegation?........	...	...	...	...	...
And, are these principles and techniques carried out most effectively in the administration of your current organization?........	...	...	...	...	...
7. To what extent do you feel that you have a thorough knowledge of and skill in the most effective use of the fundamentals of management principles and techniques?........	...	...	...	...	...
8. To what extent have you mastered the techniques of utilizing management controls most effectively—ratios, standards, and trends—as basic guides in managing your department?........	...	...	...	...	...
9. To what extent are you adequately informed regarding your organization's plans and programs; budgets and schedules that directly affect operations for which you are held accountable?........	...	...	...	...	...

What the Job of Management Requires of Every Executive *(cont'd.)*

	5	4	3	2	1
10. To what extent are you thoroughly familiar with the specialized subject matter and current developments in your present fields of management responsibility?........					
11. To what extent have you followed current progress in the development of modern facilities used in your present area of management?					
And are you adequately skilled in the utilization of these facilities to see that appropriate recommendations are made with reference to their use as needed?					
12. To what extent are you familiar with modern developments in how to plan and lay out the most effective flow of work required in your department?........					
And are these principles and techniques utilized in the organization and distribution of your present work load?........					
13. To what extent have you developed expertness in conference leadership?........					
And, do you utilize these skills and techniques in your staff meetings insofar as practicable?........					
14. Have you completed one or more training programs on "How to Instruct"?					
And, do you feel that you do as an effective job as possible in the training of your employees in the performance of their respective jobs?........					
15. To what extent do you utilize the principles and techniques of methods improvement in your areas of management?........					
16. To what extent do you carry out recognized techniques and practices in maintaining good human relations in your department?					
TOTALS					
SUMMARY RATING OF PERFORMANCE					

DO YOU/SHOULD YOU

How Much Time Do You/Should You Spend on Planning and/or Developing

ACTIVITY	IMPORTANCE TO ME			SHOULD SPEND (Check One)			HOURS PER MONTH ALLOCATED
	LITTLE	SOME	MUCH	LESS	SAME	MORE	
1. Over-all viewpoints							Present / Future
2. Objectives, goals							
3. Policies							
4. Basic controls							
5. Plans and programs							
6. Budgets							
7. Organization							
8. Personnel							
9. Growth and development							
10. Procedures and reports							
11. Operating details							
12. Self-improvement							
Summary totals							

GENERAL INDEX